THE WORLD ATLAS OF COFFEE

3RD EDITION

JAMES HOFFMANN

THE WORLD ATLAS OF COFFEE

3RD EDITION

FROM BEANS TO BREWING
– COFFEES EXPLORED, EXPLAINED
AND ENJOYED

MITCHELL BEAZLEY

Dedicated to my family

First published in Great Britain in 2014 by Mitchell Beazley,
an imprint of
Octopus Publishing Group Ltd
Carmelite House
50 Victoria Embankment
London EC4Y 0DZ
www.octopusbooks.co.uk

Revised edition 2025

An Hachette UK Company
www.hachette.co.uk

The authorized representative in the EEA is Hachette
Ireland, 8 Castlecourt Centre, Dublin 15, D15 XTP3, Ireland
(email: info@hbgi.ie)

Text copyright © James Hoffmann 2014, 2018, 2025
Design and layout copyright © Octopus Publishing Group
2025

Distributed in the US by Hachette Book Group
1290 Avenue of the Americas, 4th and 5th Floors
New York, NY 10104

Distributed in Canada by Canadian Manda Group
664 Annette St, Toronto, Ontario, Canada M6S 2C8

All rights reserved. No part of this work may be reproduced
or utilized in any form or by any means, electronic or
mechanical, including photocopying, recording or by any
information storage and retrieval system, without the prior
written permission of the publisher.

James Hoffmann asserts the moral right to be identified as
the author of this work.

ISBN: 978-1-78472-986-8
eISBN: 978-1-78472-988-2

A CIP catalogue record for this book is available from the
British Library.

Printed and bound in Italy

10 9 8 7 6 5 4 3 2 1

Publishing Director Alison Starling
Senior Editor Alex Stetter
Art Director Juliette Norsworthy
Designer Lizzie Ballantyne
Special Photography Cristian Barnett
Illustrators Grace Helmer and Claire Huntley
Cover Design and Illustration Jon Gray (gray318)
Picture Research Manager Jennifer Veall
Assistant Production Manager Allison Gonsalves

Cartography
Digital mapping by Martin Darlison,
with updates by Martin Lubikowski

James Hoffmann is the co-founder of Square Mile Coffee Roasters, a multi-award-winning coffee roasting company based in East London. He is also the World Barista Champion 2007, having won the UK Barista competition in both 2006 and 2007. He has a YouTube channel with more than 2 million subscribers, where he makes videos about anything and everything to do with coffee, and an Instagram following of more than 700k. He is the author of *The World Atlas of Coffee* (first edition 2014, second edition 2018) and the *Sunday Times* bestseller *How to Make the Best Coffee at Home* (2022).

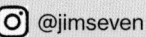 @jimseven

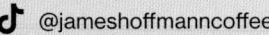 @jameshoffmanncoffee

▶ @jameshoffmann

Contents

6   Introduction

10   PART ONE: INTRODUCTION TO COFFEE

12	Arabica and Robusta	28	Harvesting Coffee	48	How Coffee is Traded
16	The Coffee Tree	32	Processing	54	A Short History of Coffee Drinking
19	The Coffee Fruit	46	Decaffeination		
22	Coffee Varieties				

58   PART TWO: FROM BEAN TO CUP

60	Coffee Roasting	81	Water for Brewing	122	Espresso Equipment
68	Buying and Storing Coffee	84	Brewing Basics	125	Espresso-Based Drinks
74	How to Taste Coffee	106	Espresso	130	Home Roasting
78	Grinding Coffee	120	Steaming Milk		

132   PART THREE: COFFEE ORIGINS

134	**AFRICA**	174	**ASIA AND OCEANIA**	212	**AMERICAS**
136	Ethiopia	176	Yemen	214	United States: Hawaii
142	Uganda	180	India	219	United States: California
146	Kenya	184	China	218	Puerto Rico
150	Tanzania	186	Myanmar	220	Cuba
154	Rwanda	188	Thailand	222	Haiti
158	Democratic Republic of the Congo	190	Vietnam	224	Dominican Republic
		194	The Philippines	226	Jamaica
162	Burundi	198	Indonesia	228	Mexico
166	Zambia	204	Papua New Guinea	232	Guatemala
168	Malawi	208	Malaysia	238	El Salvador
170	Madagascar	208	Timor-Leste	242	Honduras
170	Réunion	210	Australia	246	Nicaragua
171	Côte d'Ivoire	210	Japan	248	Costa Rica
171	Togo	211	Taiwan	254	Panama
172	Cameroon			258	Venezuela
172	St Helena			260	Colombia
				266	Ecuador
				268	Peru
				272	Brazil
				278	Bolivia

280   Glossary
282   Index
288   Acknowledgements

Introduction

'Coffee has never been better than it is today. Producers know more than ever before about growing coffee and have access to more varieties and specialist growing techniques. Coffee roasters have never before been so likely to appreciate the importance of using freshly harvested coffee beans, and their understanding of the roasting process continues to improve. There are now more and more cafés selling really good coffee, using the best equipment and training their staff more effectively.'

I wrote these words as the introduction to the first edition of this book, over ten years ago. A great deal has changed in the world of coffee since then, and speciality coffee in particular, but I'm happy to find that these words still ring true. What has changed most of all has been the audience for great coffee. It has grown in a way few of us could have imagined, and delicious coffee, which was once the realm of the hobbyist or a fringe interest, is now widely embraced, adopted and enjoyed.

The seeds of this book came from wanting to own a book that didn't exist, a guidebook to the world of coffee that gave me context, detail and explanation. It still surprises me that I got to write it, and that now I get to update and improve it with this wider audience in mind.

The coffee industry is enormous and has spread around the world. Today, our best estimate is that 125 million people depend on coffee production for their livelihood, and coffee is consumed in every part of the globe. Coffee is entwined with both the economic and cultural histories of so many countries yet very few coffee drinkers have, in the past, scratched the surface to see what is underneath. For many, coffee is what powers their work. Yet while many people may not have explored the world of coffee, a large portion of coffee drinkers are seeking out coffee that has been sourced carefully, sold traceably and brewed well.

The coffee industry can be separated into two distinct areas: commodity and speciality. In this book we will primarily be dealing with speciality coffees. The coffee industry has struggled for years to give a clear definition of 'speciality', but for me these are coffees that are defined by their quality and by how good they taste, and for this reason are sold at a premium compared to commodity coffee. Their origin is important, as this will often determine their flavour. 'Commodity coffee' is the term used to describe coffees that are not traded on their quality but are considered simply to be 'coffee'. Where they are grown doesn't matter much, nor when they were harvested or how they were processed. Commodity coffee has defined the way that much of the world thinks about coffee – a generic product from somewhere tropical; an efficient, if bitter, way to get caffeine into the bloodstream and to clear the mind in the morning.

The idea that one might drink coffee for pleasure, to delight in its complexity of flavour, has rapidly spread, especially in the last decade. Most people would accept that there is a spectrum of quality in coffee, although they may not agree on which ones are 'better'! There are many differences between the production and international trade of speciality coffees and commodity coffees as they are quite different products.

While this new world of coffee has boomed, it has remained a little intimidating. The language of coffee is foreign to most people, and many cafés are eager to

share the story of the coffee they brew: its variety, its post-harvest processing or the people behind it. This can be overwhelming or frustrating. This book is written to make sense of that language, to give context to the stories of the cups of coffee you drink, to highlight what makes each farm or cooperative different and interesting. At first, the sheer diversity of coffees and the huge volume of information available can be off-putting. However, once you start to understand a little more about coffee, the diversity of flavour and the 'why' of its differences are the very things that make it so compelling. I hope this book serves you well.

All of this is not to say that the future of coffee is simple and without significant problems that it will have to contend with. The balance in the market, between supply and demand, has been on a knife edge for some time. There is growing demand for coffee, but also for speciality coffee specifically. Meeting that demand faces some challenges – climate change continues to be deeply disruptive and challenging in coffee lands, and there is a looming crisis of labour. Already, in many producing countries, the average age of a coffee farmer is late fifties, if not sixties. Finding labour to pick coffee has always been hard, but now finding labour for farm management is also hard. People don't want to be coffee farmers; people don't want to work in coffee. Coffee has been too cheap for too long. That is going to change, and the demand being so high will make coffee much more expensive in the coming years.

This is no bad thing, but this is a moment when I cannot help but feel that we have perhaps reached a kind of 'peak coffee', specifically for the coffee drinker. There is so much choice, and the best coffee in the world is (compared to so many other things in food and drink that we cherish) relatively inexpensive compared to the worst of coffee. I do not know if this can last much longer. I think we may look back on these times fondly and realize how lucky we were to drink and enjoy coffee. That mindfulness has deepened my appreciation for coffee, and I hope it also brings a little more pleasure to every cup of coffee you drink.

Left: This 19th-century painting by Megerdich Jivanian depicts a coffee house in Constantinople, where customers are enjoying an evening of coffee, music and pipe smoking.

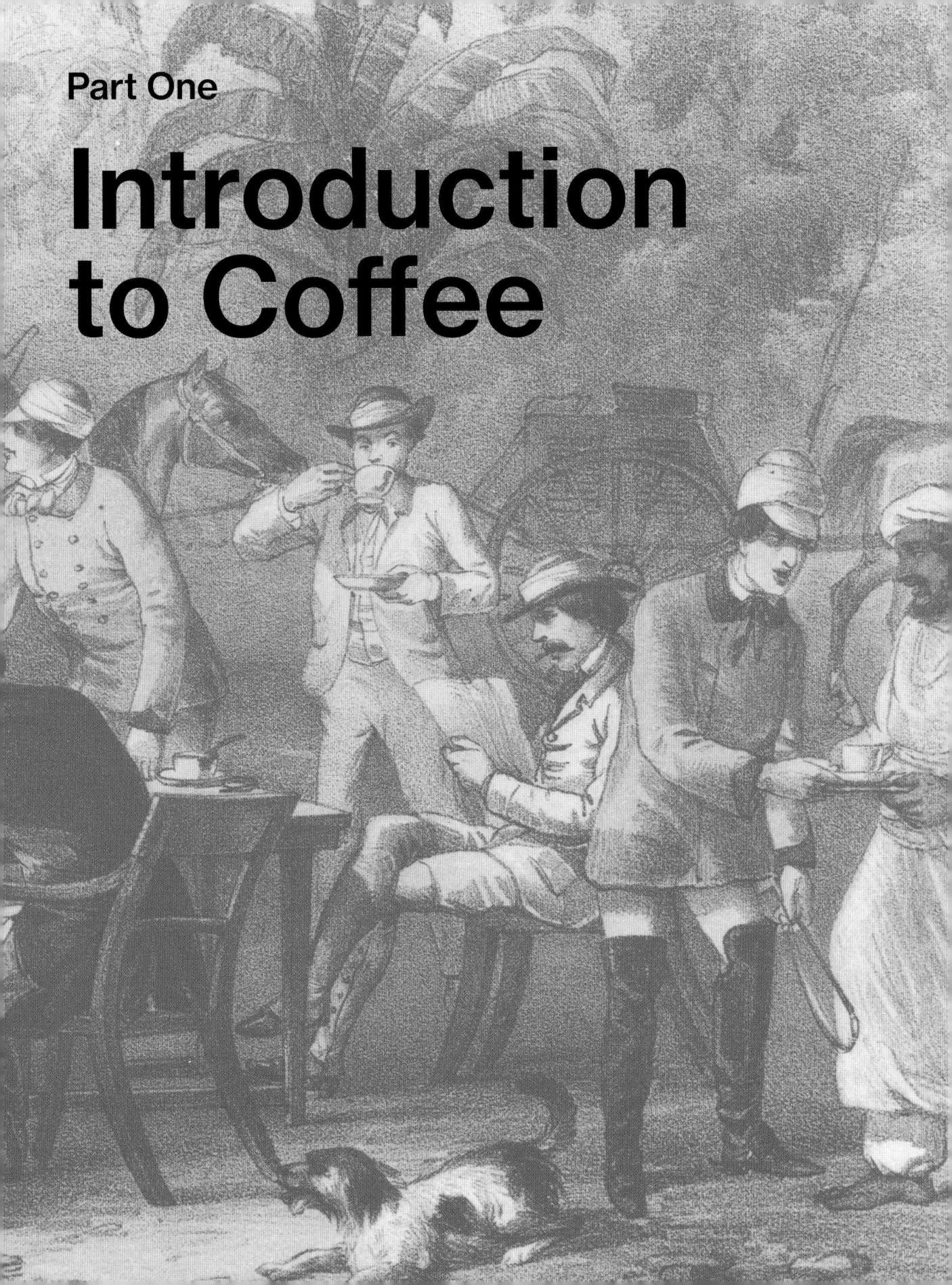

Part One
Introduction to Coffee

Arabica and Robusta

When talking about coffee, people are usually referring to the fruit from one particular species of tree: *Coffea arabica*. It is a species that most people will have heard of at some point, as it is often used in marketing by larger brands trying to establish their quality by stating a bag is '100 per cent Arabica'. Arabica makes up around 60 per cent of the coffee produced each year, and it is grown in dozens of countries between the Tropic of Capricorn and the Tropic of Cancer. It isn't the only species of coffee, however. In fact, over 120 different species have been identified to date but the only other one that is grown in significant quantities is *Coffea canephora*, a plant we commonly refer to as Robusta.

Robusta is actually something of a brand name given to the species, chosen to highlight its attributes. It was discovered in the Belgian Congo (what is now the Democratic Republic of the Congo) in the late 19th century and its commercial potential was clear. It was able to grow and fruit at lower elevations than the existing Arabica plants, in higher temperatures, and was more resistant to disease. These attributes are what still drive much of the production of Robusta today, and because of the way it is grown it is substantially cheaper to produce. There is an inevitable downside, however: it doesn't taste as good as Arabica.

Some people will make a rather unnecessary argument that a really well-produced Robusta coffee can taste better than a poor Arabica coffee, and this may be true, but it does nothing to convince us that Robusta actually tastes very good. It is generally difficult to ascribe particular tastes to coffees, but I think it would be fair to say that Robusta has a woody, burned-rubber quality in the cup that is present to a varying degree, depending on how well grown and processed it is. It usually has very little acidity but will have a heavy body and mouthfeel (see page 76). There are, of course, grades of quality within Robusta, and it is possible to produce higher-quality Robustas, and that is a trend that is steadily growing. Robusta has been a staple of the Italian espresso culture for many years, but currently most of the Robusta produced around the world ends up in large manufacturing plants destined to become instant soluble coffee.

For the soluble coffee industry, price is far more important than flavour, and the global reliance on coffee as a fast-food product means that Robusta makes up around 40 per cent of the world's coffee produced each year. This percentage is somewhat variable, driven by fluctuations in price and demand. For example, an increase in the global price of coffee may result in more Robusta production, as large multinational coffee companies may need to find cheaper alternatives to Arabica. Interestingly, in the past when roasters have substituted Robusta coffees for Arabica in big commercial blends, there has been a downward trend in coffee consumption. This might be related to flavour, or to the fact that Robusta has about twice the caffeine content of Arabica. Either way, when big brands cut corners, consumers notice – or at least change their coffee-drinking habits.

It is worth noting that Robusta production is concentrated in just a few countries. Vietnam, Brazil, Indonesia, Uganda, India and Côte d'Ivoire combine to produce about 95 per cent of the world's Robusta.

The Genetics of Coffee

The coffee industry treated Robusta like an ugly sister to Arabica until a rather interesting genetic discovery was made. Once scientists began sequencing the genes, it became clear that the two species are not cousins or siblings. Instead, it appears that Robusta is, in fact, a kind of parent of Arabica. Most likely somewhere in what is now South Sudan, Robusta crossed with another species called *Coffea eugenioides* and produced the species that is the parent to modern-day Arabica. This new species spread and really began to flourish in Ethiopia, long considered the birthplace of coffee.

Opposite: *Coffea arabica*, shown here in an illustration by Lucy T. Smith, bears less dense flower clusters than those of Robusta, and the beans are longer and narrower.

Currently, 129 species of *Coffea* have been identified, mostly through the work of the Royal Botanic Gardens, Kew, in London, though most look very different to the plants and beans we are familiar with. Many of these species are indigenous to Madagascar, though others grow in parts of Southern Asia, even as far south as Australia. In recent years there's been an increased interest in other species of coffee, and this is driven by two different forces. First, there has been an explosion of coffee-roasting companies around the world, and that has meant there is a great interest in the new and the unique. Having a rare species for sale will give a roaster a temporary advantage in their market. However, the second reason is perhaps more important: climate change poses a significant threat to coffee. Arabica is vulnerable at higher temperatures, and while Robusta's genetics do offer some potential hardiness, when crossed with Arabica, it has been hard to produce something that rivals the cup quality of Arabica. It isn't just temperature that is a threat. The way that coffee has spread around the world means we have a global crop with a common ancestry. There is little variation in the genetic make-up of coffee plants, and this exposes global coffee production to massive risk. A disease that can attack one plant can likely attack them all, something the wine industry suffered with *Phylloxera* species, insects that devastated huge swathes of grapevines across Europe in the 1860s and 1870s. As such there has been renewed interest in other coffee species, which we will discuss here.

Coffea liberica

This species of coffee was initially grown in and around its native area in West and Central Africa, and grown commercially in countries like Sierra Leone, Ghana and Liberia. It spread from there to Asia, particularly Sri Lanka, in the 1870s, as Arabica production was being destroyed by the leaf rust fungus and *Coffea liberica* was resistant. While *Coffea liberica* seeds do vary in size, it was the large seed stock that was taken across. The very large fruit was hard to process, and the yield of finished beans was relatively small from the large fruit. The difficulties with processing meant that the flavour of the resulting beans was often poor. As a result, after a brief period of popularity, *Coffea liberica* fell out of favour in many places. However, it is still grown commercially, particularly in Malaysia, but also in the Philippines and Indonesia as well as in some African countries. Today, it accounts for less than 1 per cent of global coffee production.

Coffea excelsa

Around the turn of the 20th century two new species of coffee, similar to *Coffea liberica*, were described. Their names were *Coffea dewevrei* and *Coffea excelsa*. However, from the 1940s onwards these were considered to be a single variant of *Coffea liberica*. The technical name became *Coffea liberica* var. *dewevrei* (while what we now call *Coffea liberica* was described as *Coffea liberica* var. *liberica*). But the name Excelsa persisted and is still the commonly used name to describe this variant.

Excelsa has seen an increased interest of late, particularly in Uganda. The seeds are smaller than those of Liberica, and carefully processed samples of this coffee have been relatively well received in industry tastings. It is included here because it is likely to become more widespread in the coming years, and we should see more well-processed lots offered by speciality roasters who are looking to explore new flavours and opportunities in coffee.

Coffea eugenioides

This species is indigenous to East Africa, though almost all the small production you will see today comes from Colombia. The species is the other 'parent' species to Arabica and is probably closer to it than Robusta is. In the last ten years or so, the commercial production of Eugenioides has been in very high demand and has typically been very expensive. The fact that it is a very low-yielding species adds to the cost and the scarcity. The species has a slightly lower caffeine content than Arabica, and the cups it produces are quite unusual. There is often a savoury aspect to the cups alongside the natural sweetness, which some people find delightful and others a little unsettling.

Coffea stenophylla

Another species native to West Africa, this was first recorded towards the end of the 1700s. Its name comes from its narrow leaves (in Greek, *stenos* means narrow and *phyllon* means leaf). Aside from its leaves, its fruit is also notable due to its black colour. It was

Above: This Arabica plant in Guatemala shows the white flowers shared by all species of coffee plants. Only Racemosa sometimes bears flowers with hint of pink.

grown commercially in various countries in West Africa, but from the 1940s onwards it fell out of favour. While this dwindling to low yields is not surprising, what is remarkable is that descriptions of its flavour were often very positive, with some comparing it favourably to Arabica.

In the last few years, the species has been found to be growing wild in Sierra Leone, and there is renewed interest because of its climate resilience coupled with its potential for a better cup. It has been described as a coffee that tastes as good as Arabica but which can grow where we usually grow Robusta. It is still very early days, and it will be a few more years before we are likely to see enough of the coffee grown that it makes its way to roasters around the world. I got the chance to taste an early sample, and while it was hard to discern the quality due to the relatively poor post-harvest processing, it did leave me quite excited for what we might see in the future.

Coffea racemosa and Coffea zanguebariae

I have combined these two species here, because for quite a long time there was some confusion about whether they were in fact two different species or not. It turns out they are, just closely related and sharing a number of characteristics. The most remarkable is the size of the beans, which are really very small – barely half the size of Arabica coffee beans. They come from dark-coloured fruit, and both species are grown mostly in Mozambique. *Coffea racemosa* is grown in the south of the country and also in the very north of South Africa, while *Coffea zanguebariae* grows in the north of Mozambique. They are of interest to us because they are two more examples of species that we might lean on to produce new coffee plants that are resistant to climate change. Both species grow at very low altitudes – in fact, the first Racemosa coffee I tasted had been grown at sea level. The cups aren't as good as Arabica but show potential, and small amounts of Racemosa have been offered for sale by a few speciality roasters.

The Coffee Tree

This section deals only with the most interesting of the coffee species, *Coffea arabica*. At first glance, all Arabica trees look similar: a thin trunk with numerous branches coming off it, supporting foliage and fruit. However, if you look more closely, there are many differences between trees, determined by the variety of Arabica being grown. Different varieties yield different amounts of fruit, in different colours, and some carry the fruit in clusters, while others have fruit evenly spaced down the branch. There are also big differences between the leaves of plants of different varieties, but more importantly between the cup characteristics when the seeds of these varieties are harvested and brewed.

Different varieties have different qualities of flavour and may also have different mouthfeels (see page 76). It is always important to remember that, for the vast majority of coffee producers, flavour is not the main reason they have selected a certain variety to grow. The flavour might be how coffee is marketed and sold, borrowing heavily from the success of grape variety marketing in wine, but that skews our expectations a little, too. Furthermore, while some varieties do have taste characteristics that manifest wherever you plant them, many do not. For a producer, the yield of the tree and its resistance to disease are usually of great value, because it is being grown first and foremost as a cash crop. That is not to say that all producers choose their varieties this way; some producers are exploring new varieties and are interested in planting new trees to see how they taste. However, one should bear in mind the impact of these choices on the profitability and income of the average producer.

From Seed to Tree

Most established coffee farms have a nursery in which to raise seedlings before planting them out on the farm for production. The coffee beans are first planted in rich soil and quickly germinate. The bean itself is then lifted out of the ground by the developing shoot, and at this stage they are often called 'soldiers'. They look strangely like a roasted coffee bean has been

Opposite: Most of the world's coffee is grown between the Tropics of Cancer and Capricorn, but it can also thrive just outside this 'bean belt' in places like Queensland, Australia.

Below left: Germinated coffee seeds, known as 'soldiers', are the first stage of coffee plant growth.

Below: 'Soldiers' soon burst open to reveal green leaves. Within 6–12 months the plants are fully established and can be moved from the nursery, ready for planting.

attached to the top of a thin green stem. Not long after this, the bean bursts open to reveal the first leaves. Coffee plants grow quickly and after 6–12 months they can be moved from the nursery into production. Coffee growing requires the investment of not only money but also time. A coffee farmer will usually have to wait three years for a newly planted tree to fruit properly. Making the decision to begin growing coffee is a serious one, and this also means that, if producers abandon coffee, it will be difficult to encourage them to return to the crop in the future.

Blossom and Fruit

Most coffee trees have one main harvest per year, although the trees in some countries have a second harvest, which is usually smaller and often considered to be of a slightly lower quality. The cycle is first triggered by a prolonged period of rainfall. This extra moisture causes the trees to bloom, producing lots of white blossom flowers with a strong scent that is reminiscent of jasmine.

Insects such as bees pollinate the flowers, although Arabica is able to self-pollinate, meaning that, unless they are knocked off the tree by adverse weather, the flowers will always yield fruit. It takes up to nine months until the fruits are ready to harvest. Unfortunately, coffee cherries do not ripen uniformly. The coffee producer has a difficult choice between harvesting all the fruits from each tree at the same time and having a certain quantity of unripe or overripe coffee cherries in the harvest, or paying pickers to do multiple passes of the same trees so each cherry is harvested when it is perfectly ripe.

Pests and Diseases

The coffee tree is susceptible to a variety of pests and diseases. Two of the most common are coffee leaf rust and the coffee berry borer, but cherry berry disease is worth noting as well.

Coffee Leaf Rust

Known as *roya* in many countries, this is a fungus (*Hemileia vastatrix*) that causes orange lesions on the leaves. It impairs photosynthesis, then causes the leaves to drop and eventually can kill the tree. It was first documented in East Africa in 1861, although it was not studied until it began to affect plants in Sri Lanka in 1869 where it pretty much destroyed the coffee plantations over the following ten years. It spread to Brazil in 1970, perhaps brought over from Africa with a shipment of cacao seeds, and quickly spread into Central America.

It is now found in every coffee-producing country in the world, and the higher temperatures brought about through climate change are exacerbating the situation. In 2013 several Central American countries declared a state of emergency due to the damage caused by rust, and while there have been several rust-resistant varieties produced by national breeding programmes, the disease remains a significant challenge to the coffee industry.

Coffee Berry Borer

Nicknamed *la broca del café* (coffee drill) in Latin America, this is a small beetle (*Hypothenemus hampei*) that lays its eggs inside coffee cherries. The hatching young eat the cherries, thereby reducing the quantity and quality of the crop. The beetle is native to Africa, although it is now the most harmful pest to coffee crops across the world. Research is being done into different methods of control, including chemical pesticides, traps and biological controls.

Coffee Berry Disease

This is a fungal pathogen (*Colletotrichum kahawae*) that causes dark necrosis spots to form on the fruit of the coffee tree. This can lead to the fruit dropping early, which obviously damages the harvest. It thrives in environments that are very humid, relatively warm and at high altitude. The disease primarily impacts coffee growing in Africa, although it has now been seen in other countries and continents. Prevention is usually a combination of growing a resistant variety, as well as using fungicides on the plants. Some additional management and prevention through agricultural practices by the producer can also lessen the impacts of this concerning disease.

The Coffee Fruit

Coffee is a part of our everyday lives, yet how many of us outside the coffee-producing countries have ever seen, or would even recognize, a coffee cherry?

The size of the Arabica fruit varies between varieties of coffee, but on the whole the fruits are the size of a small grape. Unlike grapes, most of the volume of the fruit is provided by the central seeds, although there is a thin layer of fruit flesh under the skin.

All cherries start out green and develop deeper colours as the fruit matures. The skin is usually a deep red when ripe, although some trees have yellow fruit, and occasionally a cross between a yellow-fruiting tree and a red-fruiting tree will yield orange fruit. While fruit colour isn't thought to influence yield, yellow-fruiting trees have often been avoided as it is harder to determine when the fruit is ripe. Red fruit starts off green, goes through a yellow stage and then turns red. This makes ripeness much easier to identify when coffee is being picked by hand.

Ripeness is tied to the quantity of sugar in the fruit, which is vitally important when trying to grow delicious coffee. Generally, the more sugar in the fruit the better. However, different producers harvest their cherries at different stages of ripeness. Some believe that a mixture of cherries at different stages of

Sweet Fruits
The flesh of the coffee fruit is surprisingly delicious when ripe, a pleasing honeydew melon sweetness, with a little refreshing acidity. The fruits are sometimes squeezed to make a drink, but even when ripe they are not particularly juicy, and you have to work to separate the flesh from the seeds.

ripeness can add complexity to a coffee, although all the cherries should be properly ripe, and none of them overripe as they eventually develop an unpleasant flavour.

The Seed

The seed, or coffee bean, is made up of several layers, most of which will be removed during processing, leaving behind the bean we grind and brew. The seed has a protective outer layer, called the parchment, with a thinner layer wrapped around the seed inside it, called the silverskin.

Most coffee cherries contain two seeds, which face each other inside the berry, becoming flattened along one side as they develop. Occasionally, only one seed inside a berry will germinate and grow and these are known as peaberries. Instead of having a flattened surface on one side, these seeds are rounded and make up around 5 per cent of the crop. These peaberries are sometimes separated from the rest of the crop, and some people believe that they have particularly desirable qualities or that they roast in a different way to the flattened beans, so you may see these marketed for sale as a separate product.

The Coffee Fruit

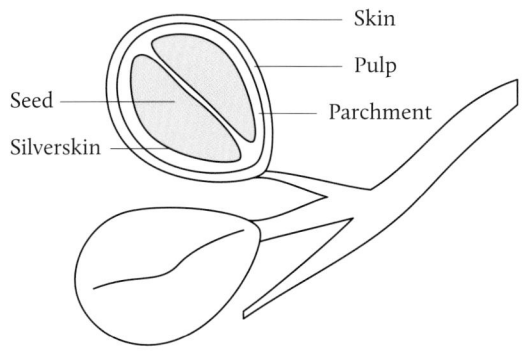

Above: Coffee seeds are extracted from the fruit and the papery parchment layer before they are roasted, ground and brewed.

Ripe coffee cherries are ready to be harvested at a coffee farm in Costa Rica.

Coffee Varieties

The first coffee trees to be cultivated originated in Ethiopia, and this same variety, Typica, is still widely grown today. Many other varieties now exist, some natural mutations and others the result of crossbreeding. Some varieties have explicit taste characteristics of their own, while others take on their characteristics from the terroir in which they are grown, the way they are cultivated and the way they are processed after harvest.

Few coffee consumers are aware that there are different varieties of the Arabica coffee tree, mainly because much of the world's coffee always has been, and still is, traded by origin. A particular lot may come from many farms, and by the time of export no one knows which varieties the contributing producers grew, only which part of the world it was grown in. This is starting to change, but we still know relatively little about how much impact the variety of the tree can have on the taste of the cup of coffee.

Please note that the descriptions of the most common varieties below will not include any specific notes on taste, unless there is something definite and distinct. So many factors influence cup quality and, coupled with the lack of organized research on the way this can be influenced by variety, it would be misleading to make any bold claims in these pages.

Varieties and Varietals

There is often some confusion over the terms 'variety' and 'varietal'. Varieties are genetically distinct variations of a single species, in this case *Coffea arabica*, that may show different characteristics in the tree structure, leaves or fruit. 'Cultivar' is another acceptable term to use here, as this is just a truncation of 'cultivated variety'. 'Varietal' should be used when referring to a specific instance of a variety. When referring to the production of one farm, for example, it would be correct to say that the crop is a 100 per cent Bourbon varietal.

Typica

This is considered the original variety from which all other varieties have mutated or been genetically selected, and in recent years the pathway it took has become clearer. The Dutch took seeds from Yemen to India, and later from India to Indonesia. These seeds are the parents of the many Typica-derived varieties we have today, as it was these seeds that were taken back to Amsterdam to grow in a botanical garden, and then taken to the Americas in the 18th century. The fruit is usually red, and Typica is capable of producing excellent cup quality, though with a relatively small yield compared to other varieties. It is still grown extensively in many different parts of the world and, as a result, is known by several different names including Criollo, Sumatra and Arabigo.

Bourbon

This was a natural mutation of a Typica-like plant (thought to be not exactly the same plant that ended up in Indonesia as discussed above), which occurred on the island of Réunion (at the time called Bourbon). The Dutch tried three times to take coffee from Yemen to the island, and it seems that the second attempt was the most successful, with those trees being the parents of what we now know as Bourbon.

The yield is higher than that of Typica, and many in the speciality industry believe that it has a distinctive sweetness, making it prized and desirable. There are various variations in the colour of the fruit: red, yellow and, occasionally, orange. This variety was grown very widely in the past, but in many producing countries it was replaced by higher-yielding varieties. This was at a time when the market had not yet matured sufficiently to reward a high enough price to compensate for the lower yields it produces compared to newer varieties.

Typica

Bourbon

Mundo Novo

Geisha or Gesha

Mundo Novo
A natural hybrid of Typica and Bourbon, this variety was named after the place in Brazil where it was discovered in the 1940s. It is grown for its relatively high yield, strength and disease resistance, and also for its success at elevations of around 1,000–1,200m (3,300–3,900ft) which are common in Brazil.

Caturra
This is a mutation of Bourbon, discovered in Brazil in 1937. Its yields are relatively high, although it has the capacity for overbearing, where the tree produces more fruit than it can sustain and succumbs to dieback. However, good farm management can avoid this situation. This variety has been especially popular in Colombia and Central America, though it is still fairly common in Brazil. Cup quality is considered good, and while quality increases with elevation, yield decreases.

There are both red and yellow variations and it is a low-growing variety, often referred to as dwarf or semi-dwarf, popular because they are easier to pick by hand.

Catuai
This is a hybrid between Caturra and Mundo Novo created by the Instituto Agronômico de Campinas in Brazil in the 1950s and 1960s. It was selected as it combined the dwarf characteristics of Caturra with the yield and strength of Mundo Novo. Like Caturra, there are red and yellow varieties.

Maragogype
One of the more easily recognized varieties, Maragogype is a mutation of Typica, first discovered in Brazil. It is notable, and often considered desirable, due to the unusually large size of its beans. The tree also has exceptionally large leaves but a relatively low yield.

This coffee is often referred to as 'Elephant' or 'Elephant Bean' coffee due to its size. The fruits usually ripen red.

SL-28
A now-prized variety, SL-28 was created in Kenya by Scott Laboratories in the 1930s, selected from a drought-resistant variety from Tanzania. The fruits are red when ripe and the beans are notably larger than average. This variety is considered to be capable of producing a cup with a distinct fruit flavour, often described as blackcurrant. It is quite susceptible to coffee leaf rust and the trees tend to perform better at higher elevations.

SL-34
This variety was selected from French Mission Bourbon, a variety brought back to Africa from Bourbon (Réunion) and first appearing in Tanzania and then in Kenya. It is also capable of distinct fruit flavours but is generally considered to be inferior to SL-28 in cup quality. It is also susceptible to coffee leaf rust, and the fruits ripen red.

Pink Bourbon

Geisha or Gesha

There is some debate over the correct name for this variety and, while Geisha is more commonly used, my preference is for Gesha, which is what is used in this book. Gesha is a town in western Ethiopia and, while the variety was brought to Panama from Costa Rica, it is believed to be Ethiopian in origin. The variety is considered to produce exceptionally aromatic/floral cups, and the demand for it has driven up prices in recent years.

It has gained prominence and popularity dramatically since 2004 when one Panamanian farm, Hacienda La Esmeralda, entered a competition with a Gesha lot. The coffee proved so unusual and distinct that it attracted an incredibly high bid of $21/lb at auction. This record bid was beaten in 2006 and 2007, reaching $130/lb – nearly one hundred times more than a commodity-grade coffee. This has since encouraged many producers in Central and South America to plant this variety. It has remained popular, and demand has kept prices for it relatively high.

Pink Bourbon

This variety has become more popular recently, although its name is actually a mistake. Initially, it was considered to have been a mutation of Bourbon, but we now know that it is an Ethiopian landrace variety that was brought to Colombia. It is not currently known how or when it was introduced to Colombia.

Sudan Rume (or Rume Sudan)

Another regional landrace variety that has spread into Colombia, this one was first cultivated on the Boma Plateau in South Sudan. It is a low-yielding variety, and so it is rare to see it cultivated and separated as a single-variety lot of coffee. It has been used in breeding programmes due to its resistance to coffee berry disease.

Wush Wush

This regional landrace is named after the area of Wushwush in south-west Ethiopia, from which it hails. It is also another variety that has found a new home in Colombia. Due to the relative scarcity of the coffee, the price remains quite high, and there isn't enough data to say whether the variety has distinct flavour characteristics although it is consistently reported to produce excellent cups.

Castillo

Castillo was developed by Cenicafé, the National Coffee Research Centre in Colombia, specifically to combat leaf rust. It was named after researcher Jaime Castillo. It was released in 2005, has come to be very popular in Colombia, and makes up a significant portion of the country's coffee. The variety was also engineered to be a 'dwarf'-size tree, making it easier to pick and to increase density and yields from farmland. Some were sceptical about its cup quality when it was

Wush Wush

Castillo

first released, but most would now consider it able to produce high-quality coffee.

Colombia
Developed by Cenicafé, and released in 1985, Colombia is a hybrid variety – a cross between Caturra and the Timor Hybrid. This was produced to be a high-yielding, disease-resistant variety. While not considered the best-tasting variety, it became incredibly important to the success of the Colombian coffee industry in the years following its release.

Sidra
There isn't a lot of clarity regarding the roots of this variety, and there are competing stories of its origins. It may be a Typica and Bourbon cross, but there are competing claims that it has genetics similar to an Ethiopian landrace. It might be both – as often different varieties can end up having the same name applied to them. Currently, Sidra production is limited, as it requires full shade and is relatively low yielding, although it is considered to produce very high-quality cups.

Jackson
This variety is derived from Bourbon and was named for a coffee farmer called Jackson who grew coffee near Mysore in India in the early 20th century. It was then brought to Africa in the 1920s as it showed leaf rust resistance. It is considered a very productive variety and is commonly found in Rwanda and Burundi. It is no longer rust resistant.

Laurina (Bourbon Pointu)
This is a variety of Bourbon, from the island of Bourbon – now Réunion. Research suggests that the mutation may have occurred a couple of hundred years ago, and it picked up the name Bourbon Pointu because of its pointed shape, though it is also called Laurina because of its similarity to a laurel tree. It is notable for having a lower caffeine content than other Arabica coffee varieties, but it has a similar caffeine content to *Coffea eugenioides*, one of the 'parent' species of Arabica.

Timor Hybrid
Even though you are extremely unlikely to drink coffee produced purely from the Timor Hybrid, it is nonetheless an important variety in coffee's history and development. This was a natural cross between Arabica and Robusta that occurred in the wild in the 1920s on the island of Timor. This natural cross provided a way for plant breeders to bring some of Robusta's genetics, and corresponding resistance, into crosses with Arabica. This led to the development of a great many varieties. However, while the Timor Hybrid was deeply influential, the varieties always carried something of the taste profile of Robusta.

Laurina

Pacas
Pacas is a natural mutation of Bourbon, discovered in El Salvador in 1949 by the Pacas family. It has red fruits, and its low-growing habit makes picking easy. Its cup quality is considered similar to Bourbon and is therefore desirable.

Villa Sarchi
Named after the town in Costa Rica where it was discovered, Villa Sarchi is another natural mutation of Bourbon that, like Pacas, exhibits dwarfism. It is currently being bred to produce very high yields, and it is capable of excellent cup quality. The fruits ripen red.

Pacamara
This cross between the Pacas and Maragogype varieties was created in El Salvador in 1958. Like Maragogype, it has extremely large leaves, fruit and coffee beans. It also has distinct cup characteristics that can be positively described. It can taste like chocolate and fruit, but also has the capacity for unpleasantly herbal, onion-like cups. The fruits ripen red.

Kent
Named after a planter who worked on a selection programme in India in the 1920s, the Kent variety was originally developed for its resistance to coffee leaf rust, although it can be destroyed by new strains of the disease.

S795
Also developed in India, this is a cross between Kent and S288, an older selection resistant to coffee leaf rust. It is widely planted in India and Indonesia, although it is now considered to have lost much of its disease resistance.

Wild Arabica Varieties
Most of the above varieties are genetically extremely similar, as they all stem from one or two varieties of Typica. Many of the coffee trees grown in Ethiopia, however, are not selected cultivars but indigenous landrace varieties. These are often referred to as 'heirloom' varieties, although many now consider this terminology incorrect, and 'regional landraces' is a preferred term for the multitude of different varieties grown in Ethiopia.

Harvesting Coffee

Careful harvesting of coffee cherries is fundamentally important to the quality of the resulting cup of coffee. Unsurprisingly, coffee beans harvested from fruit at peak ripeness generally taste the best. Many experts see the harvest as the point at which the quality of the coffee peaks, and every stage thereafter is about preserving quality rather than improving it, although there has been a growing interest in the use of fermentation to improve coffee post-harvest (see page 40).

The greatest challenge in harvesting high-quality coffee is perhaps the topography of the land on which the coffee is growing. Great coffee requires higher elevations, and the fact that many coffee farms are located on steep hills means that harvesting the trees can be difficult, if not downright dangerous. This isn't true of every coffee farm, however.

Machine Harvesting

Brazil has large areas of flat land at high elevations where coffee proliferates. The estates in these areas drive large machines down the neat rows of coffee trees to harvest the cherries. These machines essentially shake the trees until the fruit comes loose. The cherries on the branch of a coffee tree ripen at different rates, so each branch has both ripe and unripe cherries together. The machines do not differentiate and pick all the cherries at once. This means they must be sorted after harvest to separate the ripe from the unripe, and to discard the twigs and leaves that also get shaken off the tree. The cost of the coffee's production will be lower than any other harvesting method, but at the expense of the quality of the harvest as a whole.

Left: Harvesting coffee by hand, like here in Kenya, results in a higher-quality crop, as only the cherries at perfect ripeness are collected.

Strip Picking

A great deal of coffee is still harvested by hand as machines simply cannot operate in hilly areas. One of the faster methods of handpicking is to strip all the cherries off a branch together with one deft movement. Like machine harvesting, this is a quick but imprecise way to pick the cherries. It doesn't require expensive equipment or flat land but still results in a mixed bag of ripe and unripe cherries that must be sorted later.

Handpicking

For high-quality coffee, handpicking remains the most effective way of harvesting. Pickers select only the cherries that are ready for harvest, leaving the unripe fruit on the tree to be picked later. This is hard labour, and producers face the challenge of incentivizing their pickers to harvest only the ripe fruit. Pickers are paid by the weight of the fruit they pick, which encourages them to pick unripe fruit to make up additional weight. Quality-conscious producers have to work carefully with their picking teams to make sure they are also paid for uniform ripeness.

The Problems of Labour

The cost of handpicking coffee is proving a growing challenge and contributes a large part of the production costs. This is one of the primary reasons that coffees produced in developed economies – such as Kona coffees produced in Hawaii – are so expensive.

Fallen Fruit

Coffee growers collect any fruit that naturally falls off the trees – ripe or not. This is usually collected separately and will become part of the lower-quality lots that even the best farms in the world inevitably produce. Leaving fallen fruit on the ground under the trees can cause problems, as they tend to attract pests such as the coffee berry borer (see page 18).

In rapidly developing countries, people simply don't want to pick coffee for a living. Coffee farms in Central America often employ itinerant pickers who travel from country to country, as different regions harvest at slightly different times. Currently, many of these workers are from Nicaragua as it is the weakest economy in the region. In the last ten years, the challenge of finding people to pick coffee has only got harder and may be one of the fundamental barriers to further growth in speciality coffee production.

Sorting the Beans

After picking, the cherries are often sorted using a variety of different methods to prevent unripe or overripe coffee from joining the bulk of the lot. In parts of the world with relatively low labour costs, and little money available for investment in equipment, this is done by hand. In more developed countries, the cherries are often sorted using a flotation tank. The cherries are poured into a large tank of water, where the ripe fruit sinks to the bottom. They are pumped from there into the main processing section. Unripe fruit floats to the top and is skimmed off, to be processed separately.

Left: Cherries can be sorted in a flotation tank. Ripe cherries sink to the bottom of the tank and are pumped out for processing while unripe fruit floats to the top and is treated separately.

Opposite, top: Much of the coffee-producing land in Brazil is flat, allowing the use of large machines to harvest the crop. The machines shake the trees to loosen the fruit.

Opposite, bottom: A worker in El Salvador sorts hand-picked fruit, separating the ripe from unripe cherries.

Introduction to Coffee

Processing

'Processing' is the umbrella term used to describe any and all steps a coffee goes through between harvesting and being readied for export. It is a vitally important part of the process that was historically focused on preservation of quality and thus the preservation of earnings from the crop. Processes were chosen to reduce the risk of a drop in cup quality or to reduce the likelihood of a defect appearing in the coffee. Flavour was not the primary concern. The rise of speciality coffee has seen an associated rise in interest in using post-harvest processing to create or refine flavour.

In turn, this has also meant that how a coffee has been processed is often a large part of how the coffee is marketed and sold. This, I think, is a good thing because how a coffee has been processed is a much better indicator of whether someone will like it than the variety of coffee grown. While the coffee industry tried to follow the wine model of marketing for many years, this is one place that breaking away from that model has been very useful. Processing alone will not guarantee whether you will like or dislike a coffee, but it is something that I look at whenever I am making a purchase of beans or even drinking a cup of coffee in a café.

After harvest, the coffee cherries are taken first to a wet mill to separate the beans from the flesh and to dry the beans so that they are safe for storage, before then going to a dry mill just before export. If left unprocessed, coffee cherries break down very quickly and the resulting cup drops in quality, too. In addition, there is no desire to export the whole fruit at greater cost when only the seeds are of commercial interest to the rest of the world.

There are several different approaches for this, which we will cover next. Coffee beans start with a moisture content of around 60 per cent, and as part of the process should be dried to around 11–12 per cent to ensure they do not rot or develop mould while waiting to be sold and shipped. A wet mill can be anything from a small collection of equipment on an individual farm, to a very large industrialized facility for processing enormous amounts of coffee.

The wet mill processes coffee from the cherry stage to the parchment stage, when the bean is dry but still covered with its layer of parchment, or pergamino. Most believe that the coffee is well protected by this outer layer, and that it does not really begin to degrade until the coffee is hulled to remove the parchment, at the last possible moment before the coffee ships.

The term 'wet milling' is slightly misleading as some producers use very little, if any, water in their processing methods. It does, however, make the

Opposite: Cherry harvests are processed at a wet mill, where beans are separated from the flesh and then dried, ready for storage and shipping.

Defining 'Defect'

The term 'defect' is used quite specifically in coffee, describing individual beans that have developed problems that result in distinct bad flavours. Some defects can be spotted by taking a look at the raw coffee, while others come to light only when the coffee is tasted. A mild defect might be a bean that has been damaged by insects, and this is easy to spot. A more serious problem is a phenolic coffee, where the coffee has a very harsh, metallic, paint-stripper flavour, mixed with notes of sulphur (it is as bad as it sounds). The cause of this defect isn't yet well understood. Bad processing can also cause defects, including giving the coffee a fermented flavour and an unpleasantly dirty, almost boozy quality. It can also add a taste reminiscent of barnyards and rotten fruit. The more unpleasant defects are labelled Category 1 defects, and the less intense or more cosmetic defects are labelled Category 2. For a long time, a popular definition of speciality coffee involved grading a sample of the raw coffee. Here speciality coffee should have zero Category 1 defects in a 350g (just over 12oz) sample and no more than five Category 2 defects.

distinction between this initial processing and the later stage when the hulling and grading takes place, known as 'dry milling' (see page 41).

The Natural Process

Also known as the dry process, this is the oldest method of processing coffee. After harvest, the coffee cherries are spread out in a thin layer to dry in the sun. Some producers spread them out on brick patios; others use special raised drying tables, which allow a better airflow around the cherry, resulting in more even drying. The cherries must be turned regularly to avoid mould, fermentation or rotting taking place. Once the coffee is properly dry, the outer husk of skin and the dried fruit are removed mechanically, and the raw coffee is then stored before export.

The natural process itself adds certain flavours to the coffee, sometimes positive but often quite unpleasant. However, if there is no access to water, this may be the only process open to the producer and is therefore common in places like Ethiopia and also in parts of Brazil. This is a process that will be used for lower-value coffees too, such as the lower-quality overripe or underripe coffee a farm produces. The goal is to add as little cost to that coffee as possible, as it will achieve the lowest value. Historically, these kinds of coffees usually ended up in the internal market, as higher-value coffees were exported rather than consumed locally. That trend is slowly changing, as producing countries develop strong speciality coffee cultures, and there is more competition from local roasting companies for speciality quality lots.

This does not mean that all natural-process coffee is of poor quality. There are those who choose this method to process high-quality coffee, and they often find the process to be more expensive due to the additional labour involved in the attentive, careful drying of the cherries. The process will often add fruity, somewhat fermented flavours to the coffee, regardless of variety and terroir. These are usually described as hints of blueberry, strawberry or tropical fruit, but sometimes attract negative terms like 'barnyard', 'wild', 'ferment' and 'manure'. High-quality naturals have long polarized those who work in coffee. Many see value in coffees that taste spectacularly fruity, and believe they are extremely useful for showcasing the possibilities of flavour that coffee has

Drying Speed and Storage Potential

While still at an early stage, research seems to suggest that drying coffee very slowly and very evenly can have benefits not only to quality in the short term but also to how long a coffee will retain its good flavour when stored in its raw state. Coffees dried too quickly can lose their attractive qualities shortly after being delivered to the roaster, in some cases within a few months or even weeks, which is bad news for both the roaster and the end consumer. There are many iconic, perhaps romantic, images of coffee being dried on large patios. The coffee will be turned by someone pushing a large rake through the expanse of coffee, and will also need to be gathered up and protected if it rains. There is a growing consensus that patios do not produce the best-tasting outcome. The heat of the bricks dries the coffee too quickly, and raised beds that allow airflow to circulate better while drying more slowly are preferred. Those beds are a significant expense for a mill and are a less efficient use of space. Both of these are challenges that hinder wider adoption.

to offer. Others find the wild flavours unpleasant or have concerns about buyers encouraging producers to process more of their coffee through the natural process. With such an unpredictable process, a high-quality lot could be damaged irreparably and significantly reduce the producer's income.

The Washed Process

The goal of the washed process is to remove all of the sticky flesh from the coffee seed before it is dried. This greatly reduces the chance of something going wrong during drying, so the coffee is likely to be worth more. However, this process is much more expensive and resource intensive than the others.

Above: Washed coffee in parchment spread out to dry in the sun needs to be turned regularly to ensure even drying.

Left: The washed process is a less risky method than the natural process, but it requires investment in machinery and resources.

Processing

The washed process

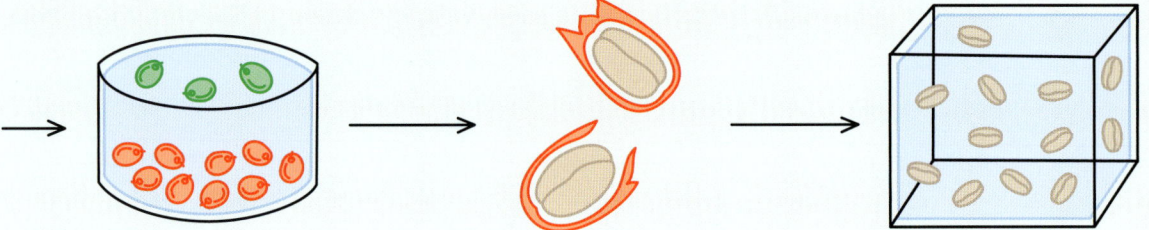

Unripe cherries removed: The harvest is placed in a flotation tank where ripe berries sink to the bottom and are removed. Unripe berries float to the top.

Pulping: Once picked, the outer skin and fruit flesh are stripped off coffee cherries by a mechanical depulper.

Fermentation: Coffee is placed in a clean trough of water where any remaining flesh is removed from the bean through a process of fermentation.

The pulped / natural process

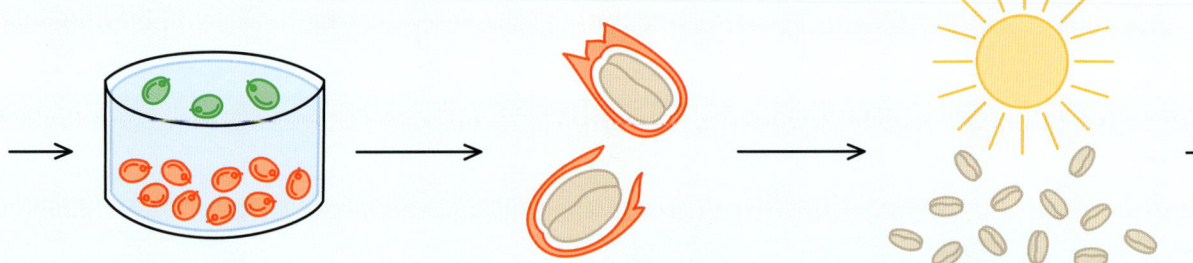

Unripe cherries removed: The harvest is placed in a flotation tank where ripe berries sink to the bottom and are removed. Unripe berries float to the top.

Pulping: Coffee is mechanically depulped to strip off all of the skin and most of the fruit flesh.

Drying: Stripped fruit is laid out on patios or drying beds where they dry quickly, increasing sweetness and body.

The natural / dry process

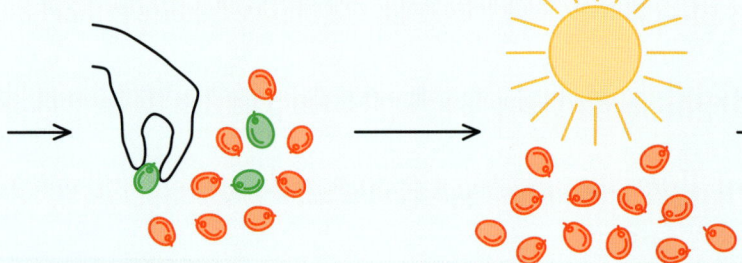

Unripe cherries removed: Picked cherries are sorted by hand to get rid of green berries from the harvest.

Drying: Ripe cherries are laid out in the sunshine and manually raked through to allow even air circulation.

Once the coffee is dry, the outer husk of skin and the dried fruit are removed mechanically.

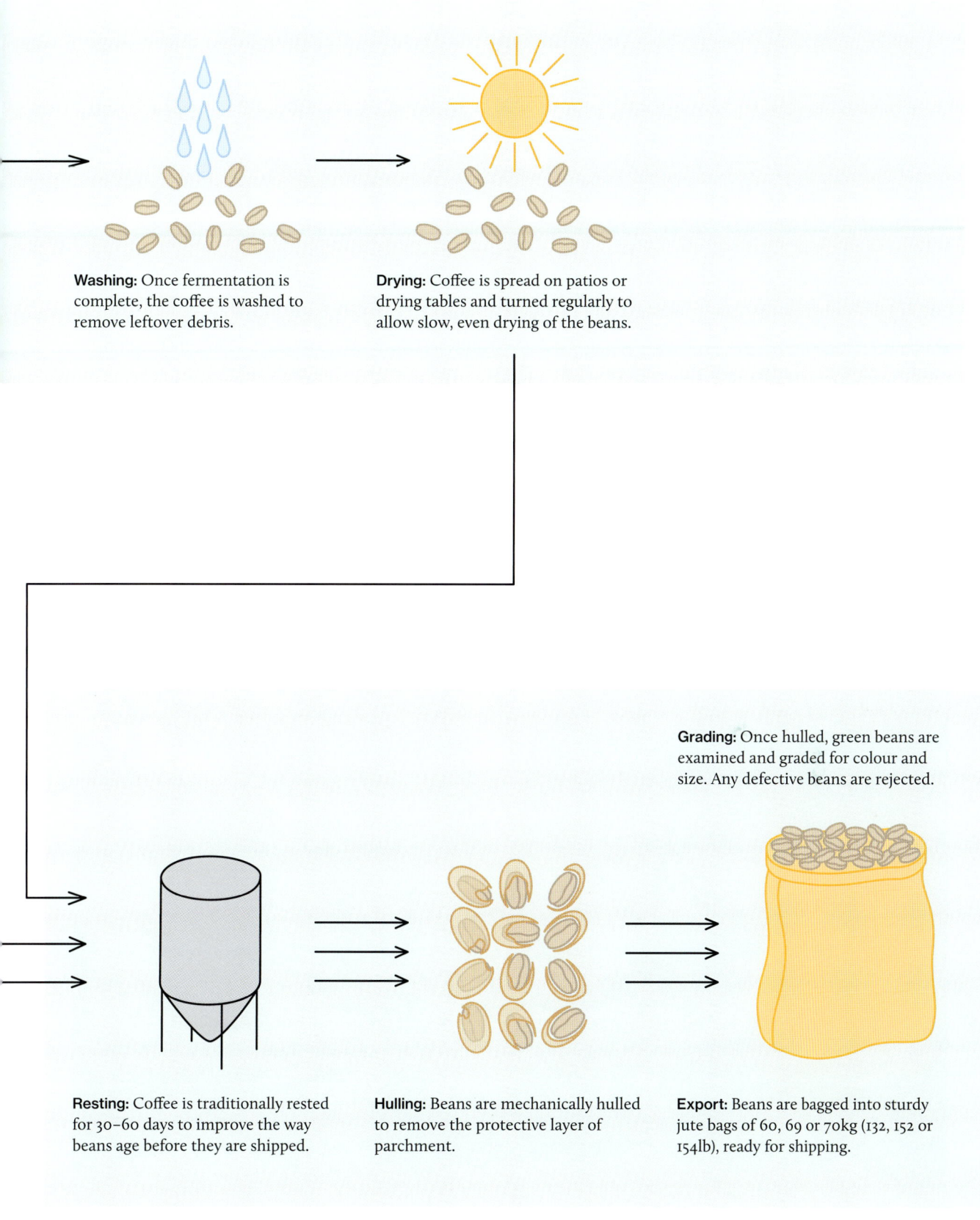

After picking, the coffee cherry has its outer skin and most of the fruit flesh stripped off using a machine called a depulper. The coffee is then moved to a clean tank or trough of water where the remainder of the flesh is removed by fermentation. There are several different approaches to this fermentation stage, which we will cover later in this chapter. The fruit flesh contains a lot of pectin and is firmly attached to the seed, but the fermentation breaks down the remaining flesh enough for it to be washed away. Different producers use different amounts of water during the fermentation stage, and there are some environmental concerns about this method, partly due to the eventual fate of the wastewater, which can be damaging if released into the environment without being correctly treated. The amount of time that fermentation takes depends on several factors including the elevation and ambient temperature. The hotter it is, the faster this process will occur. If the coffee is left too long to ferment, negative flavours can quickly creep in. There are many different methods for checking whether the process is finished. Some producers rub the coffee, as it will squeak if the fruit flesh has broken down, leaving the seed completely smooth. Others put a stick into the tank: if it stands up, supported by the slightly gelatinous water full of pectin, the process is deemed to be complete.

After fermentation, the coffee is washed to remove the leftover debris, after which it is ready to be dried. This is usually done in the sun by spreading out the coffee on brick patios or raised drying tables. In the same way as the natural method described above, the

Below: Hulled coffee is sorted for defects by hand. This process is time-consuming but creates coffee of a much higher quality.

coffee must be turned regularly with large rakes to ensure slow and even drying.

Where there is a lack of sunshine or excess humidity, some producers use mechanical dryers to dry the beans down to a moisture content of around 11–12 per cent. In terms of cup quality, mechanical drying is often considered inferior to sun drying, and it seems that even drying in the sun on a patio may be too fast to achieve the best possible quality (see box on page 35). While many producers of high-quality coffee choose the wet process in an effort to reduce defect, it can also have an impact on the cup quality. Compared to other processes, wet-processed coffees tend to present a higher level of acidity, increased complexity and what is described as a 'cleaner' cup. 'Cleanliness' is an important term used in coffee to indicate the absence of any negative flavours, such as off tastes or unusual harshness and astringency.

Hybrid Processes

The Pulped Natural Process

Developed in Brazil, and still popular there, this process is the result of experiments run by the Brazilian coffee-processing equipment manufacturer Pinhalense. The idea was to produce coffees with high cup quality using less water than that used in the washed process. After picking, the coffee is mechanically depulped, stripping all the skin and much of the fruit flesh from the beans. From here it goes straight out to dry on patios or drying beds. With less flesh surrounding the beans there is a decreased risk of defect, yet there is still enough sugar in the surrounding fruit to see a noticeable increase in body or texture in the coffee. This process still requires careful drying after depulping.

The Honey (Miel) Process

This process is very similar to the pulped natural process and is used in a number of Central American countries, including Costa Rica and El Salvador. The coffee is mechanically depulped, but the method uses even less water than the pulped natural process. The depulping machines can usually be controlled to leave a specific percentage of the flesh on the beans. The resulting coffee is then referred to as '100 per cent honey' or '20 per cent honey', for example. The term miel is the Spanish term for the fruit mucilage, meaning 'honey'. With larger quantities of flesh being left on the beans, there is a higher risk of fermentation and defect when the coffee is dried. Often, you will see the different levels of honey referred to using colours. As a very broad explanation, white and yellow honey coffees have the least mucilage left on after processing, with white being the least and yellow slightly more retained. Then, with coffees that have more mucilage, varying the drying time can yield different outcomes. The quickest drying of these is gold honey, then red and then black for the slowest drying times. Longer drying times can produce more fermented flavours in these coffees, which some people like while others can find a little off-putting, as it makes them more akin to natural-process coffees.

The Semi-Washed/Wet-Hulled Process

This process is common in Indonesia, where it is known as *giling basah* (wet-hulled). After picking, the coffee is depulped and then briefly dried. Instead of drying the coffee to a moisture content of 11–12 per cent as the other processes do, in the semi-washed process the coffee is dried only to 30–35 per cent. It is then hulled, stripping off the parchment and exposing the green coffee beans beneath. The naked beans are then dried again until they are dry enough to be stored without the risk of rotting. This second drying gives the beans a distinctive deep swamp-green colour.

The semi-washed process is the one exception to the practice of keeping the parchment on the beans until just before shipping. It is considered by many to result in a form of defect, but the market has come to associate the flavours with coffees from Indonesia and therefore does not demand an end to the practice. Semi-washed coffees have lower acidity and more body than other coffees, and the process also creates a range of flavours such as woody, earthy, musty, spicy, tobacco and leather. There is strong disagreement within the industry over whether this is desirable. Many feel that these flavours dominate the flavour of the coffee (in the same way the natural process does), and we rarely get to find out how coffees from Indonesia really taste. However, there are some Indonesian coffees that are processed by the wet method, and they are worth looking out for. It should be clear on the packaging as they should be described as 'washed' or 'fully washed'.

New and Experimental Post-Harvesting Techniques

In the last five to ten years there has been a dramatic rise in the number of experimental post-harvesting techniques. In many cases these experiments are conducted in the fermentation stage, before the coffee is dried. What follows cannot be an exhaustive list, but it may provide some guidance on understanding whether one of these coffees will be to your liking when you are shopping for something new to try. Many of these experimental techniques seek to produce extremely unusual and characterful coffees. There has been some debate as to whether they obscure the terroir, or 'taste of place', of that particular coffee. In my own opinion, it tends to boil down to ideas of 'purity' in coffee, which are problematic. Transparency and traceability are, of course, important and valuable, but there is no correct or ideal way to process coffee – other than the way that best serves both the producer of the coffee and the customer. Coffee is not native to most of the areas in which we grow it, so from the outset there is clearly a great deal of human intervention in place.

My own preferences have little place here, but it is worth noting that my experience tasting coffee with thousands of people around the world has left me with little doubt than in many cultures a significant percentage of the population can find fermented flavours in coffee challenging. This is by no means universal, and it also appears to be generational. If you developed your coffee preferences before coming across these kinds of coffees, which are now widespread, then I would consider it more likely that you might find them unsettling. However, more recent inductees into coffee tend to be more open, as coffee flavours today are far more diverse than before. Some proponents of particular techniques will ascribe a particular flavour to that fermentation or technique. These techniques certainly influence the flavour, but I haven't included matching tasting notes for them because I don't think there is sufficient consistency in outcome with the different approaches.

Aerobic and Anaerobic Fermentations

In the world of coffee fermentation, and fermentation in general, there is a divide governed by access to oxygen. In a typical aerobic environment, the pulped coffee might be fermented in water in an open-air tank. This is extremely common and requires less equipment but more active attention to the process. In an anaerobic environment the pulped coffee is typically sealed in a tank, often flushed with gas and without any access to air. There has been a lot more interest in the last few years in anaerobic fermentation, as it can produce quite distinct, unusual and potent fruit notes in the coffee. Both these kinds of fermentation can be combined with other experimental approaches.

Carbonic Maceration

This refers to one part of post-harvest processing, which is the fermentation. This process requires whole, unbroken and unprocessed coffee cherries, and places them in an airtight container. That container is then flushed with carbon dioxide to create an anaerobic environment. Typically, this is temperature controlled, too. The coffee is left in this environment for 24–48 hours and will then be processed as a washed or natural-process coffee after that.

Lactic Fermentations

Lactic fermentation is extremely common in the food world and is the driver of preservation in many pickled foods. These fermentations are anaerobic, and often salt is added to create a preferential environment to lactic acid bacteria, which are able to thrive in saline environment when other bacteria are not. For coffee, as with food, a 2 per cent saline solution is typically used for the fermentation.

Thermal Shock

This is quite a broad term, or at least one with a variety of applications. As the name suggests, this is a process that moves the coffee from hot temperatures to cold ones very rapidly. This can be done at various stages and is typically used as part of an anaerobic process. It may be that the cherries are bathed in hot water and then rapidly cooled before fermentation. In other cases, the pulped coffee is heated and cooled later. Such rapid temperature shifts require a significant investment in both equipment and energy as part of the process.

Co-Fermentations

This has become something of an umbrella term, or perhaps one used without adequate transparency.

Initially, co-fermentations were coffees that had additional ingredients added to the fermentation process to add some additional flavour. An early example was the addition of cinnamon to the tank that led to a distinct cinnamon note in the coffee. Now, these are perhaps better described as 'infused' coffees, as producers are finding more ways to add different flavours to the coffees they produce. They are somewhat controversial, or at least divisive, in the speciality industry. Some appreciate that they have a coffee with a pronounced, unmistakable flavour note in it. Others feel that these flavours are often applied with a heavy hand and can obscure the qualities of the raw coffee.

Hulling and Shipping

When they leave the wet mill, the beans are still enclosed in their layer of parchment (unless they have been processed by the semi-washed method). Now the moisture content is low enough for the coffee to be stored without risk of rotting. Traditionally, coffee is intentionally stored at this stage in reposo (at rest) for 30–60 days.

The traditional practice of holding the coffee in reposo has not been fully researched, although anecdotal evidence suggests that if this step is missed then the coffee can taste green and unpleasant until it has aged further. There is also evidence that this stage influences how well the coffee will age once shipped, probably linked to the moisture content in it.

At the end of this period the coffee is sold and then hulled to remove the parchment. Up until this point the parchment has provided a protective layer, but it also adds weight and bulk to the coffee so it is removed to make shipping less expensive.

The hulling is done mechanically in a dry mill (as opposed to a wet mill where the coffee was processed to remove the flesh and dry the beans – see page 33). Dry mills also usually have equipment to grade and sort the coffee. Once hulled, the green coffee beans can be passed through a machine that examines the colour and rejects any coffee with obvious defects. The coffee can be sorted by bean size using large shaking sieves with varying hole sizes, and finally it may be graded by hand.

This time-consuming process is performed at a large table with a central conveyor, or sometimes on

Above: After the coffee has rested for 30–60 days, it is hulled before being sorted and graded.

large patios, usually by women rather than men. They pick through their allocation of coffee and remove all the defects they can, sometimes within a given time frame controlled by an automated conveyor. This is a slow process, adding significant cost to the coffee, but also massively increasing its quality. It is undeniably a difficult, monotonous job, and it is right that high-quality coffees cost more, so that the people who do this difficult work can be better paid.

Bagging

The coffee is now ready for bagging, into either 60kg (132lb), 69kg (152lb) or 70kg (154lb) jute bags, depending on the country of origin. In some cases, the bags are lined with a protective material, such as a multilayer polyethylene, to make them resistant to moisture, or the coffee can be vacuum-packed and shipped in cardboard boxes. Jute has long remained

Workers sew up 60kg (132lb) jute bags near Yirgacheffe, a coffee-growing community in south-central Ethiopia. Their popular product is exported around the world.

the material of choice because it is cheap and accessible and has little environmental impact. However, as the speciality coffee industry is increasingly concerned with the condition of coffee during shipping and in ongoing storage, new materials are being explored.

Shipping

Coffee is generally transported from its country of origin in shipping containers. These hold up to 300 bags of coffee, although low-quality coffees are sometimes just tipped into a giant lining covering the walls of the container, as the waiting roaster will process the entire container on the day it arrives. The containers are emptied out like dump trucks into a receiving station at the roasting facility.

Transporting coffee in container ships has a relatively low impact on the environment per kilo of coffee (certainly compared to other aspects of the coffee industry) despite container ships not burning clean fuels, and it is also relatively cheap. The downside is that the coffee can be exposed to both heat and moisture that may damage its quality. Shipping is also a complicated process, with bureaucracy in many countries causing exporters, importers and roasters huge amounts of stress as containers of coffee sit for weeks or even months in hot, humid ports waiting for their paperwork. As air freight remains both an environmentally unfriendly and financially unsustainable alternative, many in the speciality coffee industry remain frustrated by this aspect of the business.

Sizing and Grading

Coffee has, in many countries, been graded by size longer than it has been graded by quality. In fact, the two things are still considered related, although technically they are not. Different countries will use different terminology around their grading (see box).

Grading is generally done with sieves, numbered to indicate the size of the perforations. Traditionally, even numbers (such as 14, 16 and 18) were used for Arabica, while odd numbers were used for Robusta.

Cherries   Cascara   Parchment

Commodity Coffee   Decaf (ethyl acetate process)   Robusta

Once the coffee is hulled, it is mechanically shaken through layers of sieves to separate out the different grades. Peaberry (PB) is a grade based on the smallest whole beans (not the broken pieces, though). Peaberries occur when a coffee berry has just one seed inside rather than two. They are considered to have a greater intensity of flavour, although this may not be universally true. It is always an interesting experience to compare the flavour of the peaberry selection of a coffee against that of the larger beans.

While larger beans aren't necessarily better, the advantage of having a relatively small size range is that roasting the coffee is easier, and the resultant roast is likely to be more uniform. This is because coffee beans of different sizes also have different densities. During roasting, the smaller coffee beans, or the less dense ones, will roast much faster than the larger or denser coffee beans. This will mean that at least a portion of the coffee in a mixed batch will not have reached the ideal roast level.

Common Size Grades

These are the most common sizing grades used in the following coffee-producing areas.

Colombia
Supremo and Excelso are very common grades. Excelso is screen sizes 14–16 and is smaller than Supremo which is sizes 16–18 (or above). Colombia pioneered how it sold its coffee and uses grades like this to emphasize its quality (see page 260).

Central America
Here the larger sizes are traditionally referred to as Superior (again, emphasizing quality through size). Peaberries are known as caracol.

Africa
The largest screen size is generally considered AA, then AB and then A. Coffee-producing countries such as Kenya have a strong focus on quality relating to size grading, and AA lots tend to sell for higher prices in their internal auction system.

Natural   Washed   Honey

Wet Hulled   Pacamara   Old Brown Java

Decaffeination

Decaffeination is a process of removing the caffeine from coffee using one of a variety of solvents. This happens before the coffee is roasted. There is not a huge number of decaffeination plants around the world, and only a few of them are in coffee-producing countries. The additional logistics involved, coupled with the additional process, is why decaffeinated coffee is often more expensive.

Caffeine is the world's most popular psychoactive drug, yet it is completely unregulated, and no one really has any idea how much of it they are taking. With a greater cultural focus on sleep quality and wellness, there has been renewed interest in decaffeinated coffee in recent years. There have been two challenges in its adoption. First, there is always going to be scepticism around a chemical process. I believe these concerns have no foundation, once you look more deeply into the science. Second, high-quality decaf has been broadly overlooked for a long time by the coffee industry. This is a great shame, as the decaf coffee drinker is perhaps the purest, most dedicated coffee drinker – choosing a cup of coffee when it offers nothing beyond flavour in return. For too long those coffee lovers have been served poor-quality coffee – inferior raw coffees, badly roasted and often badly brewed by cafés. That is changing, and there is no reason to accept a lower-quality coffee simply because it is decaffeinated.

While he was not the first to isolate caffeine from coffee, the German coffee merchant Ludwig Roselius (1874–1943) is generally credited as the inventor of decaffeination. He noticed that a shipment of coffee that had been soaked in sea water had lost much of its caffeine but little, in his opinion, of its flavour. He patented a process in 1906 and sold decaffeinated coffee through his company based in Bremen, Germany, called Kaffee Hag. The brand, if not the company, continues to this day.

There are several different methods of decaffeinating coffee, each with various pros and cons. Some methods are more commonly used with speciality coffee, and as such I will cover them in a little more detail. The most common process uses a solvent called methylene chloride. Unsurprisingly, the name of this chemical is rarely put on a bag of coffee. There is a good amount of fearmongering, because in high concentrations methylene chloride is not a safe or pleasant chemical. However, after processing, the amount legally allowed to be retained in the raw coffee is incredibly low, and even then very little of that will survive the roasting process. This does not stop periodic efforts around the world to ban the process.

There are two approaches to decaffeination: direct and indirect decaffeination. In direct decaffeination the raw coffee is mixed with a solvent to extract the caffeine. In the indirect method, water is used to dissolve everything, including the caffeine, from the coffee and that solution is decaffeinated separately, before being returned to the coffee to be absorbed into it. This is commonly used with water-based processes other than the Swiss water process (see page 47).

With all decaffeination processes the raw coffee must be steam-treated before decaffeination. This process increases the overall water content of the raw coffee and is required to 'open up' the coffee bean to make the process more efficient. After decaffeination, the coffee will have to be dried to a suitable moisture level (usually 10–12 per cent moisture, as it would be dried to for export from its country of origin). There is some loss of quality due to this part of the process, but it is relatively small. Decaf can be sweet, complex and very enjoyable coffee.

Ethyl Acetate/The Sugar Cane Process

The ethyl acetate processs is commonly used in speciality coffee because of the quality of the results as well as the fact that there is a plant operating in Colombia. Ethyl acetate is a naturally occurring compound, often found in fruits like apples and pears, and is a by-product of molasses fermentation. This is where the process picks up its common name, the sugar cane process. Ethyl acetate is an ester of ethanol (alcohol) and acetic acid (vinegar). It is used in a direct process as it is quite a selective solvent, meaning it extracts caffeine but not a lot else. After decaffeination, steam is used to heat the raw coffee to cause any

Above: This 1923 advertisement for Kaffee Hag reads, 'Firstly, quite excellent. Secondly, caffeine-free.'

remaining ethyl acetate to evaporate, as its boiling point is much lower than that of water. The coffee can then be dried, and the ethyl acetate can have the caffeine removed and thus be reused.

Carbon Dioxide

Carbon dioxide (CO_2) is a very selective solvent for caffeine, but not a very efficient one. There are a variety of approaches to using CO_2, and all will require compressing it to the point of being a liquid. Depending on the decaffeination plant, it may be subcritical or supercritical. The critical point of carbon dioxide is 31.1°C and 73.8 bars of pressure. Above this point it becomes a supercritical fluid and has the properties of both a gas and a liquid. Subcritical is below the critical point. Removing caffeine from the CO_2 is relatively easy – once it is returned to a gaseous state from a liquid, it is no longer able to hold on to the caffeine, so bubbling it through water is an effective way to offload the caffeine into a different solvent.

The Swiss Water Process

This is a notably different water-based decaffeination process because it is a direct process. First, a batch of coffee is used to create a 'green coffee extract'. This contains all the soluble material in the coffee, as well as the caffeine. This is decaffeinated, using active carbon rods, and the initial batch of raw coffee must be discarded.

Soaking new coffee in this green coffee extract will cause only the caffeine to dissolve out of the bean, because there is no osmotic pressure driving other compounds into the solution because they are already there. By constantly rotating and decaffeinating the green coffee extract you can slowly decaffeinate the coffee.

Natural Versus Synthetic Caffine

Most decaffeination plants will have a caffeine reclamation process. With anywhere between 1 and 4 per cent of the coffee, by weight, being caffeine the output of these plants can be quite large. That caffeine will be sold as 'natural caffeine' and used in a variety of products. There is now synthetic caffeine, which is cheaper to produce. The caffeine molecule is identical; it is just derived in a different way. Generally, products using natural caffeine will be labelled as such on the ingredients list.

How Coffee is Traded

It is often quoted that coffee is the second-most traded commodity in the world. It is not and, whether based on frequency or monetary value, is not even in the top five. Nonetheless, how coffee is traded has become a focus for ethical trade organizations. The relationship between the buyer and the producer is often seen as an example of where higher-income countries exploit lower-income countries. However, while there are undoubtedly those who wish to exploit the system, there are a great many who feel frustrated to participate in a system that feels endemically unfair.

The price paid for coffee is generally quoted in US dollars per pound in weight ($/lb). There is something of a global price for coffee, often referred to as the C-price. This is the price for commodity coffee (see page 6) being traded on the New York Stock Exchange. Coffee production is often discussed in terms of bags. A bag usually weighs 60kg (132lb) if it comes from Africa, Indonesia or Brazil, 69kg (152lb) if it comes from Central America, and 70kg (154lb) if from Colombia. While bags may be the units of purchase, on the macro scale coffee is usually traded by the shipping container, which contains up to 300 bags.

Contrary to popular belief, a rather small percentage of coffee is actually traded on the New York Stock Exchange, but the C-price does provide a sort of global minimum price for coffee, the minimum a producer would be willing to accept for his or her coffee. Prices for particular lots of coffee often have a differential added to the C-price, a kind of premium. Certain countries have, historically, been able to get higher differentials for their coffee, including Costa Rica and Colombia, although this type of trading is still mostly focused on commodity-grade rather than speciality coffee. The problem with basing everything on the C-price is that this price is somewhat fluid. Usually, prices are determined by supply and demand, and to some extent this is true of the C-price. As global demand increased at the end of the 2000s, the market saw an increase in price and coffee supply began to look scarce. This produced one of the highest spikes in the price of coffee, reaching above $3.00/lb in 2010. While that remains the highest price seen in recent times, since 2020 prices have been a little higher than the preceding decade's price.

This 2010 price wasn't simply about supply and demand, however; it was also influenced by other factors, not least the influx of cash into the industry from traders and hedge fund managers who saw an opportunity to make money. This produced a volatile market, the like of which had never really been seen before. From that spike, prices steadily declined again to levels that can be considered unsustainable for profit. The C-price for coffee does not reflect the cost of production, and as such producers may end up in

a position where they lose money growing coffee. It is also worth remembering that the cost of production will vary dramatically based on the size and type of farm, as well as the country the farm is in. There is no simply calculated, universal cost of production despite the fact that there is a universal price used for its sale.

There have been a number of reactions to this problem that have looked to create certifications around better pricing and better conditions on the farms as well. The most successful has been the fair trade movement – dominated by a loose association of four organizations including Fairtrade International – although there are many other sustainable coffee certification schemes, including those of the Organic Trade Association and the Rainforest Alliance.

Above: Coffee bags being loaded onto ships at the port of Santos, Brazil, in 1937. Nowadays coffee is usually transported in shipping containers, which hold around 300 bags each.

Fairtrade

Fair trade has been a successful idea, and Fair Trade or Fairtrade is a strong brand, but many consumers are not aware of what the certification precisely guarantees. The idea that coffee may be exploitative is relatively broadly understood, so many people are looking for a shorthand to a more ethical purchase. Many of them presume that the promises of Fair Trade are far wider reaching than they actually are, and that any coffee could (in theory) be certified as

Fair Trade. This is not the case. And to make matters worse, it is easy for detractors to allege that the farmer is not getting the premium passed down to him because of the complex nature of financial transactions within the coffee industry.

Fair Trade guarantees to pay a base price that it considers sustainable, or a $0.15/lb premium above the C-price if the market rises above Fair Trade's base price. Fair Trade's model is designed to work only with cooperatives of coffee growers, and as such cannot certify single estates that produce coffee. Critics complain about a lack of traceability or true guarantee that the money definitely goes to the producers and isn't diverted through corruption. Others criticize the model for providing no incentive to farmers to increase the quality of their coffee. These are not entirely justified criticisms. That the scope of the certification does not include quality, or put quality to the forefront, does not mean that the producers are not focusing on quality – especially as quality will further increase the price for the coffee that the Fair Trade guarantee goes on top of.

However, the speciality industry has not adopted these kinds of standards or certifications widely. As the primary demand made of the coffee is its quality, many feel that their interests simply do not align. In addition, speciality prices tend to be significantly higher than the typical Fair Trade price, although those coffees will also have a higher cost of production, too.

The Speciality Coffee Industry

A number of different terms are used to describe the various ways in which speciality roasters are buying their coffee and their relationships with the growers.

Relationship Coffee is used to describe an ongoing relationship between producer and roaster. There is usually a dialogue and collaboration to work towards better-quality coffee and more sustainable pricing. For this arrangement to have the desired positive impact, the roaster would have to be buying the coffee in sufficient quantities. Many smaller roasters may build relationships early on, though, hoping to bring more scale to their buying as their business grows.

Direct Trade is a term that has arisen in the last 20 or so years, where roasters wish to communicate that they bought the coffee directly from the producer. It is less popular now than it was, in part because it rarely was truly direct. To transact with a producer directly is very difficult, because coffee has a long supply chain and a producer often has to subcontract aspects of the post-harvest processing or will have already sold their coffee to someone who is doing the post-harvest processing. Many farmers do not have their own wet mills, and so part of the final price of the coffee will include the wet milling and dry milling. In addition, there are both exporters and importers and logistics companies involved in the transaction – all fulfilling

Auction Coffees

In the first two decades of the 21st century, there was a slow and steady increase in coffees sold through internet auction. The typical format for this involves holding a competition in a producing country wherein farmers can submit small lots of their best coffee. These are graded and ranked by juries of coffee tasters, usually a local jury for the first round and then an international cadre of coffee buyers who fly in for the final round. The very best coffees are sold at auction and generally achieve very high prices, especially the winning lot. Most auctions display the price paid for the coffee online, allowing full traceability behind the whole process. The most successful of these is the Cup of Excellence.

In many ways these kinds of auctions began to act as a kind of coffee roaster and coffee producer dating service, if you can forgive the metaphor. They connected those looking for great coffee with those producing it and in many cases led to the establishing of long-term coffee buying relationships. Demand and interest around these auctions are not as strong as they once were, due to the needs of both parties having been somewhat met by now. The idea of an auction has also been embraced by a small number of coffee-producing estates that have managed to build up a brand based on the quality of their coffee. Once they have sufficient interest from international buyers, they can make an auction work. This idea was pioneered by a farm in Panama called Hacienda La Esmeralda, a farm that had previously set records for the huge prices paid for its competition-winning coffees (see page 25).

vital roles. If anything, Direct Trade implies that the price paid by the roasters was agreed between the coffee buyer and the producer, although it may have been paid to someone else along the chain with the understanding that the money will flow back to the producers.

Fairly Traded is a term you see less and less, in part because speciality coffee's messaging around buying has become more widely understood, and so there is less value in slyly leveraging the brand of Fair Trade. This isn't a very commonly used term, except in situations where a customer asks whether a particular coffee is Fair Trade.

The idea behind all these buying models is for roasters to try to buy more traceably, to remove unnecessary or exploitative intermediaries from the supply chain, and to pay prices that match the increased costs of production for higher-quality coffee. However, these terms and ideas are not without their critics. Without third-party certification it can be difficult to ascertain whether a roaster is actually buying the way they say they are. Some roasters may buy coffees that have been kept traceable by importers and brokers, and claim this as a Direct Trade or Relationship Coffee.

There are no guarantees of a long-term relationship for the producers either, with some coffee buyers simply chasing the best lots of coffee they can each year. However, at least they are paying handsomely for it. This type of approach makes long-term investment in quality difficult, and it should also be noted that some intermediaries provide a valuable service, especially to those who are working on a smaller scale. The logistics of moving coffee around the world require a level of specialization and skill that many small roasters simply do not have.

As more and more companies become transparent with the prices they are paying, with coffee it is worth touching on a couple of key terms used in transparency reports or on websites displaying the information about a particular coffee.

Free on Board (FOB) Pricing is the price paid for the coffee at the point of export. The coffee has been fully processed and milled, graded and bagged for export at this point. This price does not include the costs of onward freight to the consuming country. This is not the price the farmer receives for the coffee, unless that farmer is able to process their coffee right through to an exported state. This is extremely rare, although more and more producers – speciality producers in particular – are able to wet-mill and dry their own coffee. The percentage of this price that makes it back to the producer will vary quite dramatically. A coffee roaster buying the coffee may struggle to find the exact percentage going to the producer, but this is a point of accurate traceability for them to share in their buying process. This price is what is typically used in coffee-buying contracts.

Farm Gate Pricing is a more accurate price, in terms of understanding what the producer receives. However, in order to gauge the true value of this price, you would need to know how much of the post-harvest work a producer had done. A producer receiving $3/lb as a farm gate price for their coffee that they sold to a wet mill is doing significantly better than a producer who received $3/lb for their finished dried coffee that they sold to a dry mill.

Advice to Consumers

When buying coffee, it is difficult for consumers to ascertain how ethically sourced a particular coffee really is. Some speciality roasters have now developed buying programmes certified by third parties, but most have not. It is fairly safe to presume that if the coffee has been kept traceable, has the producer's name(s) on it, or at least the name of the farm, cooperative or factory, then a better price has been paid. The level of transparency you should expect will vary country by country and is covered in more detail in each of the sections on the producing countries. If you find a roaster whose coffee you like, you should be able to ask them for more information about how they source it. Most are more than happy to share this information and are often extremely proud of the work they do.

Harvested coffee cherries are sorted and cleaned to remove unripe and overripe fruit as well as leaves, soil and twigs. This is often done by hand, using a sieve to winnow away unwanted materials.

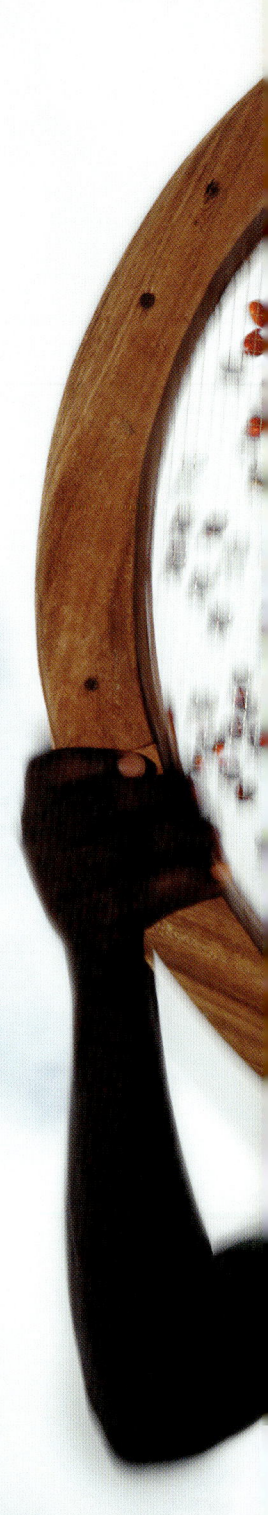

A Short History of Coffee Drinking

This book discusses the history of coffee cultivation in producing countries around the world, but it is also important to consider the growth in demand that went alongside it. Coffee is a truly global beverage, and it is common to hear the claim that it is the second most popular drink in the world after water. While there is no evidence to support this, the ubiquity of coffee in one form or another makes it at least plausible.

The origins of coffee drinking are frustratingly vague. While there is some evidence of the fruit of the coffee plant being eaten in Ethiopia going back as far as the 6th century CE, balled up with animal fat and consumed as an invigorating trail snack, we are missing a key piece of the puzzle: we have no idea who decided to take the seed of the fruit, roast it, grind it to a powder, steep that powder in hot water and drink the resulting concoction. It's an astonishing leap, and a mystery that will probably never be solved.

There is evidence of coffee drinking, as we would understand it, in the late 15th century, but little to back up the anecdote that the first coffeehouse was Kiva Han, opened in 1475 in Constantinople. If this story is true, the coffee would have been grown in Yemen, and we know that consumption did spread into the Arabian peninsula and beyond. Coffee quickly became entwined with political and religious subversion, and coffeehouses were banned in Mecca in 1511 and in Cairo in 1532. In both cases, popular demand won out and these bans were soon lifted.

Right: Cafés serving Italian-style coffee were a novelty in 1950s London. With coffee enjoying a resurgence of popularity in recent years, interest in coffee shops and how to make the perfect brew has increased again.

Above: The first coffee houses opened in Europe in the mid 1600s, and coffee soon replaced beer and wine as the breakfast drink of choice. In the New World, the popularity of coffee surged after the Boston Tea Party in 1773, when drinking coffee became a patriotic act.

Coffee Reaches Europe and Beyond

Coffee drinking wouldn't spread to Europe until the 1600s and coffee consumption, for medicinal purposes rather than for pleasure, predates coffeehouses in Europe. Coffee would have been traded through Venice in the early 1600s, but a coffeehouse didn't open there until 1645. The first coffeehouse in London opened in 1652 and began a hundred-year love affair between the drink and the city. Coffee unquestionably inspired culture, art, trade and politics and left a lasting impact on the city itself.

In France, it was the influence of fashion that spread coffee drinking. Coffee had been gifted to the court of Louis XIV (reigned 1643–1715), and its growing popularity there spread the habit of coffee drinking into Paris.

Vienna was another city that would develop a rich café culture in the late 1600s. The story of how the first café in Vienna, the Blue Bottle, used coffee beans left behind by the Ottomans fleeing after the failed siege of Vienna in 1683 is charming but probably not true; recent evidence suggests the first café there opened in 1685.

One key moment in the spread of coffee drinking and coffee culture actually revolved around tea. The Boston Tea Party in 1773, when American colonists protested against British oppression by attacking merchant ships in Boston Harbor and throwing chests of tea overboard, was not just an important rejection of the British Empire, but also marked the moment that coffee became a patriotic drink in the United States. A rapidly growing population meant a rapidly growing market and made the country increasingly influential in the coffee industry in the years to come.

Change Through Innovation

The United States was also where key innovations came from that allowed coffee to be an affordable staple in every home around the world. In 1900 a company called Hill Bros. began packing coffee into vacuum-sealed cans. Extending the shelf life this way meant fewer households would have to roast their own coffee, but made business more difficult for small local roasting companies.

A year later a Japanese chemist named Satori Kato patented his process for producing instant, or soluble, coffee. Until very recently he was thought to have been the first to produce it, but recent discoveries now credit the invention to David Strang in New Zealand in 1890. The process elevated convenience above quality, but it made coffee drinking easier for many, if not necessarily cheaper. Today instant coffee is still incredibly popular around the world.

In Europe, key innovations focused more on the café than coffee at home. There are various claimants to the first espresso machine, but patents using these principles began to be filed from 1884 onwards. The Italian mechanic Luigi Bezzera would patent his machine in 1901, and he is often credited as having invented the espresso machine.

These machines allowed café operators to make lots of cups of coffee, of a similar size and strength to filter coffee, very quickly. The great leap forward in espresso technology would come with the use of a large spring to produce very high pressures. The claim to this innovation belongs to another Italian, Achille Gaggia, in 1945, although how he acquired the patent remains a little murky. This high-pressure brewing produced espresso as we know it today: a small, concentrated cup of coffee topped with a deep brown foam, called crema.

The espresso bar boom that happened in many cities in the 1950s and 1960s was as much cultural as it was about the consumption of coffee. However, from a technical perspective, espresso brewing was perfect for cafés because one machine could now rapidly produce a whole range of drinks.

Coffee Today

It would be impossible to write about modern coffee drinking without discussing Starbucks. The company's roots were in roasting and selling coffee beans from a shop in Seattle, but it was transformed by Howard Schultz into the global phenomenon that we know today. Schultz claimed to be inspired by his travels to Italy, although the modern Starbucks experience would be unrecognizable to a native Italian. Starbucks, and businesses like it, undoubtedly paved the way for the growth in speciality coffee that we see around the world today. Starbucks made coffee an even more popular out-of-home drink and changed expectations for what a cup of coffee could cost.

What defines modern speciality coffee is the focus on where coffee comes from, and how that impacts its taste. This focus has influenced how cafés brew, sell and serve cups of coffee. Coffee drinking has evolved from simple morning stimulation into an expression of self, an expression of values or of conscious consumption. Coffee drinking is now woven into a myriad of cultures around the world.

Below: Today, there is a coffee shop for every taste, from the mass-market purveyors of sweet, creamy coffee-flavoured drinks to the craft coffee shops selling single-estate pour-overs.

Part Two

From Bean to Cup

Coffee Roasting

Roasting is one of the most fascinating aspects of the coffee industry. It takes the green coffee seed, which has almost no flavour beyond a quite unpleasant vegetal taste, and transforms it into an incredibly aromatic, astonishingly complex coffee bean. The smell of freshly roasted coffee is evocative, intoxicating and all-round delicious. This section deals with roasting on a commercial scale; see page 130 for information about home roasting.

A huge amount of research has gone into the commercial roasting of relatively low-quality coffee, most of it to do with the efficiency of the process and the methods used in producing instant soluble coffee. As these coffees aren't particularly interesting or flavoursome, very little work has been done on the development of sweetness or the retention of flavours unique to a particular coffee's terroir or variety. Speciality roasters around the world are, by and large, self-trained, and many have learned their trade through careful trial and error. Each roasting company has its own style and aesthetic, or 'roast philosophy'. For a while there was perhaps a little too much homogeneity in roasting styles within speciality coffee, but as the sheer number of roasting companies around the world has continued to increase dramatically, we have seen a greater diversity of roasting styles and approaches on offer to the customer. It is also slightly more common to see one speciality roasting company offering more than one style of roasting, although by and large most tend to roast within a fairly narrow band of styles and roast colours.

Fast or Slow, Light or Dark?

To simplify matters, it can be said that the roast of a coffee is a product of the final colour of the coffee bean (light or dark), and the time it took to get to that colour (fast or slow). To simply describe a coffee as a light roast is not enough, as the roast could have been relatively fast or it could have been quite slow. The flavour will be quite different depending on how quickly the coffee is roasted, even though the bean may look the same.

A whole host of different chemical reactions occur during roasting, and several of them reduce the weight of the coffee, not least of course the evaporation of moisture. Slow roasting (14–20 minutes) will result in a greater loss of weight (about 16–18 per cent) than faster roasting, which can be achieved in as little as 90 seconds. Generally, speciality roasting is closer to slower roasting times than to faster roasting times – although equipment choice, and the size of the batch being roasted, will play a big role in the time a roasting batch takes.

The roasting process can be controlled to determine three key aspects of how the coffee will taste: acidity, sweetness and bitterness. It is generally agreed that the longer a coffee is roasted, the less acidity it will have in the end. Conversely, bitterness will slowly increase the longer a coffee is roasted, and will definitely increase the darker a coffee is roasted. Sweetness is presented as a bell curve, peaking in between the highs of acidity and bitterness. A good roaster can manipulate where a coffee may be sweetest in relation to its roast degree, producing either a very sweet, yet also quite acidic coffee, or a very sweet, but more muted cup by using a different roast profile. However, adjusting a roast profile can never improve a poor-quality coffee.

One particularly frustrating aspect of talking about roast colour in coffee is that there are no universally agreed boundaries to roast colour. What one roaster might call 'medium', another roaster may call 'light'. Generally, speciality coffee tends to roast lighter than commercial coffee, and also have its boundaries between light, medium and dark overall a little lighter in colour.

Opposite: The roasting process affects acidity, sweetness and bitterness of bean flavours, as well as the aromas and flavours of the coffee. Roasters seek to balance these aspects through carefully controlled use of heat and timing during a roast.

The Stages of Roasting

There are several key stages during roasting, and the speed at which a particular coffee passes through each of these stages is described as its roast profile. Many coffee roasters track their roast profiles carefully so they can replicate them to within very tight boundaries of temperature and time. The stages that I will describe here are descriptions of the journey that coffee goes through, and are necessary simplifications of the underlying chemistry and physics involved.

STAGE 1: Drying

Raw coffee contains 10–12 per cent water by weight, spread evenly through the dense structure of the bean. Coffee won't turn brown in the presence of water, and in fact this is true of browning reactions when cooking anything. After the coffee is loaded into a roaster, it takes some time for the beans to absorb sufficient heat to start evaporating the water, and the drying process therefore requires a large amount of heat and energy. The coffee barely changes in look or smell for these first few minutes of roasting. Evaporating water does require a great deal of energy, and not all the water that turns to vapour is able to escape the coffee bean immediately, which can lead to a slow build-up of pressure inside the coffee bean.

STAGE 2: Yellowing

Once most of the water has been driven out of the beans, the first browning reactions can begin. At this stage, the coffee beans are still very dense and have an aroma of basmati rice; they can smell a little like bread. Soon the beans start to expand and their thin papery skins – the chaff – flakes off. The chaff is separated from the roasting beans by the air flowing through the roaster and is collected and safely removed to prevent the risk of fire. These first two roasting stages are very important: if the coffee is not properly dried, then it will not roast evenly during the next stages and while the outside of each bean is well roasted the inside will essentially be undercooked. This coffee will taste unpleasant, with a combination of bitterness from the outside, and a sour and grassy flavour coming from the underdeveloped inside. Slowing the roasting process after this will not fix the problem as different parts of the coffee will always be progressing at different rates.

STAGE 3: First Crack

Once the browning reactions begin to gather speed, there is a build-up of gases (mostly carbon dioxide) and water vapour inside the bean. Once the pressure gets too great, the bean will break open, making a popping noise and it will have started to grow in volume. From this point onwards, the familiar coffee flavours develop, and the roaster can choose to end the roast at any point. A roaster will see a decrease in the rate at which the coffee is increasing in temperature at this point, even though they may be adding a similar amount of heat. Failure to add enough heat can stall the roast and 'bake' the coffee, resulting in poor cup quality.

STAGE 4: Roast Development

After the first crack stage, the beans will be much smoother on the surface but not entirely so. This stage of the roast determines the end colour of the beans and the roast degree. Here the roaster can determine the balance of acidity and bitterness in the end product as the acids in the beans are rapidly degrading while the level of bitterness is increasing as the roast continues.

STAGE 5: Second Crack

At this point the beans begin to crack again, but now with a quieter and snappier sound. This is because the bean is much more fragile, and so gases expanding are able to break out of the bean more easily, hence the change in sound. Once you reach second crack, the oils will be driven to the surface of the coffee bean. Much of the acidity will have been lost and a new kind of flavour is developing, often referred to as the generic 'roast' flavour. This flavour doesn't depend on the kind of coffee used as it is a result of essentially charring or burning the coffee, rather than working with its intrinsic flavours. Progressing a roast significantly past the second crack can result in the beans catching fire, which is extremely dangerous, especially with large commercial roasting machines.

There are terms used in coffee roasting such as 'French roast' or 'Italian roast'. Both these terms are used to indicate very dark roasts, typically high in body and bitterness but with many of the characteristics of the raw coffees lost. While many enjoy coffees roasted in this manner, these kinds of roasts are less suitable for exploring the flavours and characteristics of high-quality coffees from different origins.

Raw Coffee
10–12 per cent moisture, no coffee flavour yet and very dense/hard.

Before First Crack
The coffee is now browning, but there is a lot of harsh acidity/plant-like flavour in the coffee beans.

Drying
Water is starting to evaporate, but no flavours/aromas developed yet.

First Crack
The coffee starts to pop and expand in size due to the build up of gas pressure inside the bean.

Yellowing
The coffee has started to roast. This stage often smells like basmati rice.

Development
The coffee now smells/tastes like coffee but may need more time to develop sweetness and ideal flavours.

Yellowing
Most of the water has now been removed and the coffee is starting to brown slightly.

Development
The beans are increasingly smooth on the outside, and the aromas are increasingly pleasant.

Yellowing
Despite starting to look brown, the aromas at this stage are more like bread than coffee.

Developed
Where a coffee achieves ideal development is often down to the opinion of a roaster. For many, this is sufficiently developed, while others may wish to roast the coffee for longer.

Coffee Roasting

Sugars in Coffee

Many people talk about sweetness when describing a coffee, and it is important to understand what happens to the naturally occurring sugars during the roasting process.

Green coffee can contain reasonable quantities of simple sugars. Not all sugars are necessarily sweet to the taste, although simple sugars usually are. Sugars are quite reactive at roasting temperatures and, once the water has evaporated out of the bean, the sugars can begin to react to the heat in different ways. Some go through caramelization reactions, creating the caramel notes found in certain coffees. It should be noted, however, that the sugars that react this way become less sweet and will eventually start to add bitterness. Other sugars react with the proteins in the coffee in what are known as Maillard reactions. This is an umbrella term covering the browning reactions

Left: Coffee vendors have plied their aromatic trade for centuries, as depicted in this 18th-century engraving of a Parisian street hawker by Anne Claude Philippe de Tubières, Comte de Caylus.

seen in roasting a piece of meat in the oven, for example, but also when roasting cocoa or coffee beans.

By the time coffee has finished the first crack stage, there are few or no simple sugars left. They will all have been involved in various reactions resulting in a huge number of aromatic compounds. You might still experience sweetness in the roasted coffee when you drink it. This sweetness is usually a different kind of sweetness from simple sugar sweetness. If you add even a gram of table sugar to a coffee, you can immediately detect that it has a different kind of sweetness to the one inherent in the coffee. Coffee is a complex olfactory experience, and that perceived sweetness comes from not only tastes in the mouth, detected by the taste buds, but also from the olfactory bulb which allows us to experience flavours.

Acids in Coffee

Green coffee contains many different types of acid, some of which are pleasant to taste and some that are not. Of particular importance to the roaster are the chlorogenic acids (CGAs). One of the key goals of roasting is to try to react these unpleasant acids away without creating negative flavours or driving off the desirable aromatic components of the coffee. Some other acids are stable throughout the roasting process, such as quinic acid, which can add a pleasing, clean finish to a coffee.

Aromatic Compounds in Coffee

Most of the aromatics in a good cup of coffee are created during roasting through one of three groups of processes: Maillard reactions, caramelization and Strecker degradation, another type of chemical reaction involving amino acids. These are all brought about by the heat during roasting and can result in the creation of over 800 different volatile aromatic compounds that flavour the cup of coffee. Although more aromatic compounds have been recorded in coffee than in wine, an individual coffee will have only a selection of these different volatiles. That said, the smell of freshly roasted coffee is so complex that all attempts to manufacture a realistic, synthetic version of this smell have failed.

Roast Profile Graph

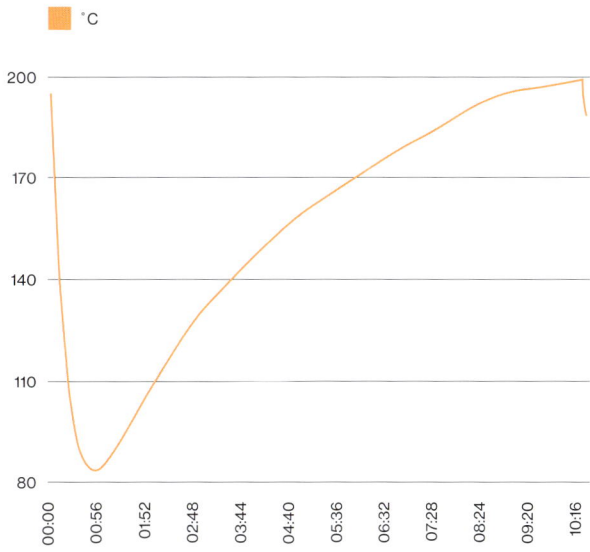

Above: The x-axis shows the time in minutes, the y-axis the temperature in Celsius. Roasters track the temperature during roasting: by changing how quickly a roast progresses at different times, they can alter the flavour of the final coffee.

Cooling and Quenching

After roasting, the coffee must be cooled quickly to prevent over-roasting or the development of negative (or 'baked') flavours. In small-batch roasting this is often achieved using a cooling tray, which rapidly draws large volumes of ambient air through the coffee to cool it down. With large batches of coffee, air alone is not effective enough: a mist of water is sprayed on to the coffee, and as it evaporates and turns to steam, it draws heat out of the beans. All of this water should immediately evaporate, and in doing so pull a lot of heat energy away from the coffee bean. Done correctly, this has no negative effect on cup quality, but the coffee will age a little more quickly. Unfortunately, however, some less scrupulous companies add more water than necessary to increase the weight of the beans and add monetary value to the batch. This is both unethical and bad for cup quality.

Types of Coffee Roasters

Coffee tends to be roasted close to where it will be consumed, as green coffee is more stable than roasted beans – coffee is at its best when used within a month of roasting. Roasting methods vary, but the two most commonly used types of machines are drum roasters and hot-air or fluid-bed roasters.

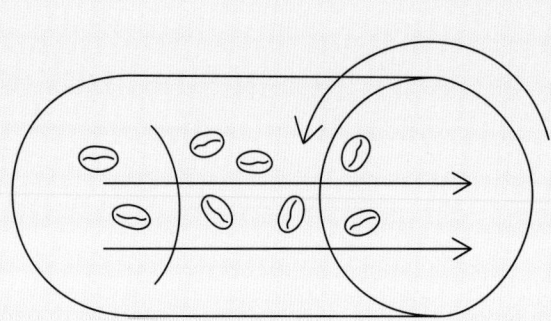

Drum Roasters
Invented around the beginning of the 20th century, drum roasters are popular with craft roasters, as they are able to roast at slower speeds. A metal drum rotates above a flame, moving the coffee beans constantly during the process to aid even roasting. The roaster can control the gas flame, and therefore the heat being applied to the drum, and can also control the flow of air through the drum, which dictates how quickly the heat is transferred to the coffee. Drum roasters come in a range of different sizes, the largest being able to roast up to around 500kg (1,100lb) per batch.

Hybrid Roasters
In speciality coffee there is an increasing usage of a kind of drum roaster that is somewhat of a hybrid of the drum roaster and fluid-bed roaster. The coffee is mixed using a drum, but the air is not heated by a flame under the drum. Usually, the heat source is away from the coffee, and the flame is also used as an afterburner, to remove smoke from the exhaust air. This means that the drum itself is not hotter than the air flowing through it, which is different from a drum roaster where the drum itself can get very hot. The result is that, with hybrid roasters, less heat is transferred via conduction. The most common roaster of this kind in speciality coffee is manufactured by American company Loring.

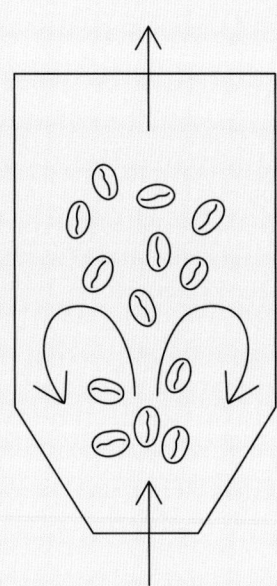

Fluid-Bed Roasters
Invented by the American engineer Michael Sivetz in the 1970s, fluid-bed roasters tumble and heat the beans by pumping jets of hot air through the machine. Roast times are significantly shorter than in a drum roaster, so the beans tend to swell a little more as a result. The higher volume of air conducts heat more quickly into the coffee, which means that this roasting process is faster than drum roasting.

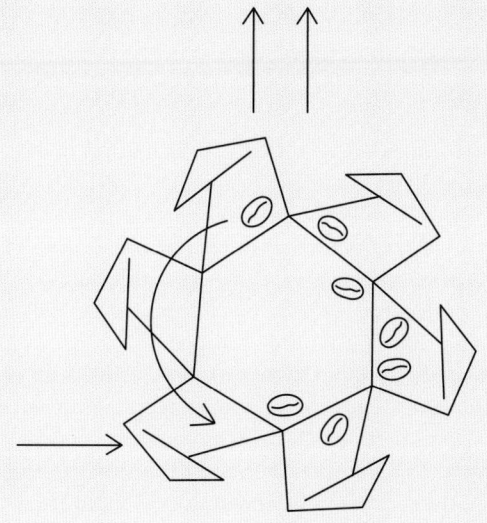

Tangential Roasters

Built by a company called Probat, tangential roasters are similar to large drum roasters but have internal shovels to mix the coffee evenly during heating, which allows a bigger batch to be roasted effectively. The capacity isn't much larger than a very large drum roaster, but this type is able to achieve faster roasting speeds.

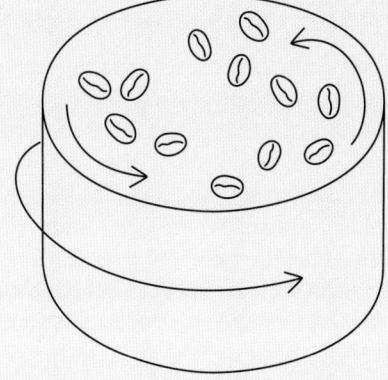

Centrifugal Roasters

Centrifugal roasters allow very large quantities of coffee to be roasted extremely quickly. The coffee is placed inside a large inverted cone, which spins to draw the coffee beans up the walls as they are heated. The beans are then flung back down into the middle of the cone to repeat their journey. Roasting times can be as little as 90 seconds using machines like this. Roasting at very high speeds minimizes weight loss and increases the amount of coffee that can be extracted from the beans, which is important when making instant soluble coffee. Roasting at these speeds is not designed to produce the best possible cup.

Buying and Storing Coffee

Coffee buying can seem complex, and the incredible breadth of choice can make it all seem a little intimidating. In addition, with prices of coffee – particularly speciality coffee – increasing, these days the stakes around buying a bag of coffee are a little higher than they used to be.

Here I will cover some key points to consider, to help you more reliably pick a bag of coffee that you will really enjoy.

Where to Buy Coffee

There are three key places you are likely to buy coffee, and each has its own advantages and disadvantages.

Direct from roasters: For speciality coffee, online retail has become the primary place that bags of coffee are sold. Buying from a roaster directly has a few advantages – the coffee will likely be very fresh, as many companies will roast to order. This is also likely to be the best price you will see for that coffee. You may however have shipping costs to cover, and it is hard to discuss your options with anyone.

From cafés: Many speciality coffee shops will carry retail bags of coffee, usually from the roaster or multiple roasters who supply the coffee they serve. Alongside online stores, this is my other recommended place to buy coffee. Chances are that you will be able to talk to someone who can give you guidance on which coffee suits your needs best. Often, cafés will throw in a free drink with a bag of coffee, which is always a welcome bonus. The borderline downside is that the coffee on those shelves may be a few days old. This, however, may be no bad thing. While coffee roasted to order is great, coffee will taste better with some rest after roasting, so if you need a bag to brew straight away this is a great option.

From supermarkets: Supermarkets remain the primary point of sale for commercial coffees but sell a much smaller percentage of speciality coffee. Some more specialized grocery companies may well offer speciality coffees alongside more commercial ones. However, they all have one key downside: the coffee can often be quite old by the time it makes it to the shelf. Commercial coffee generally won't have a 'roasted on' date on it; instead, it will usually have a 'best before' date that may be 12, 18 or 24 months from its roasting date. Generally, all speciality coffee will have a roast date, which will help you find something fresh. This is the cost of the convenience of buying coffee when grocery shopping.

When it comes to picking a bag you will like, it is worth considering what the information on the bag is implying about the taste of the coffee. In my experience there are a few key characteristics of coffee that will determine whether or not someone will like it. These are bitterness, acidity, mouthfeel, and whether or not the coffee has fermented fruit flavours. These attributes are rarely listed explicitly, so we have to interpret the label to discern the more useful information. There are no ideal flavours or tastes in coffee, simply those that you enjoy. Some people find acidity in coffee unpleasant and deeply off-putting, while others chase coffees with lots of vibrant juicy acidity. The goal for me is to help you understand the style of coffee you enjoy, and then to help you explore coffee more easily to find something you will enjoy even more!

Strength Guides

You will often see a strength guide on the side of a bag of coffee, especially those on offer in supermarkets. These have nothing to do with strength, which is really about how much coffee you use to brew a cup, but more to do with the level of bitterness you can expect to find in that particular coffee. This is usually determined by the roast level of the coffee – light-roasted coffees usually have lower strength ratings and dark-roasted coffees have higher strength ratings. Similarly, you would expect lower acidity levels in those 'higher-strength' coffees. Most of the time a strength guide is an indicator that that bag of coffee is not a speciality coffee, although this is not universal. We will cover what strength really means in the section on Brewing Basics on page 84.

Espresso Roasts Versus Filter Coffee Roasts

You will often see coffee sold with some reference to its brewing method, most commonly with coffees or coffee blends designed to be brewed as espresso. First, I should say that any coffee can be brewed using any brew method. A coffee labelled as filter coffee can be brewed as espresso and, while the recipe may need some adjustments, it can produce delicious cups. However, the espresso brewing process can benefit from a roast profile designed around its restrictions. Espresso uses a lot less water in the brew, in order to create a richer, more intense cup. The downside of having less water is that it is harder to properly extract all the flavour you want. Even with the notably finer grind, a shorter espresso brewed from lighter-roasted coffee can taste sour and unbalanced. Therefore, many roasters use a different roast profile on coffees destined to be brewed this way, usually a little slower

Above: The best cup of coffee begins with a well-chosen bean. For best results, choose freshly roasted beans from a specialist shop; they should also be able to advise you about the coffee's origins.

Golden Rules for Fresh Coffee

Everyone agrees fresh-roasted coffee is better, so I would make the following recommendations:

- Buy coffee that has a clear roast date on the packaging.
- Try to buy within two weeks of roasting.
- Buy only enough coffee for 2–4 weeks at a time.
- Buy whole beans and grind them yourself at home for best results.

Storing Coffee at Home

Once the staling process begins, there is very little that can be done to prevent it continuing. As long as you are buying fresh coffee and using it relatively quickly, the impact on your cup of coffee should be minor. However, there are ways to store coffee at home that will keep it in the best possible condition.

Keep the coffee airtight If the bag can be resealed, then make sure it is kept that way. If the bag can't be completely resealed, transfer the coffee to an airtight container, such as a plastic tub with a lid or one designed specifically for storing coffee.

Keep the coffee in a dark place Light rapidly accelerates the staling of coffee, especially sunlight. If you keep your coffee in a clear container, keep it somewhere dark.

Don't put it in the refrigerator This is a common practice, but it does not extend the life of coffee, and you can get cross-contamination of aromas if you have something particularly fragrant in the refrigerator with the coffee.

Keep it dry If you can't keep it in an airtight container, then at least avoid placing it in a humid environment.

Below: Beans last longer when stored in dry, dark place in an airtight or vacuum-sealed container.

and a little darker. This makes the coffee more soluble, and the resulting brews more balanced. These coffees will usually be labelled 'Espresso Roast' or 'Espresso Blend'. They can still be brewed as filter coffee, although the resulting cup will often have a little more body and a little more bitterness. Not every roaster feels the same way, and some believe that roasting is about creating optimal flavour, and the brew process should be tailored to the coffee, not the other way around. These roasters will offer just one roast level for all coffees. For more information on adjusting your espresso recipe around the coffee, see the chapter on Espresso on page 106.

Tasting Notes

It is now commonplace to see a few words to describe the flavour of the coffee. We will cover more about how to taste coffee in the chapter titled 'How to Taste Coffee' on page 74. Here we are going to discuss parsing those descriptors to understand what they are trying to communicate.

Fresh fruit descriptors: These will be words like 'apple', 'pear' or 'grape', or berry or citrus words. This implies relatively high levels of acidity in the coffee, particularly berry or citrus descriptors. If the coffee is also listed as a washed-process coffee, then you can be fairly confident that the coffee will carry a pleasing, complex acidity that is common in high-grown, speciality coffee. This doesn't mean the coffee will necessarily taste sour or unpleasant, unless the brews of it are less than ideal. These coffees tend also to be lighter in body. One small note on cooked fruit descriptors: these will be words like 'jammy' or something like 'candied orange'. These coffees often have a lower level of acidity and a little more body and mouthfeel, or a higher level of sweetness to offset the acidity present.

Browning descriptors: I have been looking for a better umbrella term than this for over a decade and still have yet to find something better. These are flavours that you would associate with products that are roasted or browned. These would be words like 'caramel', 'chocolate' or 'nutty'. These tend to be used with coffees that have lower levels of acidity, and those often have higher body or heavier mouthfeel, too.

Tropical fruit descriptors: These tend to be used in coffees that have a more fermented fruit taste. Some people experience these as being very tropical, while others will experience these same flavours as being very unpleasant, rotten or somewhat animal in nature. 'Mango', 'pineapple', 'strawberry' or 'blueberry' would all be classic choices to describe these coffees. These are often natural-process coffees, or more experimental fermentations. Strawberry and blueberry – the exceptions to the tropical fruit words here – are much more indicative of fermented flavours when used in this context.

Traceability

There are thousands of different coffee roasters, and hundreds of thousands of different roasts of coffee from different farms. Not all of them can be good, and variations in price and the way they are marketed can make buying fairly confusing. This book aims to explain where coffee comes from, and how and why its origin can affect its flavour. The best advice I can give is to buy as traceable a coffee as possible.

In many cases it is possible to find a coffee from one specific farm or one cooperative. However, that level of traceability is not possible in every coffee-producing country in the world. Each of the sections on the different countries offers an idea of how traceable the coffees from that country can be. Much of Latin America is able to produce coffees that are traceable down to a particular small farm because most of the coffee there is grown on small private estates. In other countries small-scale land ownership by farmers is unusual, or the trade regulations of a country may interfere with the export process, making traceability difficult.

To keep a batch of coffee traceable throughout the entire supply chain adds cost, and this investment can only be returned if the coffee is sold for a higher price. This means it is only worth keeping high-quality coffees traceable, as doing so with low-quality lots would make them uncompetitive in the marketplace. In an industry plagued by ethical concerns, and dogged by an image of exploitation of the Global South, knowing exactly where a coffee comes from is a powerful piece of information. It is now possible to follow and interact with many coffee producers across social media, and that trend only continues to grow.

Freezing Coffee

Freezing coffee has gained more traction in recent years and is an excellent choice for longer-term storage of coffee. It might be that you have bought a few different bags from one roaster and you won't get through them all fast enough, or that you would like to chop and change between them. If you need to store some coffee for a long period of time, you can use your freezer to slow down the staling process. It is important to package it in an airtight container first, and many people recommend taping over the one-way valve of the bag before freezing. In the past I've frozen single portions of coffee that I will use less often – such as decaf – in freezer bags or other containers that can be sealed. This is better than constantly opening a particular bag and pulling out a dose, as this can cause some condensation to occur on the coffee beans, which will impact longevity and quality.

You can grind the coffee straight from frozen if you are pulling out single portions. If you are going to brew a bag that you have had frozen, then the coffee may grind a little differently when frozen compared to defrosted, although this is a pretty small change –

Below: Vacuum packing isn't essential when you freeze coffee, but it can help keep it airtight and reduce staling.

more noticeable in an espresso than in filter coffee. Coffee frozen straight after roasting may still benefit from having some time to rest and degas after defrosting, although in my experience some resting and degassing will occur while it is in the freezer.

Freshness and Resting

Historically, most people have been conditioned not to think of coffee as a fresh food product. For some it is because instant coffee is what they think of as being coffee, and that doesn't really ever go stale. Coffee sold in supermarkets will often have a best-before date that is 12–24 months after the date it was roasted. This is because coffee is considered shelf stable and is safe to consume two years after roasting, although it will taste pretty terrible at that point. It is more convenient for all involved if coffee isn't treated like a fresh product, with the exception of the ultimate consumer.

For many years now, the speciality industry has repeated the idea that fresh is better, and that is true but also a little bit of a simplification. Without doubt, the aromatic complexity of fresh coffee is an incredible upgrade to the experience of stale coffee, and buying freshly roasted coffee is an essential of a great coffee experience. We should discuss the nuance of freshness, though, as the industry may have been too successful in communicating this simple idea.

After roasting, coffee beans contain a surprising amount of carbon dioxide (CO_2; see page 62). If you brew very fresh coffee, this CO_2 can interfere with the brewing process and will impact the resulting brew. The coffee will be harder to evenly extract, and the resulting brew can have a slightly unpleasant acidity due to the dissolved CO_2 creating carbonic acid. (This acidity is similar to the unpleasant tang that sparkling water has when it goes flat.) Therefore, it is recommended to 'rest' the coffee after roasting, in order to make it easier to brew and to get tastier cups from it. This resting period might be a few days, or you may see benefit from resting coffee for 2–3 weeks.

There are two key variables when it comes to determining how to rest coffee. The easiest is ambient temperature. If the coffee is stored in a cool environment, it will degas at a slower rate, while hotter environments will speed things up.

The other variable is the density of the coffee bean. This is itself impacted by both the density of the raw coffee and the roast level. With the raw coffee, this is usually determined by the elevation at which the coffee was grown. Higher-grown coffees will typically be denser. The roast level is probably the more impactful variant. Lighter roasts will degas at a much slower rate than darker roasts. However, lighter roasts will have developed less CO_2 during the roasting process than darker roasts. Very light roasts often benefit from at least 7–10 days' rest, regardless of whether they will be brewed as espresso or filter coffee. Darker roasts may need only 3–5 days' rest before they are ready to brew.

Brewing very fresh coffee is not a terrible experience; it is just not optimal. With more and more coffee roasting companies roasting the coffee they sell online to order, it is not unusual to receive coffee that is barely 24 hours old. You absolutely can brew it, but if you are disappointed by the result, then letting it rest, particularly with espresso, will often fix issues such as sourness or a borderline metallic taste.

Staling

When coffee goes stale, two main changes are occurring. The first is the slow but steady loss of aromatic compounds – the compounds that give coffee its flavour and smell. As they are volatile, these compounds slowly leach from the coffee so the older it is the less interesting it will taste.

The second change is the staling caused by oxygen and moisture which results in oxidation. This type of staling creates new flavours, often relatively unpleasant ones. As the coffee changes, it will develop a generic stale taste, and much of its original character will be lost. Stale coffees tend to taste flat, woody and vaguely of cardboard.

The darker the coffee has been roasted, the faster it will go stale. This is because the roasting process makes the coffee bean more porous, so it is easier for oxygen and moisture to penetrate and start the staling reactions.

Packing Coffee

Coffee roasters have a few choices when it comes to the packaging of their coffee. They will make this decision based not only on the preservation of the coffee, but also on the environmental impact, cost and look of the packaging.

Unsealed Craft Packaging

The coffee is packed into craft paper bags with a simple greaseproof lining to prevent any leaching of the oil from the coffee. While the bag may be rolled up at the point of sale, the coffee is still exposed to oxygen and will stale more quickly than other types of packaged coffee. Many roasters who use this kind of packaging will emphasize the importance of freshness, often suggesting the coffee be used within 7–10 days. When they retail the coffee, they must be sure that the coffee on the shelves is as fresh as possible, although this can lead to some undesirable wastage. This type of packaging is sometimes recyclable and is generally considered to have the least impact on the environment. This packaging is becoming less and less common.

Sealed Packaging

For a long time the primary material for this kind of packaging has been a triple-ply foil material that is sealed as soon as the coffee is packed to prevent fresh air getting in. Due to the limited options for recycling or reuse, this packaging isn't quite as dominant as it once was. There are more and more recyclable materials being used by coffee-roasting companies, although it is worth investigating whether that particular material is supported by your local recycling service. Unfortunately, not all materials are universally accepted, and feeding it into your domestic recycling will result in it going to landfill. There are also biodegradable options available now, although these cause trouble for the waste management industry if not disposed of properly. To properly break down, they should not go to landfill, and if added to recycling then they can contaminate a batch. They should be broken down via domestic or commercial composting.

Increasingly common in coffee packaging is a resealing strip inside the bag. I would strongly recommend using these, as they help keep the coffee in the best condition without the need to use an additional storage container.

Above: Triple-ply foil bags with a valve are common in the speciality coffee industry as they reduce staling until the package is opened.

Gas-Flushed Sealed Foil Packaging

This is the same as the above, but with one crucial difference. During the sealing process, a machine flushes the bag of coffee with an inert gas such as nitrogen to expel any oxygen from the bag, as oxygen causes staling to occur. This type of packaging slows staling down the most, although once the bag is opened the staling process will start. Despite this being the most effective way to package coffee, it is not widely used due to the additional costs of equipment, process time and the inert gas.

How to Taste Coffee

Coffee drinking is often tied into a ritual, a specific part of our day. We might drink a cup of coffee first thing in the morning, or as a break from work. Our attention is usually focused on the people we are with, or what we are reading or listening to over breakfast. Few people really concentrate on tasting the coffee they drink, but when they start to notice it, their appreciation increases rapidly.

The process of tasting happens in two different places – in our mouths and in our noses – and it is helpful to think about these two aspects of the process separately when learning to taste and talk about a coffee. The first part of the process occurs on the tongue, and it is here we detect the relatively basic tastes of acidity, sweetness, bitterness, saltiness and savouriness. These are not the only tastes we experience in the mouth – there are others like metallic tastes, astringency or spiciness. When reading the description of a coffee, we might be attracted to the flavours described, such as chocolate, berries or caramel. These flavours are actually detected the same way as smells – not in the mouth but by the olfactory bulb in the nasal cavity. This is the second aspect of the tasting process.

For most people these two separate experiences are completely intertwined, and the separation of taste and smell is extremely difficult. It gets easier if you try to focus on one particular aspect at a time, rather than trying to unpack the extremely complex taste experience all in one go.

How Professionals Taste Coffee

While we might have different goals when assessing coffee at home, compared to someone assessing a coffee they might be purchasing several tonnes of, I think the basic framework of professional tasting is worth understanding and adapting as necessary. Before it reaches the final consumer, a coffee will have been tasted a number of different times along its journey through the coffee industry. Each time it is tasted, the taster might be looking for something different. As coffee tasters work, they may record their notes on a score sheet. Different processes require different score sheets but in almost all cases a number of different attributes are being assessed, and these are all attributes it is helpful to consider when drinking and tasting coffee at home.

Comparative Tasting

The biggest advantage a coffee professional has, when it comes to developing their tasting skills and their language, is that almost all coffee tastings will be comparative ones. Roasters will regularly taste all the batches that they've roasted on a given day, and it is relatively rare that a roaster or coffee buyer would taste a single coffee with nothing to benchmark it against. Comparing different coffees side by side, even if it is just two, is a delightful experience, and there is nothing that will accelerate your own understanding of your preferences and flavour itself faster.

While I will cover the professional tasting process, called cupping, further on in this chapter (see page 77), I want to cover how to use and think about comparative tastings at home now. The brews can be two different coffees brewed the same way, as pour over or French press perhaps, or the same coffee brewed using two different methods. As long as the two cups of coffee are different in some way, they are viable for this experiment.

When tasting comparatively it is important to initially just focus on one attribute at a time. Is the first cup more, or less, acidic than the second? Is the second cup sweeter than the first? Which one do you like more? Soon you will find trends in the simple tastes, and you can start to consider flavour.

Describing flavour is the most intimidating part of learning to taste anything, be it wine or coffee or olive oil or apples. Once you are comfortable picking apart the tastes, you should start exploring flavour through connected experiences. What does it remind you of? If there is acidity, then chances are it will remind you of some fruit. Start with broad categories like 'citrus' or 'berry' rather than trying to home in on whether it is lemony or orangey. You can start with broad categories like the browning flavours – chocolate, caramel, nuts – without having to be very specific. Sometimes one particular thing will jump out at you.

Above: Each brew is affected by the origin, preparation and roasting of the beans, which create its distinct flavours.

The way that we experience flavour is quite personal. What you have tasted and experienced in life will obviously shape how you think about flavour in general. A descriptor of a coffee tasting like persimmon means nothing to someone who has never tasted a persimmon – that coffee may remind them of other flavours, of completely different experiences. Coffee is an incredibly aromatic and complex beverage. It is potentially overwhelming for the brain, which is mostly trying to assess whether consuming this thing is of benefit or is potentially a poison. Your brain will use as much other information as possible to filter out the noise and to shape the flavours you pay attention to as part of the conscious experience. The colour of a liquid or the type of acidity it has will be used to help the brain decide which of the many aromatic compounds it is detecting are of importance. This is a very long way of saying that tasting is highly subjective. If you are sharing a tasting experience with other people, no one is wrong in how they are describing what they are tasting. If a coffee reminds you of melon but someone else of mushroom – you are both right.

One of the key aspects of tasting coffee is experiencing the coffee through a range of temperatures. Our tasting apparatus is much less effective when foods or drinks are a long way from body temperature. Very hot things or very cold things are hard to taste accurately. You can start tasting a coffee when it is still hot but feels comfortable in your mouth. I would recommend tasting it all the way down to room temperature. As the temperature of the liquid drops, the coffee will appear to 'open up' and become both more complex, but also clearer and easier to describe. Even when you are enjoying a single cup of coffee, letting it cool down a little will make such a difference to your overall experience of the cup. To many the change is genuinely shocking, and when they have experienced it once they rarely go back to drinking hotter cups.

When you have finished a tasting, compare what you have written down with the roaster's description on the packet. Can you see now what they are trying to communicate about the coffee? Often, on reading the label, any frustration you have had in searching for a word will be relieved as you see a good descriptor for what you have tasted. It can suddenly seem so obvious, and this is part of building a coffee-specific vocabulary of flavours. Describing coffee gets easier and easier, although this is something even industry veterans continue to work on.

These are the initial key attributes to pay attention to – the important tastes and qualities that may appear on a coffee-tasting score sheet:

Sweetness

This is one of the standout attributes of speciality coffee, as commercial coffee rarely has much in the way of sweetness, even in a well-brewed cup. Sweetness is a complex experience in coffee, different from the simple sweetness of sugar or honey. When tasting the coffee, we should consider how much sweetness the coffee has. This is a very desirable trait in coffee, and generally the more the better.

Acidity

How acidic is the coffee? And how pleasant is this acidity? If there is a lot of unpleasant acidity, the coffee will be described as sour. A lot of pleasing acidity, however, gives the coffee a crispness or juiciness. (This is often in concert with a pleasing level of sweetness.)

For many people learning to taste coffee, acidity is a difficult attribute. They may not have expected coffee to have much acidity, and certainly would not have considered this a positive quality in the past. Apples can be a great example of positive acidity: in an apple, high acidity can be wonderful, adding a refreshing quality.

Coffee professionals tend to develop a preference for high acidity in coffees, much as beer aficionados may develop a preference for very hoppy beers. This can result in a difference of opinion between industry and consumer. In the case of coffee, unusual flavours – such as fruit notes – are determined by the density of the coffee. Generally, denser coffees are also more acidic, so coffee tasters learn to associate high acidity with quality and interesting flavours.

Mouthfeel

Does the coffee have a light, delicate, tea-like mouthfeel or is it more of a rich, creamy, heavy cup? Again, more is not necessarily better. Low-quality coffees often have quite a heavy mouthfeel, coupled with low acidity, but are not always pleasant to drink.

Balance

This is one of the most difficult aspects of a coffee to assess. A myriad of tastes and flavours occur in a mouthful of great coffee but are they harmonious? Is it like a well-mixed piece of music, or is one element too loud? Does one aspect dominate the cup?

Flavour

This is not just about describing the different flavours and aromas of a particular coffee, but also about how

Below: Professional tasters grade and rank coffee before it reaches the consumer. They will often use a score sheet like the one below to rate the different properties of a brew.

NAME ______________ # ___ DATE ______ Rnd 1 2 3 Sn 1 2 3 4 5 TBL# ___ Country __________

	ROAST COLOUR	AROMA (DRY CRUST BREAK; 3 2 1)	DEFECTS (# x i x 4 = score)	CLEAN CUP (0 4 6 7 8)	SWEET (0 4 6 7 8)	ACIDITY (0 4 6 7 8)	MOUTH FEEL (0 4 6 7 8)	FLAVOUR (0 4 6 7 8)	AFTER TASTE (0 4 6 7 8)	BALANCE (0 4 6 7 8)	OVERALL (0 4 6 7 8)	TOTAL (+36)
1.												
2.												
3.												
4.												
5.												

pleasant the taster finds them. Many new tasters find this the most frustrating aspect of coffee tasting. Each of the coffees they taste are clearly different but the language to describe them remains elusive.

Bitterness

It is strange that one of the defining characteristics of coffee is not one considered by coffee tasters. The coffee industry will act as if speciality coffee isn't bitter, which it obviously is. However, in good-quality coffees bitterness should not be front and centre in the tasting experience. The coffee industry would argue that, if bitterness is its dominant taste, then the coffee has some sort of issue or defect of roasting. Nonetheless, I think it is a helpful characteristic when comparing coffees, especially if you have a commercial-grade coffee in your comparative tasting, alongside a speciality coffee.

Professional Tasting Process

In its journey from farm to roaster a coffee will be tasted several times. It might first be tasted early on to detect any presence of defect (see page 33). It will then be tasted by a roaster as part of the purchasing process, or by a jury ranking coffees for an auction of the best lots from a particular place. It will be tasted by the roaster again as part of their quality control to make sure that the roasting process has been done correctly and then it may be tasted by a café owner selecting the range they wish to stock. Finally, it will be tasted, and hopefully enjoyed, by the consumer.

The coffee industry uses a pretty standardized practice called 'cupping' to taste coffee. The idea behind cupping is to avoid any impact on flavour from the brewing process, and to treat all coffees being tasted as equally as possible. For that reason, a very simple brewing process is used, as bad brewing can easily change the flavour of a coffee quite dramatically.

A fixed amount of coffee is weighed for each bowl. It is ground at a fixed setting and a specific amount of water, just off the boil, is added. For example, for 12g (½oz) of coffee, 200ml (7fl oz) of water might be added. The coffee is then left to steep for 4 minutes.

To end the brewing process, the layer of floating grounds on top of the bowl, called the crust, is stirred. This causes almost all the coffee grounds to fall to the bottom of the bowl where they stop extracting.

Above: It can be helpful to note your observations while doing a comparative tasting so you can refer back to them later.

Professional tasters will often get their noses down to the bowl as they break the crust, to experience the pop of flavours as trapped aromas are released. It's certainly fun to do, but in my experience this is not particularly useful information for a tasting, unless a very obvious defect is present in the coffee. After breaking the crust, any grounds and foam that remain on top can be skimmed off.

Once the coffee has cooled to a safe temperature, tasting begins. Coffee tasters use a spoon to get a small sample of coffee, which they then aggressively slurp from the spoon. This slurping process aerates the coffee and sprays it across the palate. It is not essential to tasting but does make tasting a little easier. In the last few years, it has become less common to have everyone use their own spoon at a communal tasting. Instead, one spoon is used to get the liquid from the bowl, and the liquid is then transferred to either another spoon or a small cup for tasting. Many of us look back at the older process as astonishingly and unpleasantly unsanitary – even if it was more convenient than the double spoon or transfer method.

Grinding Coffee

The smell of freshly ground coffee is evocative, heady and indescribable, and in some ways it is worth paying for a coffee grinder for this alone. However, grinding your own beans at home will also make an enormous difference to the quality of your cup, compared to buying pre-ground coffee.

The aim of grinding the beans before brewing is to expose enough surface area to extract enough of the flavour locked inside the beans to make a good cup of coffee. If you brewed whole beans, you would end up with a very weak brew. The finer the beans are ground, the more surface area is exposed and, in theory, the faster the coffee can be brewed because the water has more access to it. This is important when considering how finely the coffee should be ground for different brew methods. The fact that the size of the coffee grounds changes the speed at which the coffee brews also makes it very important that we try to make all the pieces the same size when grinding coffee. Finally, grinding the coffee exposes more of it to the air, which means that the coffee will go stale more quickly, so it should ideally only be ground just before brewing.

There are two main types of coffee grinder available for domestic use:

The (Whirly) Blade Grinder

These are common and inexpensive electric grinders. They have a metal blade attached to a motor that spins and smashes the coffee to pieces. The biggest problem

Below: A blade grinder (left) smashes the coffee beans, resulting in an uneven grind, whereas a burr grinder (right) cuts beans into evenly sized pieces.

is that this smashing action produces some very fine powder and some very large pieces. When you brew coffee ground like this, the tiny pieces will quickly add a bitter flavour to the brew, while the larger pieces will add an unpleasant sourness. This uneven brew won't be very enjoyable.

There are a couple of additional steps you can take to improve the quality of coffee from blade grounders, although I will admit that both are a little time intensive. The first is to pass the resulting coffee through a sieve. This will remove any very large pieces of coffee, which the coffee industry often describes as 'boulders'. These can easily make up a significant percentage of your grounds, and they won't brew properly. Brewing with them results in a weaker cup that is often sourer. You can regrind them after sieving them out, which is better than throwing them away or using them as they are.

To try to reduce the very fine, bitter particles you can spread the grounds out onto some paper kitchen towel. A good amount of the finer pieces will get caught up in the paper and you can tip the grounds from the paper towel to the brewer. There is obviously the waste of a piece of paper towel, and the time involved, but it will help reduce the bitterness from those tiny pieces.

The Burr Grinder

These are increasingly common and available as electric or hand-cranked grinders. They have two cutting discs, called burrs, facing each other, and you can adjust the distance between them to change the size of the grounds of coffee produced. Because the coffee grounds can't escape until they have been cut down to the size of the gap between the burrs, the resulting grounds are more even in size. Uniformity is important, but burr grinders are especially useful because you can adjust the burr gap and so get the right grind size for the particular coffee and particular brew method you are using.

Burr grinders are more expensive than blade grinders, but the manual models are relatively cheap and easy to use. If you enjoy coffee, a burr grinder will prove to be an invaluable investment, especially if you are brewing espresso. However, because grind size is so important in espresso – variations of a few hundredths of a millimetre make a difference – it is

Above: Beans ground in a blade grinder (left) will be of a more uneven size and make a less palatable brew than those milled from a burr grinder (right), which has two cutting discs that can be adjusted to determine grind size.

important to buy a burr grinder designed for espresso. This means that it is built with a good motor capable of grinding the beans very fine, and that it allows you to make very small adjustments to the grind size.

Different manufacturers use different materials to make the burrs, such as steel or ceramic. Over time, the cutting teeth on the burrs will start to dull and the machine will start to mill the coffee rather than cut it cleanly, producing a lot of tiny pieces that make the coffee taste flat and bitter. Follow the manufacturer's recommendations for how often to change the burrs – new burrs are a small but worthwhile investment in your coffee-brewing setup. Most modern metal burrs easily grind 300–500kg (approximately 660–1,100lb) of coffee before having issues.

Many people who enjoy coffee as a hobby like to upgrade their equipment from time to time. I would strongly recommend investing in a better grinder first. More expensive grinders have better motors and cutting burrs capable of a more uniform grind size. You will make a better cup of coffee with a high-end grinder and a small domestic espresso machine than with a cheap grinder and a top-of-the-range commercial espresso machine.

One final note on burr grinders is to flag the kinds of machines known as 'false burr' grinders. Generally, these are cheap electric grinders with ceramic discs shaped to look like burrs rather than properly cut metal burrs. They produce poor-quality ground coffee and should be avoided.

Density and Grind Size

Unfortunately, not all coffees should be treated equally in the grinder. Darker roasts are more brittle in the grinder, and you may need to grind a little more coarsely. Equally, if the coffee is from a much higher elevation than you typically drink – for example, you've been drinking a delicious coffee from Brazil, and then you switch to a coffee from Kenya – you may need to go finer in your grinder for the high-grown coffee. Once you have made the switch a few times, you can make a well-educated guess when changing coffees and prevent too many bad brews.

Very Fine

Fine

Medium

Coarse

Grind Size

Communicating grind size is not easy. Terms such as 'coarse', 'medium' and 'fine' aren't particularly helpful because they are relative. There is no common setting among grinder manufacturers either, so setting one grinder to a numerical setting of 5, for example, won't replicate the grind of another grinder set to the same setting. Occasionally, you will see people reference a grind size in microns. This is not particularly helpful either, despite seeming extremely precise. Saying that the coffee is ground at 450 microns implies that the largest peak of particles occurs at that grind size. Not all particles will be this size, and the variance in that size is tied to the way the burr cuts coffee. Conical grinders will often have a peak in grind size at a larger micron than flat burr grinders, particularly for espresso. To further muddy the waters, some grinder manufacturers are starting to put the gap between the burrs onto the grinder. So, a grinder might let you grind at a burr gap of 450 microns, but that doesn't necessarily mean that the peak in grind particle size will be at a matching size. These numbers are not without merit – they let you understand something of the size and scale of adjustments you are making, and if a manufacturer is properly calibrating the grinders then two people with the same model will be able to accurately communicate the grind they are using to each other.

Above are some different expressions of grind size, with the accompanying photographs shown at life size. This should get you close to the perfect grind, then with a little experimentation each morning you should be able to achieve a much more delicious cup of coffee very quickly.

Water for Brewing

The role of water in the brewing process is crucial in creating a great cup of coffee. For reasons that will become clear, I really wish this were not the case. I wish that great coffee brewed well with any water, and that the mineral composition had no impact whatsoever. When thinking about water for coffee, we have two things to consider: will the coffee taste good and will my equipment be impacted by this water?

At first glance the recommendations below may seem somewhat excessive, but making a little effort with water will bring enormous returns. If you come to the end of this chapter feeling sceptical, then I would recommend a simple experiment. Get a bottle of water that has a high mineral content, and a high bicarbonate content, and brew a cup of coffee. Then brew that exact same coffee using the same recipe and technique with much softer water. The difference is huge and hopefully will be enough to prompt a little curiosity about how you can get the most out of the coffee you're buying by paying just a little attention to the water you use to brew it.

The Role of Water

Water is a vital ingredient in a cup of coffee as it makes up around 90 per cent of an espresso and 98.5 per cent of a cup of filter coffee. If the water doesn't taste good to start with, neither will the cup of coffee in the end. And if you can taste the chlorine, the resulting cup of coffee will be terrible. In many cases a simple water filter jug that contains active carbon (such as a Brita filter) will do a good job of removing negative tastes, but it still might not produce the perfect water for brewing coffee.

Water acts as a solvent, but the minerals in it are involved in the work of extracting the flavours in the ground coffee during the brewing process. This is where the composition of the water plays a major role, as the hardness and the mineral content can significantly affect how the coffee brews.

Hardness

Water hardness is a measure of how much limescale (calcium carbonate) is dissolved in the water, and this is determined by the bedrock in the local area. Heating hard water causes the limescale to come out of solution and accumulate over time as a chalky white build-up. Those who live in hard water areas struggle with the frustrations of limescale affecting kettles, showers and washing machines.

Water's interaction with coffee is maddeningly complex, and so I am going to simplify it to help you think about it in a relatively straightforward way. If this turns out to be of interest, then there are a lot of resources online to help you go more deeply into the topic than is possible here.

The hardness strongly influences the way the hot water and the ground coffee interact. Calcium helps the water to extract more from the coffee, but more doesn't always equal better. Brews with high levels of hardness can often feel heavy, almost chalky. Calcium is not the only mineral to consider here, as magnesium also plays a role in hardness. While magnesium can precipitate out of solution as a form of scale, it is quite different from calcium carbonate and tends not to stick to things the way calcium carbonate (limescale) does. We will discuss how to change the composition of your water later in the chapter, but for now we just want to think about the relative impact of the minerals. They help extract flavour, but calcium in particular will cause limescale and that can cause serious problems in a coffee machine, requiring regular descaling if the water is hard.

The other part of this equation is the bicarbonate in the water. This impacts coffee in a couple of ways. Obviously, it needs to be present to have limescale form. Water could have high levels of calcium but low bicarbonate levels, and in that case it would not form very much limescale. Bicarbonate plays another role, particularly when it comes to the taste of coffee. It acts as a buffer, which is a term in chemistry for a compound that mitigates changes in acidity. In our bodies we use a bicarbonate buffer system to maintain the pH of our blood, which has to be held in a very narrow band to avoid death.

From a simple taste perspective – the more bicarbonate that is present, the more buffer there will be and the less acidity you will experience. The mineral content will help extract soluble material, a lot of which is acidic, and the bicarbonate will help balance this out in terms of flavour and experienced acidity. This means that most recommendations for ideal water composition will have a somewhat balanced ratio of minerals to bicarbonate. Brewing with low-bicarbonate water can produce a brew that has a harsh and intense acidity, and brewing coffee with a lot of buffer will produce a flat, boring and characterless cup.

How Do I Know if My Water is Good?

While I do not recommend bottled water for regular coffee brewing, simply from a waste impact alone, it can be useful to experiment with on occasion. In many parts of the world, it is required to show the mineral composition of bottled water, which will give you numbers for calcium, magnesium and bicarbonate. There are obviously other minerals in many waters, but these are the ones we are most concerned with.

Many countries' local water authorities and suppliers will publish the mineral content of the tap water they provide. There are often fluctuations around this number, but they provide a good guide as to whether you are in the ballpark of good water.

Finally, there are a lot of relatively inexpensive test kits available. Many of these are sold as aquarium test kits – because regulating water in those environments is, of course, extremely important. These are usually dropper kits that will give you reasonably accurate numbers, certainly enough to understand the overall suitability of your water for coffee.

Ideal Brewing Water

In the past there was often thought to be an ideal water composition for brewing coffee, but as we have come to experiment with water more, I think it is fair to say that the target has expanded quite dramatically. Personal preference plays a huge role, and many people have good experiences with water that is outside the 'official' recommendations of organizations such as the Specialty Coffee Association (SCA). What is common to most of the recommended water compositions is a balance between hardness and bicarbonate. Those who prefer more acidic brews may prefer a little less bicarbonate, and the opposite is true for people who like less acidity. Below is a chart showing a number of recommendations.

Guidelines for the Perfect Water for Coffee Brewing

	Target	Acceptable Range
Odour	Clean, fresh, odour-free	
Colour	Clear	
Total Chlorine	0mg/l	0mg/l
Calcium	80ppm (ideal for filter coffee) 40ppm (ideal for espresso coffee)	50–150ppm
Total Alkalinity	40ppm (ideal for filter coffee) 80ppm (ideal for espresso coffee)	20–100ppm
pH	7.0 (ideal)	6.5–7.5

How to Get Better Water

If all of this seems very intimidating, and if you are in an area with harder water, then a simple domestic water filter is a good start. You will get a notable improvement in your coffee, although be mindful that domestic water filters should be changed every month to prevent bacterial growth, regardless of usage. These filters usually carry out a two-step process. There will be some ion exchange occurring in the filter, swapping out the calcium and replacing it with a sodium ion. They also have active carbon in there to remove any negative tastes from the water. They are particularly good for better-tasting drinking water, if you have some slightly off tastes in your tap water.

I would argue that a filter like this will get you 50 per cent of the way there, or to put it another way – whatever improvement you experience you can expect to experience again when you get into ideal coffee water. The world of home-made, customized water sounds utterly absurd, but it is actually increasingly practical and worthwhile when investing in some truly excellent coffee.

Custom-made water is usually done by taking deionized (essentially 'pure') water and adding minerals to it. Several companies now offer simple remineralization solutions. In some cases, you might mix a little sachet of powder into a few litres of

Above left and right: Some coffee consumers customize the water they use for brewing. It is possible to buy sachets of minerals (left) or dropper kits (right) to add to deionized water to create the perfect composition for your needs.

distilled water. Other solutions might allow you to make even smaller batches of water, using dropper kits of different minerals and buffers. You can either buy deionized water or you can use a filter jug designed to take the water back to as close to pure as possible.

There is one additional advantage. You can often create a different water for espresso than for filter. There are two reasons for this. First, from a taste perspective it is often beneficial to have a little more buffer in water for espresso, because espresso is more concentrated and so the acidity can easily be more potent – so this balances that out. Second, you can use water that is less likely to cause limescale inside an espresso machine, without compromising on the water's ability to make good coffee. This is usually done by using more magnesium, rather than calcium, in the recipe.

This is a little bit of work, and perhaps the point at which many an outsider would consider that someone had become absurdly fanatical about their coffee. My best advice is to suggest you give it a try once and see whether you find the benefits worth the effort. For an increasing number of people, it is an easy part of their coffee-making ritual.

A note on TDS meters

You will often come across people talking about TDS (total dissolved solids) when it comes to brew water. I don't consider TDS a particularly useful indicator of a water's composition or suitability. For a long time people recommended water based on TDS, but now we would consider that unhelpful. A TDS meter typically measures conductivity in the water, and converts that to a number in milligrams per litre (mg/L) of all dissolved solids. However, some dissolved solids are not accurately measured this way, and it tells you nothing about that composition. There are uses for TDS meters, but selecting water quality based on TDS can easily take you in the wrong direction when it comes to coffee.

Brewing Basics

A key moment in the journey from crop to cup is the process of brewing. All the hard work up until this point, all the potential and deliciousness locked within the coffee, can be obscured by bad brewing. It is upsetting how easy it is to brew coffee badly, but understanding the basic principles can simplify things, make the whole process more enjoyable and, of course, lead to better results.

When we brew coffee, we are dissolving some of the grounds into the brew water. However, most of the coffee grounds are not soluble. You could brew them endlessly, and there would still be some spent grounds to throw away. Good brewing is about getting the right amount of the soluble material out of the grounds because not everything that we can get from the coffee tastes good.

From the 1960s onwards, there has been ongoing research into measuring how much of the coffee we want to extract for the resulting cup to taste good. If you don't take enough from the grounds, then the cup of coffee will not only be weak but will often also be sour and astringent. This is called 'under-extraction'. And if we take too much from the grounds then the cup of coffee will taste bitter, harsh and ashy. This is what we call 'over-extraction'.

It is possible to calculate whether we have extracted as much as we want from the coffee. In the past this was done relatively simply: the grounds were weighed before brewing, then after brewing the spent grounds were placed in a low oven until they were completely dry. When they were weighed again, the difference in weight would indicate how much of the coffee had been extracted during the brewing process. Now a combination of a specialized refractometer and software allows us quickly to calculate how much has been extracted from the grounds. For a long time it was agreed that a good cup of coffee contains 18–22 per cent by weight of the ground coffee used to brew it, but in the last decade the upper limit has increased with better grinding technology and a better understanding of brewing. The exact figures are not important to most people at home, but understanding how to adjust different parameters to improve the cup is useful. There is no need for most people to worry about the exact level of extraction, because everything is really going to be built around what tastes best to them personally.

Strength

This is an important term when talking about a cup of coffee, but one that has been quite widely misused. The term is commonly used on bags of coffee sold in the supermarket, and in this instance it is completely inappropriate. What they are trying to communicate here is how dark the roast of the coffee is, and how intense the bitterness will be.

The word 'strength' when used to describe a cup of coffee should be used in the same way it is used to describe alcoholic drinks. A beer that is 4 per cent strength means that 4 per cent of what you drink is alcohol. In the same way, a strong cup of coffee has a higher percentage of dissolved ground coffee in the hot water than a weak cup. When it comes to strength in coffee there is no right and wrong – there is only individual preference.

There are two ways to control strength, and the first and most common way is by varying the ratio of coffee to water. The more coffee used to brew a cup, the stronger the resulting cup is likely to be. When talking about brewing, we tend to communicate something about the desired strength by the number of grams of coffee per litre of water, for example 60g/l. To brew a cup of coffee of this strength, you would first decide how much coffee you want to brew, for example 500ml. You would then use the ratio to calculate how much coffee to use, in this case 30g.

The preferred ratio of coffee to water varies around the world from around 40g/l up to nearly 100g/l in Brazil and Scandinavia. Generally, people find a ratio that they enjoy and they stick to it for most brew methods. I would recommend 60g/l as a starting point for almost everyone, but once you are comfortable brewing this way you should absolutely

Opposite: Brewing a good cup of coffee at home is a matter of preference, but an important factor to understand is the ratio of water to coffee.

experiment with your preferred ratio. I would recommend moving in steps of 5g/l as this will make a surprising difference to the resulting cup. Changing the coffee to water ratio is how most people at home change the strength of their brews, but it is not always the best way.

The other way to change strength is to change the level of extraction. This is primarily done through changing the way coffee is ground. The finer you grind coffee the more of its surface area you expose. Water will not penetrate the middle of a large coffee ground as effectively as a smaller one, and so finer ground coffee will produce stronger cups.

Alongside grind size, there is also time. As we steep coffee in a French press, the water is slowly taking more and more out of the coffee, and the resulting drink is getting stronger and stronger as it brews, although the rate does slow down over the course of the brew.

The challenge is to control the level of extraction so we take enough from the grounds that it tastes good, before we start to extract bitter and unpleasant flavours. Many people don't think about changing the level of extraction when they get a poor cup of coffee, but an error of extraction can certainly lead to a disappointing cup. If you brew a French press with very coarsely ground coffee, then the resulting brew will likely taste very weak, even when using a suitable ratio of coffee to water. Often, the obvious solution to people would be to use more coffee to get a stronger cup. That will be the outcome, but they have fixed the wrong variable. The cup brewed from the higher ratio will be stronger, but it will still not be properly extracted so it will likely taste a little sour and unpleasant. Adjusting the grind would have been a more suitable solution to the initial problem.

As we discuss each of the brewing methods in this chapter, we will often focus on grind size, brew time and also technique. Many of the goals with brewing technique are focused on trying to extract the coffee evenly. One of the ways that brews go wrong is that the water does not pass evenly through the coffee. This is a particular issue with pressurized brewing, like espresso, and so we will go into greater detail there. However, it is still an issue in all percolation methods (a brew where water passes through a bed of coffee, rather than an immersion or infusion brew, where all the coffee and water spend a period of time together).

Exact Measurements

Small changes in how coffee is brewed can have a big impact on taste. One of the biggest variables is how much water you use, and being consistent is one of the most important aspects of brewing. It is a good idea to put the coffee brewer on scales so you can measure exactly how much boiling water you are adding. Remember than each millilitre of water weighs a gram. This will give you a lot more control and massively improve the quality and consistency of your brews. A set of simple digital scales is not expensive, and many people already have one in the kitchen. While it seems a little obsessive at first, once you start brewing this way you will never want to go back. In addition, I don't do my best guessing and estimating before I have had my morning coffee, so using a scale allows me to skip thinking too much about it, and I can just easily make the correct recipe without much strain on my un-caffeinated brain.

Opposite: Well-foamed milk brings a richer, creamier texture to milk-based coffee drinks, and with practice can be used to pour latte art.
Below: A set of digital scales is a worthwhile investment for anyone interested in making consistently good coffee.

Milk, Cream and Sugar

For a long time the addition of milk, cream and sugar to speciality coffee was the source of some tension between the coffee industry and the coffee consumer. The coffee industry treated these 'adulterations' as somewhat taboo, or at least a little disrespectful to the coffee they had brewed. In this they may have lacked a little empathy and were rightly branded snobs for it. (I may have been as guilty of this as anyone!)

What is often forgotten by the professionals is that most coffee served in the world requires something to help make it more drinkable. Cheap commodity coffee that has been poorly roasted or badly brewed is often incredibly bitter and lacks any sweetness. Milk and, even more so, cream do a great job of blocking some of the bitterness, and sugar makes it more palatable. Many people get accustomed to the taste of milk and sugar in coffee and will then add them almost as a default to what is already an interesting cup of coffee that has been brewed with care. This may well cause a little frustration for the barista, the professional roaster or any person simply passionate about great coffee and for good reason.

Excellent coffee should have its own sweetness, and instead of suppressing bitterness that isn't really there, the milk will obscure the flavour characteristics of the coffee, hiding the work of the producer and the ultimate character of that coffee. I would always recommend trying a coffee before adding anything to it. If it is not sufficiently palatable, then add milk or sugar so you enjoy the cup. However, exploring the wonderful world of speciality coffee is extremely difficult if you drink it in any other way than black, and the investment of time and effort learning to appreciate it this way will be extremely rewarding. I would also say that speciality coffee tastes quite odd and a little unpleasant when sweetened, almost to the point that if I had to drink sweetened black coffee then I would rather drink more commercial coffee with sugar than speciality coffee with sugar.

The French Press

The French press, also known as a cafetière or coffee plunger, is probably the most underrated method of brewing coffee and certainly one of my favourites. It is cheap, easy and repeatable, and just about everyone has one at home. However, many people associate it with a sludgy, silty cup of coffee that has nice mouthfeel but a terrible final mouthful. It doesn't have to be this way...

Considering its name, it seems somewhat surprising to discover that the most familiar version of the French press was invented and patented by an Italian named Attilio Calimani in 1929. However, a very similar brewer had been patented first by two Frenchmen, Henri-Otto Mayer and Jacques-Victor Delforge, in 1852.

A French press is an infusion brewer, which helps produce a more uniform extraction. The other notable aspect of the French press is the way that it filters the grounds from the brewing liquid: by using a metal mesh. Due to the relatively large holes in the mesh, more of the non-soluble material from the coffee gets into the cup. The advantage of this is you get a little of the coffee oil and some tiny suspended pieces of coffee in the cup, which gives the resulting brew a bigger, richer body and texture. The disadvantage is what puts many people off the French press: the sludge.

The brewing method described opposite is designed to achieve a great brew with the minimum amount of sludge. It requires a little more work and patience, but you will be rewarded with a great cup of coffee that will give you easy access to all the unique flavours and characteristics of the bean. This method is based on the way that coffee professionals taste coffee – a technique called cupping, which I explained in more detail on page 77.

Left: Brewing coffee in a French press results in a drink of uniform extraction. The metal mesh allows for small particles to flavour the water, creating a rich body and texture.

The French Press Method

Ratio: 60–70g/l. I recommend a slightly higher ratio of coffee to water when using an infusion brewer if you want to produce a brew with a strength similar to that of a pour-over brewer. I might start at 60g/l and increase the dose if you feel like you want more from the coffee. The upside of this brew method is that increasing the dose doesn't require a matching change in grind setting; you can keep the grind consistent and still see good results. However, if you go all the way to 70g/l, then I might extend the brew time by 1 minute before stirring the crust.

Grind: Medium (caster/superfine sugar) (see page 80). Many people grind their beans very coarsely when brewing in a French press, but I don't think this is necessary unless your grinder produces a lot of very fine pieces and your brews quickly turn bitter. Most recommendations on commercial grinders (as you sometimes find in supermarkets, where you can grind the beans you're buying) are too coarse in my opinion, and that's also true of many domestic grinder setting recommendations. Something closer to the recommended setting for a pour over will yield far better results unless brewing very dark roasts.

1 Grind the coffee just before you start brewing. Don't forget to weigh the coffee beans first.

2 Boil a kettle of fresh water suitable for brewing coffee.

3 Put the ground coffee in the French press and place it on the scales. **A**

4 Pour in the correct amount of water, weighing as you pour so you achieve the ratio of 60–70g/l. Pour relatively quickly and try to get all the coffee wet. **B**

5 Leave the coffee to steep for 4 minutes. During this time the coffee will float to the top to form a crust-like layer on the water.

6 After 4 minutes, take a large spoon and stir the crust at the top. This will cause most of the coffee to fall to the bottom of the brewer. **C**

7 A little foam and some floating grounds will remain on the top. About 30 seconds after stirring the brew, use the spoon to scoop them off and discard them. **D**

8 Wait another 5 minutes. The coffee would be too hot to drink anyway, and leaving it in the brewer allows more and more of the coffee and fine particles to sink to the bottom of the press.

9 Place the mesh plunger in the top of the beaker, but *do not plunge*. Plunging will create turbulence, which will stir up all the silty coffee at the bottom. I tend to lower the plunger just to the top of the liquid inside, to make sure it doesn't fall out while pouring.

10 Pour the coffee slowly through the mesh into the cup(s). Until you get close to the bottom, this liquid will have very little silt in it. If you can resist pouring out the very last bit, you will end up with a delicious, flavourful brew of coffee that has very little silt. **E**

11 Allow the coffee to cool in the cup(s) a little, then enjoy.

Pour-Over or Filter Brewers

The term 'pour over' is used to describe a host of different brew methods. The common factor is that each brews by percolation, which means that the water passes through a bed of coffee, extracting flavour along the way. Usually there is some sort of material to filter the grounds from the resulting drink, and this can be made of anything from paper to cloth to a fine metal mesh.

Simple cup-top filter brewers have probably been used since coffee brewing began, but the innovations on the theme came relatively late. Interestingly, the first filters were made of cloth; the invention of the paper filter is credited to a German entrepreneur, Melitta Bentz, in 1908. Now controlled by her descendants, the Melitta Group still sells filter papers, coffee and coffee machines today.

The invention of paper filters encouraged the move away from the electric percolator, a terrible brewer which recirculated hot water through the grounds, brewing an incredibly bitter cup. The final death knell for the percolator was the next major innovation in drip-coffee brewing, the electric coffee machine. The invention can be credited to another German company, Wigomat. Variations on the electric filter coffee machine are still incredibly popular today, although not all produce good coffee (see page 96).

Currently there is a huge range of different brewers, brands and devices on offer, all designed to do this same job and each with its own advantages and idiosyncrasies. There are an astonishing number of

Pouring Kettles

When using the pour-over method to brew coffee, the rate at which you add the water plays a role in the brewing process. Pouring slowly and carefully from a standard tea kettle is difficult to do, and now coffee-focused pouring kettles are relatively widespread and available at a range of price points. The simple versions designed to go on a cooktop were often used in coffee shops, where they would be filled from a water boiler. Now, certainly at home, electric pour-over kettles are far more common. Many of them will also offer some level of temperature control. For light to medium roasts, I would just recommend setting them to boil. For darker roasts, I would set them lower – to 90°C (194°F). The shared design trait of all of them is that the spout is very narrow, so they issue a very slow, steady stream of water on to the coffee. Again, some pour more slowly than others but that isn't always ideal. If you are just making pour-over coffee with the kettle, then this is fine, but if you want to make tea or even brew immersion-style brews with coffee, then a faster pour-over spout may be preferable for you.

Despite their popularity in the industry, I have been hesitant to label pouring kettles as essential. They do make pouring easier, but they aren't cheap and few of us have space in our lives for yet another single-use kitchen appliance. As such, I have always sought out techniques that are viable with a standard tea kettle. Brewing this way won't be quite as easy, but it can be done and with good results. However, I confess I still use a pouring kettle myself every time I brew a pour over.

different shapes and geometries but, if I'm to be honest, there is perhaps more success in creating novelty than there is in brewing innovation. The good news is that the principle behind this method of brewing is universal and the technique is easily adapted to different brewers.

The Key Principles

When coffee is brewed in this way, four big variables affect the resulting cup of coffee. Unfortunately, they are not independent of each other, which is why precise measurement of both coffee and water is so useful, especially if you are bleary eyed when making the coffee first thing in the morning.

1. **The grind of the coffee.** The finer the coffee, the more is extracted from it as the water passes through. This is because there is a greater surface area, and because water flows through finer coffee more slowly so there will be more contact time. However, going too fine may prevent even extraction, as the water may find or create channels in the coffee bed, which will produce an uneven extraction.
2. **The contact time.** This is not only how quickly the water flows through the coffee, but also how long it takes us to add the water. We can extend the brew time by adding the water very slowly to increase the extraction of the coffee.
3. **The amount of coffee.** The more coffee there is, the longer the water will take to flow through and the longer the contact time, but the more work the water will have to do to properly extract all the flavour from the grounds.
4. **The evenness of the brew.** In a pour over, a number of the steps we will take will be focused on making sure that the brew is as even as possible. It really does make a big impact on the taste.

To replicate a good brew, these four variables must be kept as consistent as possible. If, for example, someone reduces the amount of coffee by accident, they might assume that the reason the coffee did not brew long enough was due to the grind being wrong. If we do not pay attention, it is very easy to get confused and start to make bad coffee.

Above: The strength of a pour-over coffee will depend on the grind size, and the timing and speed of the water flowing through it.

The Bloom

This is the common practice of adding just a little water to the coffee at the start of the brew, usually just enough to get all the coffee wet. When you add the hot water, the grounds start to release the trapped carbon dioxide and the bed of coffee will swell like dough rising. It is typical to wait at least 30 seconds before starting to add the rest of the brew water.

Despite the widespread nature of this practice, there isn't a lot of science to justify it, even though there has been a lot of testing and experimentation. It might be that releasing some of the carbon dioxide helps make the coffee easier to extract, and some studies seem to support this. I think it also adds a pleasant moment to the morning coffee ritual as watching the grounds bloom is a little mesmerizing.

Pour-Over or Filter Brewer Method

It is hard to provide a singular technique that works on all shapes and sizes of pour-over brewers, which can brew anywhere from 12g to 60g of coffee at a time. For smaller brews I have a different approach, because grinding too fine can produce a less even brew. This technique is therefore focused on extending the brew time by adding water in small increments. With larger brews this is less of a concern, and so the focus is on adding more water to keep the thermal mass high during the duration of the brew. See overleaf for a brew method for two or more cups.

Ratio: 60g/l. I recommend this as a starting point for all pour-over and filter methods, but be sure to experiment to find your preference.

Grind: Medium (caster/superfine sugar) (see page 80) would be suitable for brewing around 30g coffee to 500ml water. You will need to grind the beans more finely if you are brewing a single cup, and more coarsely if you want to brew more.

A Brew Method for One Cup

1 Grind the coffee just before you start brewing. Be sure to weigh the coffee first – in this example we will use 15g coffee.

2 Boil a kettle of fresh water suitable for brewing coffee.

3 While the kettle is boiling, place the paper filter in the brewer and rinse briefly under the hot tap. This helps to reduce any taste the paper might impart to the coffee, and also warms up the brewing device.

4 Add the coffee to the brewer, place the brewer on top of the cup or jug, and place on the scales. **A**

5 As soon as the kettle has boiled begin to pour the water.

6 Using the scales as a guide, pour a little water on to the coffee, about twice as much as the coffee by weight – in this case, approximately 30–40g. I like to pick the cone up and give it a little swirl to make sure all the coffee is wet. Careful stirring with a spoon is another option, and preferable if your grinder is an entry-level one that tends to produce more fine

particles. Wait 45 seconds before starting to pour more water. **B**

7 Slowly pour an additional 60–70g water, until the total amount added to the brew from the start is 100g. The timer should show about 1 minute of total brewing at this point.

8 Wait 10 seconds and slowly add another 50g water. This should take up to 10 seconds.

9 Wait another 10 seconds and then add another 50g. (The total weight should now be 200g.) **C**

10 After another 10 seconds' wait, add the final 50g water for a total weight of 250g. Give the liquid in the top of the cone a gentle stir with a spoon, or gently pick up and swirl the brewer. **D**

11 Allow it to drain out completely. The bed of spent grounds should be pretty flat at the end of the brew. **E**

12 Serve, allow to cool a little, and enjoy.

Brewing Basics

A Brew Method for Two or More Cups

You can use this brew method for ground coffee doses from 30g up to 60g. With very large brews, the brewer may not be big enough to pour two main pours and so I would split the overall brew into three or even four. I have yet to see a pour-over brewer that I would recommend using with more than 60g coffee, or for trying to brew with more than a litre of water.

Troubleshooting

If you are not happy with the resulting cup of coffee, think about what you want to change. I would recommend using the grind to change the flavour of the coffee. If the coffee is bitter, it may be over-extracted so you should try your next brew using a slightly coarser grind. If it is weak, sour or astringent, try grinding the coffee more finely for the next brew. Very quickly you will know the best grind settings for the coffees you enjoy.

1 Grind the coffee just before you start brewing. Be sure to weigh the coffee first; in this example we will use 30g coffee.

2 Boil a kettle of fresh water suitable for brewing coffee.

3 While the kettle is boiling, place the paper filter in the brewer and rinse briefly under the hot tap. This helps to reduce any taste the paper might impart to the coffee, and also warms up the brewing device.

4 Add the coffee to the brewer, place the brewer on top of the cup or carafe and place on the scales. **A**

5 As soon as the kettle has boiled, begin to pour the water.

6 Using the scales as a guide, pour a little water on to the coffee, about twice as much as the coffee by weight. In this case, approximately 60–80g. I like to pick the cone up and give it a little swirl to make sure all the coffee is wet. Careful stirring with a spoon is another option, and preferable if your grinder is an entry-level one that tends to produce more fine particles. Wait 45 seconds before starting to pour more water. **B**

7 Slowly pour water across the coffee bed, using a circular motion to cover all the coffee equally, until you have added a total of 60 per cent of the water for the entire brew – the scale should show 300g in this example. The cone is likely to be relatively full, and if it is too full, then you've likely poured the water in a little too quickly.

8 Wait around 15 seconds.

9 Slowly pour the remaining water in. You should poor slowly enough that the cone fills very slowly. If it fills quickly and you cannot add all the water as part of a slow, steady stream, then you may have added the water too fast, or the coffee may be a little too finely ground. **C**

10 After you pour wait 10–15 seconds, and then give the cone a little swirl if the level has dropped sufficiently for you to do this safely. Otherwise, use a spoon and give it a gentle stir. **D**

11 Allow it to drain out completely. The bed of spent grounds should be pretty flat at the end of the brew. **E**

12 Serve, allow to cool a little, and enjoy.

Different Kinds of Filter

There are three main types of filter used in pour-over and filter coffee brewing. Each affects the resulting brew by straining out different things.

Metal

Like the French press, metal filters remove only the larger pieces of ground coffee. The resulting brew will have some silty sediment and will look a little cloudy. It will have the added body from both the suspended grounds and the oils from the coffee, and many people enjoy a cup like this. Metal filters can be used for years as long as they are kept clean and washed regularly, as failure to do so will allow oils to build up and become rancid. Metal filters that have not been properly maintained may benefit from cleaning in a little espresso machine cleaner and/or with an ultrasonic cleaner – similar to the ones used to clean jewellery.

Cloth

Cloth has been used to filter coffee for a very long time. Like paper, it strains out the suspended pieces of coffee, but it does allow some of the oil to come through. The resulting cup is very clean, with a richer, fuller mouthfeel than that achieved with a paper filter. After use, immediately rinse a cloth filter as thoroughly as possible, then dry it quickly. If you leave the cloth to dry slowly it will develop unpleasant flavours, similar to the smell of laundry that has been left in the washing machine too long. If you use the cloth regularly, you can store it wet in a glass of water in the refrigerator. If you plan to store a cloth for a long time, you can put it wet into a zipper storage bag and freeze it. Repeatedly freezing and thawing it will cause the cloth to degrade a little quicker, however.

The cloth shouldn't be allowed to get too stained. For cleaning I would recommend a product called Cafiza, made by Urnex. While this is marketed as an espresso machine cleaner, the original formula was developed to clean the cloths used in very large filter brewers. Dissolve a small amount in hot water and soak the cloth in it, then rinse thoroughly and store.

Paper

Paper filters are the most common type of filter and produce the cleanest cup of coffee. They strain out all the suspended material, as well as any oils that may have ended up in the brew. The resulting cup is a fairly clear liquid, often with a reddish hue. There has been an explosion in options for those looking for a different kind of paper for their pour-over brewer. In addition, sometimes a manufacturer might use different factories to produce its papers, and so there can even be variation between the different pack sizes. Some papers brew a little faster than others, and, generally speaking, slower papers offer more clarity in the brew, although they do require an adjustment in brewing. There are papers specifically sold as being faster flowing, and others focused on different roast levels. It is hard to make broad recommendations here beyond always recommending bleached white papers (look for chlorine-free, oxygen-bleached ones), as the unbleached brown papers tend to impart an unpleasant papery taste to the coffee.

Metal

Cloth

Paper

Electric Filter Machine

An electric coffee machine takes away a lot of the guesswork and adds plenty of repeatability. We still have to be consistent in how much coffee we use, and how much cold water we put into the machine, but aside from that we can mostly trust it to do its job.

However, most domestic filter coffee machines have historically tended to make pretty bad coffee – certainly the cheaper units. The way that the cheaper units heat water produces a mixture of undesirable temperatures. The first water hitting the coffee is often quite a bit too cool, which is not a great way to start the brew. By the end of the brew, by contrast, the brew water tends to be too hot. In addition, this heating element sits under the carafe which keeps the coffee hot after brewing. Keeping coffee hot like this effectively cooks the coffee and quickly transforms it into a harsher, less enjoyable brew.

Thankfully, there has been a good amount of innovation in these kinds of machines, and for relatively modest sums of money you can upgrade to something far better. If you are shopping for a new one, make sure it has been certified to reach suitable temperatures. I would recommend buying a machine endorsed by an organization such as the Specialty Coffee Association or the European Coffee Brewing Centre. Many of these use a thermal carafe instead of a hotplate, which is a great improvement. Do pay attention to the state of your thermal carafe, though, as they can quickly develop an unpleasant patina of old coffee if not cleaned quickly. If this does happen, then soaking the carafe in some espresso machine cleaner, such as Cafiza from Urnex, does a good job of making it look (and work) like new!

For most people, the appeal of a filter coffee machine is not having to interact with the brew, by just loading it up and pushing a button. That said, if you want to squeeze every drop of quality out of your brews, after providing a method that applies to most machines, we also give you a few extra tips, including some for getting better results from cheaper units.

The Electric Filter Machine Method

Ratio: 60g/l. I recommend this as a starting point for all pour-over and filter coffee methods, but be sure to experiment to find your preference.

Grind: Medium (caster/superfine sugar) (see page 80), if making between 500ml and 1 litre of coffee. You will need to grind the beans more coarsely if brewing large volumes, as many machines can brew up to a litre at a time, if not more. As in the pour-over method (see page 93), adjusting the grind size is a better way to change the flavour than adjusting the amount of coffee if you are not happy with your cup.

1 Grind the coffee just before you start brewing. Be sure to weigh the coffee first.
2 Put the filter paper in the brewing basket, then rinse under the hot tap. Add the coffee.
3 Place the brewing basket in the machine, then add fresh water that is suitable for brewing coffee.
4 Switch on the machine and start the brew.
5 Allow the brew to finish.
6 Discard the paper and grounds, and enjoy your coffee.

A few tips

- Some machines have a function where they bloom the coffee, similar to a pour over. Whether or not your machine does this, as soon as the first water is added, it's worth giving the slurry of coffee and water a quick stir to make sure all the grounds are saturated evenly from the get-go.
- Once the brew ends, you can also achieve a small bump in quality by giving the brew a stir to help the last of the water draw down evenly through the coffee.
- If you are brewing a lighter roast in a cheap machine, try loading hot water into the reservoir so that the first water to hit the coffee will be of a suitable temperature. Having to do this regularly is probably a sign to upgrade your machine, but it's a nice hack to use when you are away from home and a cheap machine is all you have access to.

The AeroPress

The AeroPress is a rather unusual coffee maker, but I have yet to meet someone who has one and does not love using it. It was invented in 2005 by Alan Adler, the inventor of the Aerobie throwing ring – hence its name. It is a cheap, durable and very portable brewer that many coffee professionals take with them when they travel around the world. In addition, this brewer is very easy to clean.

The AeroPress combines two different brewing methods. Initially, the water and coffee steep together, as they would in a French press. To complete the brew, a piston is used to push the water through the grounds and then through a paper filter – a little like an espresso machine and a little like a filter coffee maker.

Compared with other kinds of brewer, the number of different recipes and techniques that can be used with the AeroPress is enormous. There is even a competition each year for the best technique, which started in Norway but has ended up growing into an international event dubbed the World AeroPress Championships. Each year the organizers publish the top three methods from the competition on the championship website, which should give you an idea of how variable these brewers can be. I would, however, argue against any claims that the AeroPress can be used to produce espresso or anything like it. It can make small, strong cups of coffee, but a person pushing down on a plunger simply cannot replicate the very high pressures used in an espresso machine.

Ratio and Grind Size

The relationship between grind size, brew time and the amount of brewing water used is incredibly important here. For best results with an AeroPress, you should first decide what kind of coffee you want to drink.

If you want to brew something short and strong, or you want something to make iced coffee with, then I suggest starting with a ratio of 100g/l. If you want to brew a little more quickly, then you will need to grind relatively fine, but I would generally recommend longer brews of at least 2 minutes' steep time. You can use a coarser grind if you choose, but you will need to extend the brewing time for best results.

My opinion on the ideal ratio has changed quite a lot over the years. I would now recommend starting at 55g/l and increasing the amount of coffee if you prefer a stronger cup.

Left: The Aeropress is like a hand-operated cross between an espresso machine and a filter coffee maker: a piston is used to push water through the grounds and then through a paper filter.

The Traditional AeroPress Method

This technique is a great place to start with the AeroPress to produce a balanced, sweet and complex cup of coffee. You may need to grind slightly finer than you expect, and if your first brews are a little weak and empty then this is likely the reason why.

1 Grind 11g of coffee just before you start brewing. Be sure to weigh the coffee first.

2 Put a filter paper into the filter holder and lock into the body of the brewer.

3 Place a mug on your digital scales, put the main part of the brewer on top and add the coffee. **A**

4 Boil a kettle of fresh water suitable for brewing coffee.

5 As soon as the kettle has boiled, add 200g of water to the coffee in the brewer. Immediately insert the top plunger just a little to help create an airlock. Make sure you get all the coffee wet when adding the water. **B**

6 Wait 2 minutes. During this time you can remove the scales, as you don't need them anymore. If you have the time, extending this up to 4–5 minutes can be worthwhile. Do not worry about over-extraction.

7 Keeping one hand on each section of the brewer, pick it up and give it a gentle swirl. This will cause the crust of coffee in the brewer to break and start to sink to the bottom.

8 Wait 30 seconds.

9 Gently press the plunger all the way to the bottom. Once the plunger has reached the bottom, pull it back a couple of centimetres to help prevent drips when you lift the brewer off the cup. **C**

Inverted AeroPress Method

In the past I covered a technique for the inverted method, a technique that brews with the brewer upside down to prevent any liquid dripping through the filter. I have long been hesitant to recommend it, because you need to flip the brewer over to finish the brew and the potential for a hot, painful and messy accident is a little too high for my comfort. In addition, there are now several alternative caps for the AeroPress that make the technique unnecessary. These have a way of holding back the liquid until you push. Sometimes these are marketed as allowing you to produce a higher-pressure extraction, and therefore something close to espresso, but this isn't the case. They do work well at holding back any liquid, so you don't have to worry about getting the plunger in to create the airlock. They are not very expensive, and if you really wish to avoid any liquid dripping through, despite a fairly negligible impact on the extraction, then these are a good investment.

Steep and Release Brewers

There are two steep and release brewers commonly used in coffee. The first is called the Clever Dripper, and the second is a brewer called the Switch that is made by Hario. Both are relatively recent inventions, although the Clever does predate the Switch.

The Clever uses a Melitta-style filter, while the Switch is the same shape as Hario's V60 and so uses the same papers. These brewers look like pour-over cones, but at the base of the cone there is a valve. This means that the coffee and water can be held together for as long as you like, before you open the valve to filter the grounds through a paper and have the coffee drip into the cup or carafe below.

I like these kinds of brewers a lot, as they are easy to use and produce a similar cup to a pour over but with less emphasis on technique and no need for additional equipment like a pouring kettle.

Above: Steep and release brewers like the Clever Dripper produce reliable results with minimum fuss.

The Steep and Release Method

Generally, the limit of the larger sizes of these brewers is around 30g coffee and 500ml water. However, they will be very full at this kind of level. For this example, we will brew a single cup.

Ratio: 60g/l.

Grind: Medium (caster/superfine sugar) (see page 80). A similar grind size to pour over is a good place to start.

1 Grind 15g of coffee just before you start brewing. Be sure to weigh the coffee beans first.

2 Put a filter paper into the brewer and rinse with hot water, making sure to open the valve to discard any water hidden beneath the filter paper.

3 Place the brewer onto a digital scale. **A**

4 Boil a kettle of fresh water suitable for coffee brewing.

5 As soon as the water has boiled, pour 250g water into the brewer.

6 Add the coffee to the brewer. **B**

7 Stir in the coffee. **C**

8 Wait for 2 minutes. **D**

9 Gently stir the coffee to break up the crust of grounds that has formed on the surface. **E**

10 Wait 30 seconds.

11 Put the brewer onto a cup or carafe to open the valve.

12 Allow to drain fully. **F**

13 Allow the coffee to cool and then enjoy.

Stovetop Moka Pot

The moka pot is one of the most iconic coffee brewers, and perhaps one of the most iconic kitchen appliances of all time. While they are still extremely popular in Italy, they have also become a staple in many households around the world. For many people the downsides are offset by the romance of the brewer coupled with the ability to make very strong coffee – even if it is isn't espresso strong.

The patent for the moka pot belongs to Alfonso Bialetti, who invented it in 1933. The Bialetti company continues to produce very popular brewers today. Moka pots are often still made from aluminium (about which there was a false scare story some years ago), although it is possible, and more desirable, to buy a stainless-steel model.

The method below is a little different from the way most people use their moka pot, but the advice may help even those who are already happy with the coffee they produce from it. My biggest issue with this type of coffee maker is that the brewing water reaches temperatures so high that you start to extract very bitter compounds from the coffee. Some people treasure the bitterness of a moka pot brew, others utterly hate the device because of it. The technique below has helped people find a new respect for their long-forgotten brewer and enjoy their coffee a different way.

However, because of the high coffee to water ratio, and because the brew time is quite fast, it is still difficult to make light-roasted, dense or particularly acidic and juicy coffees taste good using this brewing method. I would recommend using a light espresso roast, or perhaps a coffee that is grown at lower elevations. I would steer away from dark roasts because of the propensity of this method to produce a bitter cup.

Left: To get the best results from your stove-top moka pot, choose a light espresso roast or coffee grown at lower altitudes. This will avoid making an overly bitter brew.

A few tips

- Make sure the brewer has cooled down to a safe temperature before taking it apart for cleaning. It must be completely dry before you put it away. Avoid storing it locked fully into position, as this will cause the rubber seal to age more quickly.
- Please clean your moka pot. There is a lingering idea that there should be some sort of patina on it for it to function well. Any coffee-coloured patina is likely to be made of oxidized, dehydrated coffee and will taste bad. A sparkling clean moka pot makes lovely coffee with minimal unnecessary bitterness.

The Stovetop Moka Method

Ratio: 100g/l. In most cases, you do not have much control over the ratio. You simply fill up the ground coffee holder and then fill the unit with water until it reaches just below the overpressure valve, so there is little room for manoeuvre.

Grind: Medium/fine (see page 80). I do not recommend using a very fine (espresso) grind – admittedly, a somewhat controversial stance. I prefer a slightly coarser grind than most people would choose because I prefer to minimize the bitterness in the resulting cup.

1 Grind the coffee just before you start brewing, and fill the basket so it is even and level. Do not compress the coffee. **A**

2 Boil a kettle of fresh water suitable for brewing coffee. The advantage of starting with hot water is that the pot is on the heat for less time and the ground coffee doesn't get as hot before the brew starts, which helps reduce the bitterness.

3 Fill the bottom section of the brewer with hot water to just below the small valve. Do not cover it with water; it is a safety valve which prevents too much pressure from building up.

4 Put the coffee basket in place. Make sure the circular rubber gasket is completely clean, then carefully assemble the brewer. If this does not seal properly, the brewer will not work properly.

5 Put the pot on a low to medium heat, leaving the lid up. When the water starts to boil in the lower chamber, the pressure created by the steam pushes the water through the tube that feeds it to the coffee. This part of the brew is crucial! The faster and harder you boil the water, the more pressure you will create and the faster the brew process will be – you don't want to go too quickly.

6 Coffee should slowly start to appear in the top chamber. Reduce the heat as low as possible, without causing the brew to stall. This may take some trial and error, depending on your heat source. You want to apply as little heat as possible to keep the coffee flowing. **B**

7 Listen carefully. Once you start to hear bubbling and gurgling, the steam is starting to bubble up through the coffee. This means that the coffee is now much hotter than you want it to be if it is to taste good. This is a good time to stop the brewing process.

8 To stop the brew, run the base of the brewer under cold running water. This drop in temperature will cause the steam to condense and the pressure to disappear. **C**

9 The body of the moka pot tends to get hot, so I prefer not to keep coffee in it for long as it can cause the flavour to degrade quite rapidly. Pouring it into your cup(s) straight away is a good idea.

The Vacuum Pot

The vacuum coffee pot, also now known as the syphon brewer, is a very old and exceedingly entertaining way to make coffee. It is, however, also extremely annoying in many respects and sufficiently frustrating that many people relegate their brewer to a cupboard or a shelf as a display piece.

Vacuum coffee pots first appeared in Germany in the 1830s. A patent was issued for one in 1838 to a French woman, Jeanne Richard. The design has not really changed a great deal since its conception. The brewer has two chambers, the lower of which is filled with water and heated to boiling point. The upper chamber, which contains the coffee grounds, is then placed on top, creating a seal and allowing steam to build up in the lower chamber. This trapped steam pushes the water from the bottom chamber up through a tube and a filter into the upper chamber. The water is, at this point, just below boiling point and suitable for making coffee. The brew is left to steep for the desired amount of time; it is important to keep heating the lower chamber while the coffee steeps.

To finish the brew, the vacuum pot is removed from the heat source. As the steam cools, it condenses back into water and creates a vacuum, which sucks the coffee from the upper chamber back through the filter into the bottom chamber. The grounds remain trapped and separate in the upper section and the coffee can be poured from the bottom carafe. The whole process is a pleasing application of physics and is often likened to a classroom experiment. Unfortunately, it is sufficiently difficult to get right that most people try a couple of times and then give up, which is a shame.

Additional Tools

An independent heat source is required for this brewing method. Some vacuum coffee pots are designed to sit directly on a kitchen stove; others come with their own alcohol-burning candle. These candles are best replaced with a very small butane camping stove. In Japan and in some specialist coffee shops, the preferred heat source is a halogen lamp placed under the brewer. This is not the most efficient source of heat, and typically very expensive, but it does look fantastic.

Some people use small bamboo paddles to stir the coffee, but these do nothing special and a spoon works equally well. While I cannot deny there is pleasure in acquiring and using a special set of tools for a ritual, I won't claim they make any difference to the coffee.

The Filter

Most traditional vacuum pots use a cloth filter, which is wrapped around a metal disc. It is important to keep this cloth clean. After every use, clean the cloth as thoroughly as possible under a hot tap. If it is not going to be used for a few days, clean it with a suitable detergent. (For more information about cleaning and storing cloth filters, see page 95.) There are alternatives to cloth, such as paper or metal, but these often need special adapters.

The Vacuum Pot Method

Ratio: 75g/l. Some people prefer to use a little more coffee than this for syphon brewing, especially in Japan where this method is commonly used.

Grind: Medium (caster/superfine sugar) (see page 80).

Because this is an immersion method, you can match your brew time to the grind size. Don't go too fine as you can stall the draw-down process to end the brewing. A very coarse grind will mean a long brew time at higher temperatures, which can make the brew rather bitter.

1 Grind the coffee just before you start brewing. Be sure to weigh the coffee first.

2 Boil a kettle of fresh water suitable for brewing coffee.

3 Fit the filter into the upper chamber, making sure it is completely flush.

4 Place the lower chamber on your digital scales and pour in your calculated amount of hot water, following your desired ratio.

5 Transfer the lower chamber to your heat source (a small butane burner, an alcohol burner or a halogen lamp, as shown here), using the handle to move it.

6 Place the upper chamber on top, but do not seal it yet. If you put the seal on too soon, the expanding gases will push the water up into the top chamber before it is the right temperature, making your coffee taste bad.

7 When the water starts to boil, seal the top chamber on top of the lower chamber. If you are using a controllable heat source, reduce the heat to low at this point. The boiling water will now start pushing up into the top chamber. Look directly down on the filter to make sure it is centred: if it isn't, you will see lots of bubbles flowing from one side. Use your paddle or a spoon to push the filter carefully into place so it is correctly positioned.

8 Initially the bubbling in the top chamber will be quite aggressive, with large bubbles. Once the bubbles become smaller, you are ready to brew. Add the coffee to the water and stir it in until it is completely wet, then start a timer. **A**

9 A crust will form on top. After 30 seconds, give it a gentle stir to knock the floating coffee back into the brew. **B**

10 After another 30 seconds, turn off the heat source. Once the coffee begins to be drawn down into the lower chamber, stir it gently once clockwise and then once anticlockwise to prevent it sticking to the walls of the brewer. If you stir too much, you will get a large dome of coffee at the end of the brew, which suggests uneven extraction.

11 Allow the coffee to draw down completely. A slightly domed bed of grounds will be left in the top chamber. Pour the coffee into a coffee pot, as the retained heat from the carafe can give the coffee a cooked taste. **C**

12 Let the coffee cool. This brewing method produces an incredibly hot cup of coffee.

Opposite: Vacuum coffee pots are an elaborate way to make coffee by immersion. Steam rises from the lower chamber and steeps the coffee grounds held above, then condenses the brew into the lower carafe.

Espresso

For a long time espresso was seen as the ultimate brewing method, a kind of pinnacle in the coffee world. This was likely due to a romantic view of Italian espresso and espresso culture, coupled with the fact that an espresso machine is a fast and flexible solution for a coffee shop. In most of the world, the most popular coffee drinks are all espresso based. Filter coffee was long seen as a poor cousin, sometimes offered at a cheaper price than an espresso, even though it used more ground coffee and was a larger drink.

Making espresso is both incredibly frustrating and very rewarding, and this is part of its charm. There is a mystique around espresso and espresso making – that it is a mountain to be conquered – and this has only added to the romance of the whole thing.

I must offer a word of caution here: do not invest in an espresso machine at home unless you want a new hobby. The fantasy of quickly whipping up a couple of delicious cappuccinos to drink on a lazy Sunday morning while reading the paper is a very long way away from the work involved in preparing the drinks (and cleaning up afterwards). If you just want the drinks and not the work, then do what I do and pop out to a local café where someone else can deal with it all. However, I accept that, for many of us, great coffee is not available locally and this is a good reason to master the art of espresso brewing at home.

The Invention of Espresso

As we have already seen, when you brew coffee, the grind size is very important. The finer you grind the beans, the easier it will be to extract the coffee, and the less water you will require to do so. This means you can produce a stronger cup of coffee. The problem starts when you try to grind the beans so fine that gravity alone cannot push the water through the bed of coffee. This puts a limit on how strong a cup of coffee you can produce without some mechanical assistance.

This problem has been recognized for a very long time, and the first solution in an espresso machine used the pressure of trapped steam to push water through the coffee. Initially, this early espresso machine was simply used by cafés to make regular-strength coffee much more quickly, hence the name. However, the pressure you can generate from steam alone, without endangering lives, is actually relatively low, so various other methods such as air pressure or mains water pressure were tried.

The big breakthrough came with Achille Gaggia's invention in 1938. This used a large lever, pulled by the operator, to compress a spring. When the spring was released, the pressure forced the very hot water through the coffee. The sudden jump in pressure was dramatic and allowed the use of a much finer grind of coffee to produce a much smaller, stronger, but well-extracted cup.

Crema

For most coffee drinkers, one of the key features of espresso is not just the strength of the cup but also the layer of dense foam that tops the drink. Crema is simply Italian for cream and refers to the natural head of foam that forms on top of the coffee, much like a head appears on a pint of beer. The term is credited to Achille Gaggia, whose initial customers were put off by the foam on top. He described it as 'crema caffè naturale' (natural coffee cream) and the word has stuck ever since.

The reason this hazelnut brown, velvety foam forms is that when water is under very high pressure it is able to dissolve more carbon dioxide, the gas present in coffee that is produced as a by-product of the roasting process. Inside the brewing basket the pressure of the water may reach up to around 8 atmospheres. When the brewed liquid gets back to normal atmospheric pressure on its way to the cup, the liquid can no longer hold on to all the gas, so it comes out of solution as innumerable tiny bubbles. These bubbles become trapped in the coffee liquid and appear as a stable foam.

For a long time crema was considered important, but in fact it can only tell you two things: first, whether the coffee is relatively fresh – the longer ago it was roasted, the less carbon dioxide it will contain so the less foam it will produce; and second, whether the cup of espresso is strong or weak. The darker in colour the foam, the stronger the liquid will be. This is because crema is just a foam of the liquid, lighter in colour because of the way the bubbles refract light, so the colour of the coffee determines the colour of the crema. For this reason, coffee that has been roasted darker will also produce a darker crema. The crema cannot tell you if the raw coffee is good, or has been well roasted, or if the equipment used to make the espresso is clean – all key factors in a delicious cup of coffee.

Right: Patented in 1905, this La Pavoni two-group Ideale model was the first machine of its kind to be marketed. It introduced the concept of quickly brewing coffee by the cup to Europe and, later, to the rest of the world.

The Basic Technique

To brew espresso, the ground coffee is placed in a small metal basket held in a handle. The basket has tiny holes that allow the liquid to pass through but prevent any of the pieces of ground coffee, except for the tiniest particles, from making it into the cup.

The coffee in the basket is compressed (tamped) so it is flat. The handle containing the coffee is locked into the espresso machine and the machine is then activated. The machine pumps near-boiling water through the coffee; the liquid then drips into the waiting cup below. With some machines the operator decides when to switch off the pump to finish brewing, either gauging the end of the brew by eye or by weighing the coffee as it comes out to make sure the desired amount of water has

Espresso 107

Above: Gaggia have been producing quality espresso machines since the 1940s and this 1950 model, the Esportazione, is one of the most beautiful. This is a two-group model.

been used. Other machines dispense a specific amount of water and then stop automatically. So far, so simple, but espresso might be one of the most complex and challenging culinary preparations.

Great espresso is about recipe, and good coffee roasters will supply you with plenty of information about how to brew their coffee to get great results. A good recipe is about accurate measurements and should include the following:
- the weight of ground coffee to use in grams (g)
- the amount of liquid you should produce from that coffee, ideally expressed in grams or at least expressed in volume (ml)
- how long the brewing process should take
- how hot the water should be for brewing
- any adjustments to brewing pressure away from the industry standard.

Rather than just give a basic guide, I want to offer some information that will help produce genuinely excellent espresso at home, techniques that I have taught to baristas around the world for years and that I believe are key to brewing espresso as well as is currently possible.

Pressure and Resistance

The aim when learning to brew an espresso is to have the machine produce a desired amount of liquid in a certain time frame. For example, the recipe might state that we want to brew 18g of ground coffee and produce around 40g of liquid in 27–29 seconds. In order to achieve this, what we need to control is how quickly the water flows through the ground coffee.

The speed at which the water flows through the coffee determines how much flavour is extracted, in part because this controls the contact time and in part because the grind size will determine the surface area of ground coffee available for extraction by the brew water. For a long time the dominant thinking was that if the contact time was too long then you would extract negative flavours, as the cup could be harsh, bitter and astringent; this was called over-extraction. Similarly, a flow that was too fast was considered a problem because it would not properly capture all the wanted flavours, and the resulting sour, thin brew was described as under-extracted. Our understanding is now more nuanced, and this change of thinking has opened up new styles of espresso and also made the whole process a little easier and more flexible. What had been missing from our thinking was a focus on how evenly the water was passing through the puck of ground coffee.

For a fixed dose of coffee, the primary control for a brew is the grind size. The finer you grind, the better the pieces fit together and the harder it is to have the water pass through the coffee bed. If you took two jars and filled one with sand and one with the same weight of pebbles, water would flow through the pebbles much faster than through the sand. In the same way, the coarser we grind coffee, the faster the machine can push the water through it. In addition, the depth of the coffee bed – as determined by the weight of the ground coffee used – has an obvious impact. The more coffee there is, the more resistance there will be and so the slower the flow will be.

In order to simply the process, we typically stick to a consistent dose. This means that consistent changes in flow rate are the result of just the grind. If you aren't consistent in your dose, then you don't really know which variable to fix if your espresso doesn't taste good. If you keep your dose consistent, you know that if your espresso brewed faster than you want then you need to grind finer and try again.

This was the traditional approach to espresso brewing, and this has evolved recently as people widened their definitions of how an espresso should be brewed. The focus has moved from the puck to the water involved – both the amount used, which we will describe with the term 'brew ratio', as well as the way that it moves through the puck.

Brew Ratio

There are many different styles of espresso, and people have different preferences for how long or strong they like their espresso to be. Commercially, we tend to talk about the brew ratio: how much liquid should you be brewing from a fixed weight of ground coffee? This ratio is explicitly about the *weight* of the ground coffee and the *weight* of the liquid espresso. A common recipe might suggest 18g of ground coffee, to produce 40g of liquid. This is a ratio of 1:2.2.

The amount of water used turns out be extremely important in brewing espresso. It will determine the strength of the final drink – if you use less water, then the resulting espresso will be more concentrated and more intense and will have a heavier mouthfeel. For many people these are desirable things. The challenge is that the water is the solvent, and the more of it you have the more extraction you can do. To some extent, you can match the ratio to the grind. If you have less water, then grinding finer will expose more surface area and allow a higher extraction. This is true until suddenly it isn't.

Evenness and Channeling

One of the big changes in how people are brewing espresso has come from a focus on getting an even extraction from the whole coffee bed. It is agreed that the more even the extraction, the better the resulting espresso will taste. However, it is very difficult to prepare a bed of coffee that is truly uniform in its resistance, so there will always be some unevenness of flow. At the most extreme, the water is able to find a shortcut through the coffee. This weak spot produces what we call a 'channel' in the puck. More water, proportionally, will flow through this weak point, as the water is looking for the path of least resistance. The coffee around this channel will be very over-extracted, and the rest of the coffee will be somewhat under-extracted. The finer you grind coffee the higher the likelihood of channels in the puck forming. This is why you can't always grind finer to overcome the problem of having less water when making a shorter and stronger espresso. That espresso, brewed from very finely ground coffee, will often simply taste bad.

This realization opened up a different way of thinking about espresso brewing. If you were to keep your dose constant, and your grind slightly coarser, you would have a more even flow through the puck. The one variable you would need to change would be that you would need to use more water in the brew to compensate for that coarser grind size. This resulted in a growing trend of people brewing longer espressos, and with less of a focus on brew time. There is always compromise, so while this technique will produce great flavour it will also produce an espresso with less body and mouthfeel.

Puck Preparation

Before you compress, or tamp, the coffee in the basket you should make sure that it is as evenly distributed as possible. As a minimum you would want to make sure that there isn't a large mound of grounds, either in the centre or off to one side. Most people will solve this with a little tapping of the portafilter. Other people prefer to distribute the coffee around the basket by hand, often using a device called a needle distribution tool, also known as a WDT (Weiss Distribution Technique) tool – named for the person (John Weiss) who popularized it.

For most home grinders, I would recommend avoiding grinding straight from the grinder into the portafilter. Many grinders will provide the option as a point of convenience, but this doesn't set you up for success as well as grinding into a catch cup and giving the coffee a shake before dosing it into the portafilter. Many home grinders will produce quite clumpy grounds and will also tend to give you a large central mound of coffee. Using a dosing cup overcomes these two issues, both of which can cause uneven extraction.

Tamping

'Tamping' is the term used for the compression of the ground coffee before brewing. We do this because ground coffee is fluffy, and if we put uncompressed coffee into the machine the high-pressure water would find the air pockets between the coffee grounds and pass through quickly, skipping much of the coffee.

Many people place a great deal of importance on tamping, but I do not believe it is as important as people think. The goal is simply to push the air out of the coffee bed and to make sure the bed is level and even before brewing. How hard you compress the coffee doesn't make an enormous difference to how

quickly the water passes through it. Once you push all the air out, there is little to no reward for pushing any harder. The espresso machine pushes the water on to the coffee at 9 bars or 130psi (pounds of force per square inch), and this is much more forceful than a human can push down. The goal is simply to produce an even coffee bed, and do no more.

If they notice a little coffee stuck to the walls of the basket, some people will use the tamper to tap the handle to loosen them so they can be tamped down into the coffee bed. Don't tap. If you tap the handle,

you may knock the puck of coffee loose from the walls of the basket, allowing the shot to channel. Also, you may damage your tamper, and the nice ones are beautiful objects in their own right.

My final piece of advice is to hold the tamper properly. It should be held like a flashlight or a screwdriver, with your thumb pointing straight down. When you apply pressure to the coffee, your elbow should be directly above it and your wrist should be straight. If you imagine a screw sticking directly up out of the workbench, you should put your arm in this same position as you push down, so that you protect your wrist (see page 112). Repeatedly performing this action incorrectly has given a huge number of professional baristas trouble with their wrists.

Above: Coffee was first discovered in 9th-century Ethiopia, and the Tomoca coffee shop in Addis Ababa is the oldest surviving café in the country. The later influence of Italian rule is seen in the sleek espresso machines.

The Espresso Method

In this process we are going to make two shots of espresso. These could go into two separate cups, or into one cup as a double espresso.

1 Fill the reservoir in the espresso machine with water suitable for brewing in an espresso machine, then switch on the machine to heat the water.

2 Grind the coffee just before you start brewing. Be sure to weigh the coffee first. **A**

3 Make sure the basket is clean. Wipe it with a small dry cloth to make sure it is dry and to remove any leftover grounds once you have tapped out the puck of coffee from the last brew. The cloth will help remove the oily residue from the last brew as well.

4 If you can, place the entire brew handle (also called the portafilter) on the scales to weigh out the coffee. If this is not possible, remove the basket from the handle and place it on the scales.

5 If your scales are accurate enough, weigh the ground coffee to within 0.1g of your recipe, whether it is your own recipe carefully honed over time, or the recipe given to you by the roaster. This level of accuracy may seem like overkill, but digital scales are now relatively cheap, and I promise that using a set of scales will help you make more delicious coffee more often. **B**

6 Remove the handle from the scales and tamp the coffee flat in the basket, keeping your wrist straight, to make sure the coffee bed is even. Leave the tamper on top of the coffee – observing the angle of the handle will show you whether or not it is sufficiently flat. **C**

7 Place the cup(s) you are going to brew into onto your scale, and zero it.

8 Turn on the machine to flush some water through the group head. This will help to stabilize the temperature of the brew water, as well as rinse off any coffee grounds remaining from the previous brew.

9 Carefully lock the handle into the machine and arrange the cup(s) in place to receive the coffee.

10 Get your timing device ready. If the machine doesn't have a time display showing you how long the shot has been brewing, use the stopwatch on your mobile phone or a kitchen timer.

11 As soon as possible, start brewing the coffee. When you start to brew, start the watch. Record the brew time.

12 When the desired brew weight is reached, stop the machine. With many machines and scales I would recommend stopping around 2g early, as some additional liquid will flow after you stop the machine.

Judging the Results

If the brew time is close to the roaster's recommendation, or is within the range of 30 seconds plus or minus 5 seconds, then you should taste the coffee. If the brew happened too quickly, you may wish to grind the next dose of coffee finer. If the brew was too slow, you should grind coarser. If the brew was too fast, you have the option of using more water next time, should changing the grind not be desirable.

For many people this kind of precision seems a little extreme, and some prefer to use volume in the cup (gauged by eye) instead of weight. The challenge of volume in espresso is that a significant percentage of that volume is made up of crema, which is a foam. The fresher the coffee, the more crema it will produce. So, if you keep the volume fixed as the coffee ages, you will slowly be changing the actual brewing ratio by using more and more water as less and less of the espresso's volume will be made up of crema.

When it comes to tasting espresso, the first quality I would focus on would be acidity. If the acidity is dominant and unpleasant, then you likely haven't extracted the coffee properly. You may need to grind finer or use more water.

Then there is sweetness and the finish. A shot that has channelled will tend to lack sweetness and have a harsh and unpleasant finish to it. Either you need to improve the puck prep, or you need to grind a little coarser and use more water.

Below: Caffè Florian on St Mark's Square, Venice, has been serving coffee since 1720.

Changing the Grind

With espresso, you really need to grind the coffee yourself with a burr grinder that allows you to adjust the grind size easily. When you start brewing a new bag of coffee you will need to set the grinder for it. The term we use for this in the industry is 'dialling in'.

Just about every grinder has some ground coffee left inside it after grinding. This means that, if you change the grind setting, the first coffee it will push out will actually be the old grind size. A common practice is to purge the grinder by grinding a few extra grams of beans at the new size to push out the old grounds, and then to throw this coffee away. If you change the grind size but don't see a change in the brewing process, it is likely you did not purge enough coffee from the grinder. Many modern grind-to-order grinders have focused on reducing retained coffee, and so with newer grinders this is less important.

I would always recommend making small changes when adjusting a grinder. When you get a new grinder, it is a good idea to buy some cheap (though ideally fresh) coffee to play with to make sure you understand how big an effect a small change in the grind setting has on the brewing process. Most grinders have numbers on the settings. The actual value of the numbers is meaningless, but if you want to grind finer, turn the dial to a smaller number and vice versa. Many grinders have marked steps that you can select, sometimes whole numbers and sometimes divisions of numbers. Start by changing the setting by a single step when the grind is wrong.

Brew Ratios and Espresso Styles

While there is no official standard for what constitutes an espresso, there are some broad definitions that are helpful when it comes to describing styles of espresso by their brew ratios:

Ristretto: this is a shorter espresso, the Italian word translating as 'restricted', with a ratio of 1:1 to 1:2.
Espresso/Normale: this is a standard, traditional espresso, with a ratio of 1:2 to 1:3.
Lungo: this is a longer espresso, as the Italian word suggests, with a ratio of 1:3 to 1:5.

There is some debate around the boundaries of these styles, of course, and they have also changed over time and will also vary a little by country or coffee culture.

Brew Temperature

The coffee industry is only now recovering from an obsession with the stability of brew temperature in espresso brewing. Changing the brew temperature does have an effect on the extraction and the taste of the coffee, but I don't believe it is as important as many make it out to be. The hotter the brew water, the more effective it will be at extracting flavour. So, for lighter roasts I would recommend a higher brew temperature than for darker roasts, which give up their flavours more easily.

There are claims that a change in temperature of 0.1°C (0.18°F) will change the taste of the coffee. I believe that to be nonsense. I think 1°C (1.8°F) creates the smallest change that most of us can detect, and in my experience a slightly incorrect brew temperature is so rarely the cause of a flawed espresso.

If you can control the temperature on your espresso machine, I would recommend a water temperature of between 92°C (198°F) and 95°C (203°F) for most light to medium roasts of speciality coffee. If the espresso does not taste right, try adjusting other aspects of the recipe first. However, if there is a persistent negative taste (such as a constant sourness) try increasing the temperature, and if there is a persistent bitterness, try decreasing the temperature (after you have checked your equipment is properly clean). For dark roasts I would suggest brewing between 85°C (185°F) and 90°C (194°F).

Brew Pressure

The first espresso machines created pressure using a compressed spring to push the water through the coffee. As the spring expanded, the pressure it produced would decline, so it started with a very high pressure and ended up relatively low. When electric pumps became common, they needed to be set at a constant pressure. Some say that the setting of 9 bars (130 psi) was chosen because it was the approximate average of the varying pressure created by the springs on older machines.

Luckily, this also appears to be the pressure at which we get the best flow rate. At pressures below 9 bars, the coffee bed provides so much resistance that the flow rate drops. At pressures above 9 bars, the coffee bed becomes so compacted that the flow rate drops again. As long as your machine produces roughly the right pressure, you should have no trouble. Lower pressures can produce better-tasting espresso for many people, due to the decrease in channelling. If you have a cheaper grinder and machine, and you can adjust the pressure, then dropping to 6 bars may improve your coffee. I wouldn't recommend going above 9 bars. At very high pressures, there can be a strange woody bitterness to the espresso that is not enjoyable, and channelling is very likely.

Some control or ability to vary the pressure while making espresso has become more popular, often termed 'pressure profiling'. Varying the pressure is a great way to introduce a variable that will make your espresso taste different, but rarely better. It often feels like it can make a difficult thing (making espresso) more difficult. However, if you are beginning to explore it, then there are two areas that I think offer the most rewards.

Using low pressures at the start of the shot, in a process called pre-infusion, is helpful. Letting the water soak through the puck before the full pressure hits allows you to use a finer grind and get better results. Some machines have pre-infusion built in mechanically, while others allow you to control it. I would avoid machines that engage the pump, turn it off and wait, then turn it back on again. This is very disruptive to the puck of coffee.

The other place that I see benefit to changing the pressure is the second half of the shot. As the water extracts the coffee puck, it is also eroding it. Channelling becomes more likely in the last third of the espresso's brew time, and so reducing the pressure towards the end of the shot can help with this.

There is no small irony that a traditional lever machine does both of these things. When the level is first pulled down, the water is under the pressure of the boiler, usually just above a bar. So, there is a period of pre-infusion. As the lever shot progresses and the spring expands, it produces less force and so there is a decline in pressure. However, we now have more complex solutions for controlling and modulating pressure during the espresso. These can replicate a traditional lever profile, but can also produce other pressure profiles too.

Cleaning and Maintenance

I would estimate that the majority of commercial coffee machines throughout the world are not cleaned properly, and this is one of the reasons people are served disappointing, bitter and unpleasant coffee every day. I think speciality coffee shops are far better at maintaining clean equipment, but they are still far from the majority of places serving coffee. There is no such thing as too clean, and although it requires a little bit of work each time you finish making coffee, a clean machine will make your coffee taste consistently sweet and clean.

- When you finish making coffee, remove the basket from the handle and clean underneath it with soapy water and a scourer. If you don't do this, an unpleasant patina of dried coffee will accumulate there and it will smell and taste awful.
- Espresso machines dispense water through a mesh screen. If this is easily removable on your machine, take it out and clean it. Also clean the water dispersion block it sits against.
- While the dispersion screen is out, clean the rubber gasket. If coffee builds here, the basket

Below: Here the coffee is flowing more readily out of one side of the portafilter, suggesting channelling in the puck.

won't make a seal against the machine and water will leak out during brewing, often dripping down the sides of the brew handle into the cup.
- Remove the brew basket from the handle and replace with the cleaning basket. This is the basket with no holes in it that will have been supplied with your machine.
- I recommend using a commercial espresso machine cleaner at the end of every session of coffee making. This will clean out any liquid coffee left inside the machine, which will turn increasingly rancid and unpleasant over time. Follow the manufacturer's instructions for how to use a cleaning powder on your machine.
- Make sure the steam wand is clean if you have used it. Avoid soaking the wand in water. If the tip becomes clogged, it can usually be removed for cleaning separately.

Some people claim that a machine can taste too clean, and that you need to brew an espresso or two to 'season' it after cleaning to take away the metallic taste. I have never found this to be the case, and as long as your machine is properly warmed up (add at least 10–15 minutes on top of the manufacturer's recommendation), it should make great coffee straight away after cleaning.

I recommend keeping the machine switched off when not in use. Use a timer to make sure it is ready to make coffee when you want it, but turn it off when you have finished. Espresso machines use quite a lot of power, and it is a waste to leave them on if they are not being used. I am pleased that there is a growing trend towards espresso machines that heat very rapidly and so are less wasteful of heat energy through long warm-up periods.

To keep your machine in good working order, make sure the water you use is suitable. If you use hard water, limescale will build up quickly in the machine and cause it to malfunction. Many manufacturers offer advice for descaling, as some limescale will form even in soft water areas (it will just take a lot longer). Err on the side of caution because, if you let your machine scale up completely, it may be difficult to descale without help from a professional (and a bill to go with it).

Over time, the rubber gasket in the group head may need changing. When you lock in your brew handle, it should stick out at 90 degrees to the machine. If it starts to twist much farther across, the rubber may be wearing and it should be replaced. If it starts to leak, replace it immediately.

Coffees Roasted for Espresso

Espresso is quite different from the other brewing methods, and because of the small amounts of water being used, it is often a challenge to fully extract the coffee. Additionally, because the concentration is so high (the coffee being so strong), balance is very important. A coffee that may taste delicious and balanced as a weaker brew can become dominated by overpowering acidity when consumed as a stronger cup.

For that reason, many roasters change how they roast their coffee when they know it is going to be used for espresso. Although this practice is not universal, I would certainly recommend a slightly slower and slightly darker roast for espresso than I would recommend for a coffee being brewed with a filter, unless you are looking to experiment with much longer brew ratios for your espresso.

However, roasters around the world disagree strongly about what the right level of roast is for espresso, and there is a wide spectrum on offer from relatively light through to a much darker roast. Personally, I prefer lighter roasts because they allow the characteristics of the raw coffee to be appreciated. Darker roasts often carry a more generic 'roasted coffee' flavour, and also a higher level of bitterness, which I don't enjoy. What I prefer is really only important to me, however, and everyone has their own preference.

The darker the roast of coffee, the easier it is to extract. This is because the coffee bean becomes increasingly porous and brittle as it is roasted. This means that less water is required in the brewing process to properly extract the coffee. If body and mouthfeel are important to you, you might prefer slightly darker roasts brewed at a 1:1.5 brew ratio. If sweetness and clarity of flavour are important, I would recommend a lighter espresso roast brewed at a ratio of 1:2 to 1:2.5.

Customers congregate around baristas at London's first espresso bar, the Moka Bar at 29 Frith Street, which was established in 1953 and opened by the Italian actress Gina Lollobrigida.

Steaming Milk

Well-steamed milk combined with well-brewed espresso is a wonderful experience. Great milk foam is like liquid marshmallow: soft, velvety and undeniably enjoyable to drink. The goal is to create bubbles so small that they are almost invisible (often called 'microfoam'). Foam like this is elastic and pourable and adds a wonderful lift to the texture of drinks like cappuccino and caffè latte.

It is important to use fresh milk for steaming. As it reaches its use-by date, milk tastes fine and is still safe to drink but it starts to lose its ability to create a stable foam. It will foam as normal when you steam it, but the bubbles will soon break down. If you lift the jug of foamed milk to your ear, you will hear it fizzing like a freshly poured soda as the air escapes.

When we steam milk we have two separate tasks to accomplish: we must whip in air to create the bubbles and we must heat the milk. With most steam wands it is best to tackle one task at a time, so the first thing to focus on is creating the bubbles. Then, when we have added enough air to the milk and it is the desired volume, we can focus solely on heating it to the desired temperature.

The Right Temperature

The ideal temperature for milk, when combined with coffee, is a subject of some contention between many coffee shops and their customers. Milk begins to irreversibly degrade in flavour and texture above 68°C (154°F). This is because the heat alters and denatures the proteins, creating new flavours, though not always good ones. The smell of cooked milk reminds me of eggs at best, and baby sick at worst.

A very hot cappuccino will lack the texture, flavour and sweetness of a drink made with milk that has been heated to 60°C (140°F). It is impossible to produce good microfoam when the milk has been heated to boiling point. Unfortunately, this is the nature of milk – we can either have a very hot or a very delicious drink. This is not to say that all drinks should be served lukewarm, instead that they should be enjoyed as soon as they are made.

Whole Milk, Skimmed and Non-Dariy Alternatives

It is the protein in the milk that supports the bubbles, so dairy milk will foam well regardless of whether it is skimmed or whole. However, the fat content does play a role: it not only adds a wonderful texture to the drink but also changes the way flavour is released. A cappuccino made with skimmed milk has an immediate, intense coffee flavour which does not linger. If the cappuccino is made with whole milk, the flavours will be less intense but will last longer. I always recommend using whole milk, but I also prefer relatively small milk drinks. I think a small, rich cappuccino is a delight.

Non-dairy milks, in particular oat-based milks, have become a very popular choice. While it took some time, many brands now have coffee-specific versions of their products which will foam very well, pour well and taste quite neutral and pleasant when combined with coffee. In the past avoiding dairy was something of a compromise in experience. That is no longer the case.

The Steaming Milk Method

This technique is suitable for traditional steam wands. If your machine has a range of attachments or automatic frothing functions, follow the manufacturer's instructions.

1 Start by pointing the steam wand over the drip tray or into a cloth and briefly opening the valve. This will get rid of any condensation inside the wand. This is known as purging. **A**

2 Pour cold fresh milk into a clean stainless-steel steaming pitcher. It should not be more than 50 per cent full.

3 Dip the steam wand into the milk so just the tip is submerged. Ideally, the wand should be at a 45-degree angle, and as you look into the jug the wand should be off centre in the milk. **B**

4 Open the valve to full flow and gently lower the pitcher until the wand is almost out of the milk. Listen carefully: you want to hear the slurping sound of the steam wand start to whip air into the milk. As the milk expands, lower the pitcher a little more to bring it back to the surface if you wish to add more air.

5 When you have your desired amount of foam, which should ideally happen before the milk feels warm to the touch, then submerge the steam tip again to start heating the foam – you want it to be just under the surface, not at the bottom of the pitcher. Position it slightly to one side and you will see the milk start to spin and churn. The process should now be relatively quiet.

6 To test whether the milk is warm enough, place your free hand on the bottom of the jug. Continue to heat the milk until the jug becomes uncomfortable to touch. At this point the milk will be about 55°C (131°F). Remove your hand from the bottom of the jug and continue to steam for 3–5 seconds, depending on how hot you like your milk. If you don't feel confident doing this, you can dip a milk-specific digital thermometer into the milk. I would recommend this over an analogue one, which will tend to lag quite badly.

7 Close the steam valve fully and put the milk pitcher down. Wipe the steam wand with a clean, damp cloth and purge the wand into the cloth to remove any leftover milk from inside the wand.

8 Don't worry if your foam contains a few large, ugly bubbles. If you let it sit for a few seconds, the milk will drain off the surface of the larger bubbles, making them very brittle. A couple of gentle taps of the steaming pitcher on the counter will usually pop them.

9 If you want to pour a combination of milk and foam into your drink, which I strongly recommend, you must make sure that they are fully combined. After the tapping, swirl the milk and foam together, much like you might swirl wine in a glass before smelling it. You can be quite aggressive, as you want to make sure that the liquid milk is fully combined with the wonderful microfoam. Swirl until the milk foam has a glossy finish, then pour it into your drink. **C**

Steaming Milk

Espresso Equipment

There are espresso machines to suit almost any budget, from cheap units with which you can make a start, to smarter machines that can cost as much as a small car. All of them are designed to do the same thing: heat water, then push it forwards at high pressure.

The more money you pay, the more the machines improve in build quality, control and consistency. Most of this consistency concerns how the machine heats water, and how it creates water pressure, and different types of espresso machine achieve this in different ways.

Thermoblock Machines

The cheapest domestic espresso machines use this technology to produce espresso. There is a single unit inside the machine with an element to heat the metal block that in turn heats the water as it passes through a tube snaking through the metal. Most of these machines have two settings: one to heat the water up to a suitable temperature for brewing coffee, and the other to boil water to generate steam. This means that the machine can only perform one function at a time, and I would recommend brewing coffee first, and then heating up the machine to steam milk.

Broadly speaking, thermoblock machines do not produce a very consistent water temperature, and the lack of ability to perform both brewing and steaming at once limits how many drinks the machine can practically make, which can be frustrating for the user. There are higher-end machines using better versions

A Word of Advice

A great espresso machine can be a beautiful object, a satisfying tool and a technical marvel, but it will be a waste of money if you are pairing it with anything but an excellent coffee grinder.

I would always recommend upgrading your coffee grinder first, rather than your espresso machine. A good grinder and a thermoblock machine will make better coffee than a cheap grinder and a top-of-the-line dual-boiler espresso machine. Spending money on a grinder gives a greater return on investment when it comes to how good your coffee will taste at home.

Finally, I would recommend descaling your equipment regularly if the water you use is medium to hard. Allowing scale to build up over time will reduce the quality of your coffee, and you won't realize you have a problem until you have a failure that comes with an annoying bill because a professional needs to fix it. There are plenty of espresso-specific descalers out there, but food-grade citric acid is often an excellent choice, and very cheap to purchase.

Above: A look inside a dual boiler machine – the smaller boiler close to the group head produces water at a temperature suitable for espresso brewing, while the larger boiler produces boiling water and steam.

of this technology, but those are the minority. However, when paired with a good grinder, a typical machine can certainly produce good espresso.

Thermoblock machines usually use a vibration pump to generate pressure. These have two disadvantages: they are quite noisy, and they are rarely accurately set. The desired pressure for espresso is around 9 bars (130psi). These pumps are usually set much higher, and manufacturers will often proudly boast that their machine can produce 15 bars (220psi) of pressure, as if more is somehow better.

The machines have an overpressure valve that should open at 9 bars (130psi) to alleviate the excess pressure. These valves are not usually very well calibrated and may need adjustment over time. While there is a lot of guidance available online, I do not recommend opening up your machine yourself, as you will probably invalidate your warranty, and in any case – and more importantly – unless you know what you're doing, it's always best to leave electrical appliances alone.

Heat-Exchange Machines

Although it is still common in commercial espresso machines, this technology is available in home machines, too. The machine still has a single element, but it heats a small boiler of water to around 110–120°C (230–248°F). This generates plenty of steam, which is always available for foaming milk. However, the water in this boiler is too hot to brew coffee, so the machine pumps fresh cold water through what is called a heat exchange. This is usually some sort of tube that passes through the steam boiler. While the coffee-brewing water is kept separate from the boiler water, heat from the boiler is quickly passed to the brewing water to bring it up to the desired temperature.

These kinds of machine are often referred to as 'prosumer', as they straddle the divide between consumer prices and professional performance. The disadvantage of heat-exchange machines, certainly domestic ones, is that changes in the boiler temperature will affect the temperature of the brew water. If you want more steam, you have to increase the boiler temperature, which will also increase the brew temperature. If you want to noticeably reduce the brew temperature, your steaming performance may suff as a result.

Many of these machines use mechanical thermostats to control the boiler temperature and this can result in some variation. Better machines have more reliable control over the boiler temperature.

Heat-exchange machines can be fitted with either a vibration pump (see above) or a rotary pump. Rotary pumps are used on commercial equipment and are quieter and easier to adjust, but there is not a lot of difference in performance between the different types of pump if they are set to the same pressure.

Temperature Surfing

With many machines, both heat exchangers and dual boilers, there can be benefits from learning how to 'temperature surf'. When the machines have been sitting idle for a while it is possible for some of the brew water, or the group head itself, to get too hot. Running the group without the portafilter in place will evacuate the hot water, replacing it with cooler water. Then a short wait allows the system to stabilize before you brew the shot. This helps produce more consistent, and often more desirable, brew temperatures from the machine. Each machine does work a little differently, but a combination of a little research and a little experimentation can yield some noticeable improvements in your espresso.

Dual Boiler Machines

The idea here is to separate the coffee brew water entirely from the water used to generate steam, and as the name suggests the machine does this by having one boiler and element for the brewing water, and then a separate larger boiler that heats its water up to a higher temperature for producing steam and boiling water for tea or americanos, for example.

The temperature in the coffee boiler is usually very finely tuned with digital controls, allowing easy adjustments of temperature and greater levels of stability. These machines can undeniably produce coffee as good as any commercial machine, but they often come with price tags to match.

Lever Machines

There has been a resurgence in interest in these kinds of machine in the last decade for a few reasons. In a lever machine the pressure that forces the water through the coffee is generated via a lever. This is either done directly, where you are forcing the water through by direct force, or indirectly, where the lever is pulled down to compress a spring which, when released, pushes a piston down that applies pressure to the water to push it through the coffee.

Lever machines can be great entry points to coffee making. They can be entirely mechanical, so you add freshly boiled water and they need no power supply. They can make excellent coffee, although they usually require a bit of extra work to fully pre-heat everything. There are also traditional electric versions. These usually have a single boiler that produces hot water and steam. Lifting the lever draws water into the group and then you or the spring do the rest. These machines are prone to overheating, and typically have sealed boilers, meaning you have to cool the machine to add more water to it. They are a little more work, but can still produce great espresso in a way that can feel particularly satisfying.

Espresso Grinders

A grinder suitable for use with an espresso machine will need to do two key things: it must be able to grind the coffee finely enough to make good espresso, and it must be easily adjustable to make very small changes in the grind size.

More expensive grinders tend to have better control over the grind setting, and a more powerful motor inside, which will be quieter. At the top end are the burr grinders with cutting discs inside, which produce fewer very tiny pieces of coffee that can add bitterness to the cup.

In the last decade, no sector of the coffee equipment market has seen the same level of innovation and new product release. A good espresso grinder was once a very significant investment, but you can get truly excellent results from grinders that now cost as little as $200 (£160). That's no small sum, but they are still a great deal cheaper than they used to be. There is now a great, perhaps overwhelming, level of choice for espresso grinders. I would still factor in things like after-sales support, and a history of reliability, as much as I would be worrying about the little differences in grind profiles.

Left: A manual lever machine is a simple but satisfying way to make an excellent cup of espresso. The lever forces boiling water through the coffee using either a spring or arm power alone.

Espresso-Based Drinks

Whether they are long, short, milky or dark, there is a wide variety of coffee drinks that start with an espresso as their base.

Espresso

There are many definitions for what makes an espresso an espresso, some extremely precise and some more general. I would define an espresso as a small, strong drink made using finely ground coffee under high water pressure. I would also add that an espresso should have crema. More precisely, I would say the ratio of the weight of ground coffee to the weight of the finished beverage is about 1:2 to 1:2.5. I would rather have an open definition and treat espresso as a broad church than be overly prescriptive about what is right and wrong.

Ristretto

This translates from the Italian as 'restricted', and the idea is to produce an even smaller and stronger cup of coffee than an espresso, something with a ratio of 1:2 or lower. This is done by using less brewing water for the same amount of ground coffee. The grind of the coffee should be finer so the brew time remains long enough to extract all the desirable aromatics from the coffee. Brewing a good ristretto is difficult, and if you love this style of espresso then picking both the right coffee to start with, alongside the right equipment, is important in achieving the best results. Generally, a slightly darker and more developed roast will be easier to work with, and a good-quality grinder is essential.

Lungo

The lungo, or 'long', coffee was until recently considered deeply unfashionable in the speciality coffee world. It was usually brewed using an espresso machine but with three to four times the amount of water to the same weight of coffee to make a much larger drink. The resulting cup was much weaker and, while a longer-lasting experience for the consumer, it was considered inferior due to the lack of body and mouthfeel. Until recently most lungos served in cafés were often done so by accident, and tended to taste ashy, harsh and bitter.

However, recently there has been a movement within the speciality coffee industry to brew lighter-roasted coffees this way, resulting in a complex and balanced brew that I think can be delicious. If ever you are struggling to balance the acidity in an espresso blend, try making it into a longer drink by adding more water to the same amount of coffee. The grind will need to be made a little coarser to allow a faster flow and prevent uneven extraction.

Macchiato

This drink takes its name from the idea of 'marking' or 'staining' an espresso with some milk foam. In Italy it is not unusual to see a busy barista line up several cups of espresso on the bar for the customers. If one of them likes just a drop of milk in their drink, it is important to add a small dollop of milk foam as well to mark which cup it is. If you pour just a little milk into a freshly made espresso, it will disappear under the crema, and you won't be able to spot it.

In the last decade or so, many quality-focused coffee shops have done something quite different with the drink. They have turned a macchiato into an espresso topped up with foamed milk. This is often done at the request of the customer, who wants a longer, milkier and sweeter drink. Sometimes, to be honest, it is done because the barista likes to show off and pour latte art in very small cups.

To further confuse matters, Starbucks has a drink called a Caramel Macchiato. This is an entirely different drink, much closer to a caffè latte that has been 'marked' or 'stained' by caramel syrup. This has created some customer confusion, especially in North America, so it is now common to see coffee shops refer to what they offer as a 'traditional macchiato'.

Cappuccino

There remain a great many myths around the cappuccino. One to get out of the way quickly is that the name has something to do with the *hoods* of Capuchin friars' robes or the bald spot on their heads. The original name for the drink was a *Kapuziner*, and it was a Viennese drink in the 19th century. It was a small brewed coffee mixed with milk or cream until it attained the same shade of brown as the Capuchin friars' robes. Essentially the name implies the strength of the drink.

Another recent myth surrounding the cappuccino is the rule of thirds. The rule of thirds is passed around to this day and describes a traditional cappuccino as being one-third espresso, one-third milk and one-third foam. I was taught this very early on in my coffee career, but this recipe has no root in tradition. I have read quite a few books about coffee and the first reference to the cappuccino rule of thirds I can find was written in the 1950s. It describes cappuccino as 'an espresso mixed with equal amounts of milk and foam'. This sentence appears almost verbatim several times in the book. The phrase is a little ambiguous as it could be saying that only the milk and foam are in equal quantities, or that all three ingredients are. So instead of the recipe being 1:1:1, the author could easily have meant it was 1:2:2.

The 150–175ml cappuccino made with a single shot of espresso in the ratio of 1:2:2 does have a long tradition and is still widely served in much of Italy and the parts of Europe that haven't yet succumbed to more generous portions of coffee as fast-food retail. This drink is, when well made, absolutely delicious.

I think a great cappuccino is the pinnacle of milk-based espresso drinks. A rich layer of dense, creamy foam combined with sweet, warming milk and the flavours of a well-brewed espresso are an absolute delight. Often, a great milk drink is served under the name of the cappuccino, but it really does need a good layer of silky, marshmallowy microfoam to offer the peak experience of the cappuccino. The closer to lukewarm you can enjoy a cappuccino, the sweeter it will be, and I confess that the best ones I have drunk disappeared in a few greedy mouthfuls – impossible if the drink is too warm.

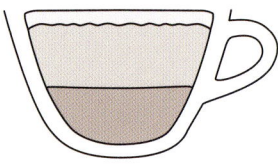

Caffè Latte

This drink did not originate in Italy. When espresso first spread around the world, it was a bitter, intense and extraordinary coffee experience for most. For some people, the bitterness was a problem, so they added hot milk to make the drink sweeter and less bitter. The caffè latte was created to satisfy the customers who wanted the coffee experience with less intensity.

Typically, there is more liquid milk in a caffè latte than in a cappuccino, making the coffee flavour less intense. It is also traditional to have less foam in the milk.

I am always careful to describe this drink as a caffè latte, rather than just a latte, because many people travel to Italy and if they order a latte there, they will suffer the humiliation of simply receiving a glass of milk.

One Cappuccino a Day

There is a tradition in Italy of having just one cappuccino in the morning, then drinking only espresso for the rest of the day. I believe this is a fascinating example of culture reflecting diet. Like most Southern Europeans, many Italians are lactose intolerant. However, a lactose-intolerant person can consume a small amount of milk without a problem, hence the daily cappuccino. A second or third cappuccino, however, even a small Italian one, could result in some gastric distress, so Italian culture prevents the excessive consumption of milk by making it a small cultural taboo to keep drinking cappuccino throughout the day.

Flat White

Different coffee cultures around the world have contributed different drinks, and while the argument continues over whether the flat white was invented in Australia or New Zealand, it is undeniably from Australasia and has been spread by those who have travelled to Europe and North America to open businesses there. In the UK, the name first became synonymous with the offerings of quality-focused cafés, to the point that it was adopted by the major chains and put on their menus. The drink probably had lowlier origins, however. By the 1990s it was common, almost everywhere outside Italy, for a cappuccino to come with an enormous head of dry, meringue-like foam. Sometimes this would rise up from the top of the cup like a mountain, carefully dusted with chocolate powder.

Many consumers were frustrated to be sold a cup of coffee that seemed to be mostly air and began to ask for a flat, white coffee. No foam, just coffee and milk. These became sufficiently part of the culture there that when people started focusing on quality more and more, and on better milk texture and latte art, the flat white was remade as something delicious.

The best description I can offer is that a flat white is like a small, strong latte. It should have a strong coffee flavour and is usually made with a double ristretto or a double espresso, topped up with hot milk to make a 150–175ml drink. The milk has a little foam added to it, but not very much. This makes it relatively easy to pour intricate patterns, known as latte art, into the drink.

Americano

The story goes that the American soldiers stationed in Italy after World War II found the espresso too strong. They often asked for their espresso to be served with some hot water, or diluted down to the point that it resembled the coffee they were used to at home. This style of drink picked up the name *caffè americano*.

Although it resembles a cup of filter coffee, I think the americano – while very enjoyable – is rarely as complex or sweet as well-brewed filter coffee. However, it remains popular with café owners because it allows them to serve filter-coffee-strength brews without having to buy additional equipment.

My recommendations for making an americano are simple. Pour some fresh, clean hot water into a cup, then brew a double espresso on top. If your espresso machine has a steam boiler, it should be able to deliver the hot water, although if you have not taken water from the machine for a while it may taste unpleasant. Some people claim that you should never add very hot water to an espresso and always brew the espresso on top of the hot water. I don't think it makes a great deal of difference; I just find the resulting coffee is cleaner and looks better.

The one disadvantage of diluting espresso is that you increase the perceived bitterness slightly. For that reason, as soon as you finish brewing the americano, I would recommend scooping the crema off the top of the drink and discarding it. Crema is delightful to look at, but there are many tiny pieces of ground coffee trapped in the foam, so the crema contributes additional bitterness to the drink. Removing the crema before stirring and drinking improves the flavour of an americano. (I would also recommend tasting an espresso after you remove the crema – the difference in flavour is dramatic. While I prefer the taste of an espresso without crema, I don't want the extra work and am happy enough to enjoy it as it is. With an americano, however, I really do think the extra work is worthwhile.)

Cortado

This is one of the few coffee-based drinks that does not have Italian origins. In fact, it comes from Spain, most likely Madrid, where it is commonly served. Traditionally, the Spanish brew their espresso slightly longer, and often a little weaker, than the Italians. To make a cortado, about 30ml of espresso is combined with an equal quantity of steamed milk. This is traditionally served in a glass. The drink seems to have spread and has been reinterpreted in a few different ways, but this is the basic idea behind it.

Home Roasting

In the past it was not uncommon for people to buy raw coffee and roast it at home. Since the mid-20th century, however, the trend has undeniably favoured convenience. Roasting coffee at home is fun and relatively inexpensive, although it is a considerable challenge to achieve the same quality of roasted coffee as the very best commercial roasters.

Home roasting allows you to roast smaller batches of raw coffees than you might be able to buy roasted, so you can explore a greater number of green coffees and learn as you go. Like any hobby, there will probably be terrible failures and surprise successes along the way. It is important to consider roasting coffee as a new hobby, not as a way to save money on buying roasted coffee beans. The time invested, as well as the equipment, means that you should be enjoying the time spent roasting and learning, rather than seeing it as a chore.

An increasing number of companies are selling green coffee online. While raw coffee does have a longer shelf life than roasted coffee, I would caution against buying in bulk. Raw coffee does fade over time, and you would certainly want to use any beans you buy within 3–6 months. Freezing in vacuum-sealed bags will probably add some additional lifespan to the coffee, but the few commercial roasters who freeze raw coffee for long-term storage tend to use temperatures lower than domestic freezers can achieve (that is to say, −40°C/−40°F)

When it comes to selecting raw coffees, I would recommend making sure what you are buying is genuinely traceable (see sections on individual countries for guidance). I would also recommend occasionally buying green coffee from a company that sells the same coffee roasted. This will allow you to benchmark your own roasting by comparing your roasted beans with the commercially roasted beans and thus see how you are progressing.

Home-Roasting Machines

It is possible to roast coffee in almost anything that generates enough heat: you can put raw coffee on a baking sheet and bake it in the oven until browned, but the results will be pretty terrible. The coffee will be unevenly roasted, and the part of the coffee in contact with the tray may be scorched. Roasting this way highlights the need for the movement and agitation of coffee beans during the roasting process, to get an even result. Roasting coffee in a wok is possible, but the amount of stirring required quickly makes the process tiresome and frustrating.

Many people start out with something a bit more sophisticated, such as using a heat gun and agitating the coffee beans regularly as they roast, or using a modified electric popcorn machine. Second-hand popcorn machines can be acquired cheaply and do a reasonable job of roasting coffee: they will usually roast a small batch of coffee quite quickly – in around 4–5 minutes – but they don't do a great job of producing even results at lighter roasts. People who prefer darker, more developed roasts seem to have more success with them. Bear in mind that this is not the use these machines were designed for, and some models may not have enough power to roast coffee properly.

If you really want to roast coffee at home successfully, you will need a machine specifically

The Perfect Roast

Ideally, a roast in a hot-air roaster should last for 8–12 minutes. Drum roasts tend to be a little slower, more like 10–15 minutes, depending on the size of the batch of coffee. If the resulting coffee tastes very bitter, you may have roasted too dark. If it lacks flavours and sweetness, you may have roasted too slowly. If it tastes very sour, astringent and grassy, you have probably roasted the coffee too quickly. A combination of lots of tasting and a little trial and error is a healthy part of the process and will allow you to understand your own preferences more and more. There are plenty of resources freely available now, including roast logging and profiling software that can be added to most machines, and there are active online communities discussing the delightful minutiae of roasting your own coffee.

designed for the purpose. Start small and decide whether you enjoy the ritual, the regularity of it and the overall process. Starting this way is easy and fun, and there is no regret if you decide you would rather leave this part of the process to the professionals.

There are two main types of machine available to the home roaster: hot-air roasters and drum roasters.

Hot-Air Roasters

Hot-air roasters mimic, on a much smaller scale, commercial fluid-bed roasters (see page 66). They work rather like powerful popcorn poppers: the hot air agitates and moves the beans around in the roasting chamber to produce an even roast, as well as providing the necessary heat to turn them brown. You have some level of control over the amount of heat and the fan speed, so you can speed up or slow down the process as necessary. Cheaper than drum roasters, these machines are a great starting point for someone looking to dip a toe in the home-roasting process.

Some machines do a better job than others of dealing with the smoke and smells produced during roasting, but I would still recommend roasting in a well-ventilated area. However, if you roast outside in the cold, roasting times may be slower than you want.

Drum Roasters

Home drum roasters are similar in design to commercial drum roasters. While the entry-level units are not built with the same quality and weight of materials as professional roasting machines, there has been something of a boom in semi-professional roasting machines with a capacity up to around 1kg (just under 2¼lb). These roasters are often expensive but excellent, and some are finding homes in commercial roasting businesses where very small batch sizes may be needed. Similar in design to larger-scale roasters, the coffee is tumbled around in a heated drum, which is designed to keep the beans moving to allow even browning while having the hot air moving through the drum do most of the heat transfer work.

Some drum machines offer more programming functions, allowing you to create your own roast profiles. The intensity of the heat can be varied during the roast, and the machine can automate the process to allow easy replication of your favourite roasts.

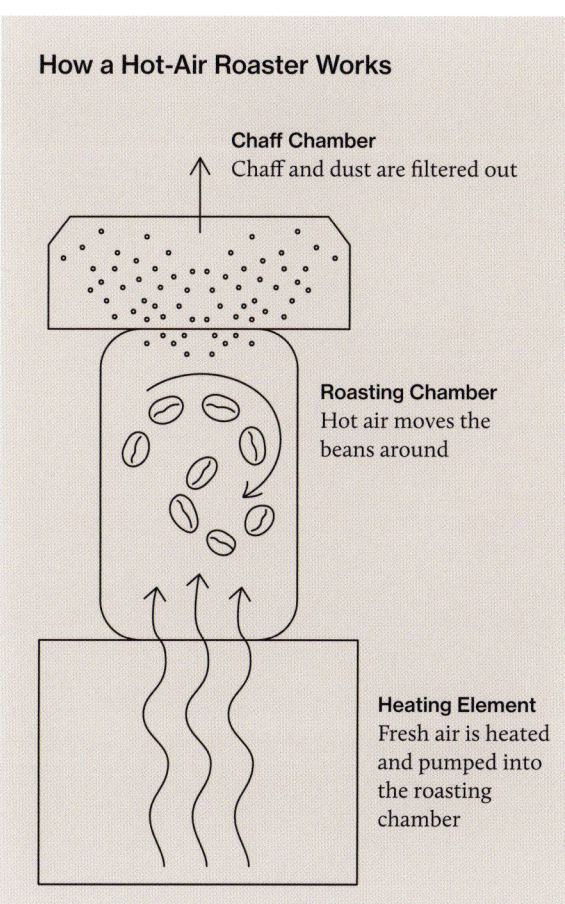

How a Hot-Air Roaster Works

Chaff Chamber
Chaff and dust are filtered out

Roasting Chamber
Hot air moves the beans around

Heating Element
Fresh air is heated and pumped into the roasting chamber

Above: Roasting coffee beans at home will have some failures and surprise successes, but it is worth trying if you are interested in exploring coffee as a hobby in a deeper way.

Part Three
Coffee Origins

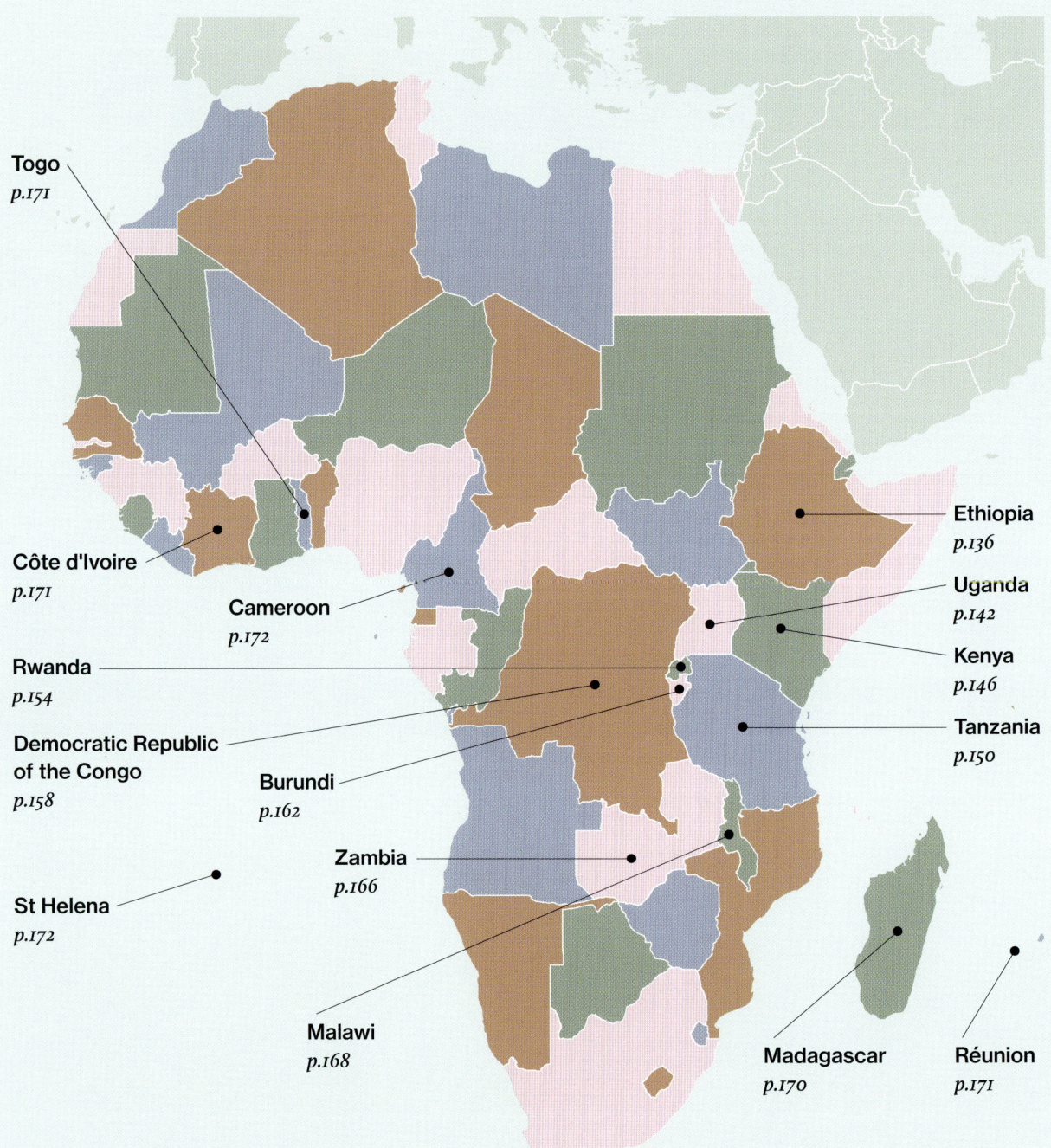

Africa

While Ethiopia is commonly recognized as the birthplace of coffee, significant coffee crops are also grown in Central and East Africa. There are established export markets for beans from Kenya, Burundi, Malawi, Rwanda, Tanzania and Zambia. Each country has its own techniques and varieties, creating a diverse selection for buyers. This section discusses key coffee-growing regions within each country and highlights the typical harvest process, taste profile and traceability of beans.

While the focus is on East Africa, due to the fact that these are the origins you are likely to see if you are buying speciality coffee, it should be noted that West Africa has long been home to substantial coffee production – but this production has been Robusta and so not within the scope of this book. Countries like Angola, Côte d'Ivoire, Cameroon, the Central African Republic, Ghana, Guinea and Togo produce significant quantities of coffee.

Ethiopia

Of all the coffee-producing countries, Ethiopia is perhaps the most compelling. Its fascination stems not only from the unusual, astonishing coffees it produces, but from the mystery that shrouds so much of it. The explosively floral and fruity coffees from Ethiopia have opened many a coffee professional's eyes to the diversity of flavour that coffee can have.

Ethiopia is referred to as the birthplace of coffee, although this should come with some caveats. It is likely *Coffea arabica* first appeared in what is now South Sudan, but it only flourished once it had spread into Ethiopia. It was here that it was first consumed by humans, initially as a fruit rather than a beverage. Yemen was the first country to grow coffee as a crop, but it had been harvested from the wild in Ethiopia long before. Coffee was probably first exported from Ethiopia in the 1600s. Interest from European traders was often rebuffed, and it then waned as coffee plantations began to appear in Yemen, Java and, ultimately, the Americas. Coffee production in Ethiopia at the time was essentially the harvest of wild coffee trees that grew in the former province of Kaffa and Buno, rather than from plantations.

Interest returned to Ethiopian coffee in the early 1800s, when there is a record of the export of one hundred quintals of coffee from Enerea, an area of modern-day Ethiopia. In the 19th century there were

Ethiopia's Production Systems

Ethiopia's coffees can be divided into three main categories, depending on their method of production.

Forest Coffees
These come from the wild coffee trees growing mostly in the south-west of the country. These trees usually have a mix of natural shade plants around them, and themselves are a broad mixture of different varieties. The productivity and yield of these trees is low compared to more purposefully cultivated plants.

Garden Coffees
These are coffees from trees typically planted around a homestead or other dwelling. There is less natural shade and more management of the shade trees, such as regular pruning to prevent too much shading. Many producers use some fertilizer on their plants. This type of coffee makes up the bulk of Ethiopia's production.

Plantation Coffees
These coffees come from trees grown intensively on large farms. Standard agricultural practices are used here, including pruning, mulching, use of fertilizers and the selection of disease-resistant varieties.

Above: Ethiopia is commonly accepted as the birthplace of coffee. This Ethiopian woman performs an age-old coffee ceremony in Wollo, Lalibella.

two common grades of Ethiopian coffee: Harrar (cultivated around the town of Harrar, often spelled Harar) and Abyssinia (grown in the wild in the rest of the country). For this reason, Harrar has a long-standing reputation for being desirable and of high quality (which it does not always earn).

The 1950s were a time of increased structure in the Ethiopian coffee industry, and a new grading system was introduced. In 1957 the National Coffee Board of Ethiopia was formed. The overthrow of Emperor Haile Selassie brought change in the 1970s, however. This wasn't a peasant uprising, more a coup from the elite class tired of famine and conflict. The vacuum of power was filled by the military, which was strongly influenced by socialist ideals. Until that point the country had been close, in some ways, to a feudal system of government. Among the new ideals was the redistribution of land, and the government quickly began to nationalize it. Some argue that this move was hugely beneficial to the population, increasing the earnings of the rural poor by up to 50 per cent. Strict Marxist rules prevented land ownership or hired labour, and this had a huge impact on the coffee industry. Large-scale farming was abandoned, and Ethiopia went back to harvesting its coffee from the wild. The 1980s was a decade of famine, affecting 8 million people and killing 1 million of them.

The Move Towards Democracy

In 1991 the Ethiopian People's Revolutionary Democratic Front overthrew the military junta. This began a process of liberalization and moved the country towards democracy. International markets opened up for Ethiopia, but with them came the effects of fluctuating market prices. Coffee farmers in Ethiopia, in particular, have had to cope with large, uncontrollable price swings. This has given rise to the formation of cooperatives, offering support to their members, in the form of funding, market information and transport, for example.

The Ethiopian Commodity Exchange

The largest change to the trade of Ethiopian coffee in recent years, and one of great concern to speciality coffee buyers, was the introduction of the Ethiopian Commodity Exchange (ECX) in 2008. The ECX was created for various commodities in Ethiopia with the aim of creating an efficient trading system that protected both sellers and buyers alike. However, the system frustrated those who wished to buy a distinct, traceable product rather than a commoditized one. Coffees were delivered to the ECX warehouse where they were allocated a numerical denomination of regional origin for washed coffees (from 1 to 10). All natural-process coffees were marked 11. The coffees were then graded for quality and assigned a number from 1 to 9, or labelled UG for ungraded. The process prevents coffee moving without authorization between different regions, to prevent smuggling and to retain traceability.

This process stripped the coffee of its exact traceability before auction, but on the positive side farmers did receive payment for their coffee sooner than they had before. The system also restricted which coffees could be offered on the international market and increased the financial transparency in contracts.

Today there are increasing opportunities to work outside the constraints of the ECX model, and more and more high-quality and traceable coffees are reaching consumers abroad.

Traceability

It is possible to find Ethiopian coffees from a single estate, although they are relatively rare. Traceability is more likely to lead back to a specific cooperative. However, a coffee roaster may simply have bought a coffee that has come through the ECX and it could still be astonishing despite its lack of transparency. These coffees have so much to offer, so I would recommend finding a roaster whose coffees you already enjoy and asking them for guidance on what is excellent.

Left: The Kafa Biosphere Reserve in south-west Ethiopia is purported to contain nearly 5,000 varieties of wild coffee plants growing in its rainforests.

Taste Profile

The flavours of Ethiopian coffees are notably diverse – from citrus, often bergamot and florals through to candied fruit or even tropical fruit flavours. The best washed coffees can be incredibly elegant, complex and delicious, and the best naturally processed ones can be wildly fruity and enchantingly unusual.

Growing Regions

Population: 102,374,000

Number of 60kg (132lb) bags in 2023: 6,600,000

The growing regions of Ethiopia are among the most recognizable names in coffee and are used to sell the coffee today and probably for the foreseeable future. The genetic potential of the indigenous and wild varieties of Arabica makes the future of coffee in Ethiopia an exciting one, too.

There is some challenge in the presentation of the growing regions of Ethiopia. The coffee industry has a preference for presenting certain regions or naming conventions, but there isn't a great deal of consistency in it all. For example, Yirgacheffe is often used as a growing region, as is Sidamo. However, as Yirgacheffe is inside Sidamo this could be considered confusing. Previous editions of this atlas were guilty of this, too. I have now changed the description of regions so that the five main coffee regions – North, South-West, Rift, South-East and Harrar – are covered, and sub-regions or zones within those regions are also described. This follows the description of the regions published in *The Coffee Atlas of Ethiopia* by Aaron P. Davis, Tim Wilkinson and Zeleke Kebebew Challa (Kew Publishing, 2018). However, due to the speciality coffee industry's focus on Yirgacheffe in particular, I have added more specific detail to that sub-region of Sidamo.

Coffee Varieties in Ethiopia

As Arabica can be said to have originally flourished in Ethiopia, it can be no surprise that there is huge genetic diversity. There are a great many different varieties growing here, with both wild and cultivated populations of Arabica. In the past the coffee industry tended to hand-wave away questions of variety in Ethiopian coffee lots by saying that they were 'heirloom' varieties. This term isn't particularly meaningful or correct. A better term would be to describe them as 'regional landraces'. I have omitted this from each regional section below, as the repetition makes it redundant, but these broad terms should not imply that producers don't know what they are growing. A great deal of work has been done to categorize and understand the varieties growing in Ethiopia, and more and more lots are making it to market with the individual variety information available – so you can expect more information than 'regional landraces' on a bag of coffee sourced from the country.

NORTH

AMHARA

One of the two small and relatively remote areas in the north of Ethiopia that produce coffee. The region is home to Lake Tana, which is the source of the Blue Nile. Coffee is not indigenous to the zone and was likely brought from the south-west of the country about 200–300 years ago.

Elevation: 1,700–2,200m (5,600–7,200ft)
Harvest: October–January

BENISHANGUL GUMUZ

This is the smallest of the coffee zones in Ethiopia, although perhaps we may see more coffee from this northern region as climate change expands its capacity for production.

Elevation: 1,700–2,200m (5,600–7,200ft)
Harvest: October–January

SOUTH-WEST

WELLEGA

Wellega covers three zones of coffee production in the south-west of the country: Kelem Wellega, West Wellega and East Wellega. Many coffees exported from here will carry the names of the towns of Ghimbi and Lekempti, or be called Nekemti after the town of Nekemte. These names may not accurately reflect the precise location the coffee is grown.

Elevation: 1,300–2,100m (4,300–6,900ft)
Harvest: October–January

ILLUBABOR

This is not an area that many buyers or consumers are particularly focused on, despite its potential for great-quality coffee. The ECX system tends to allocate these coffees under the name of Limu (if washed) and Jimma (if natural process). The area in south-western Ethiopia is home to a wide array of varieties, many of which are not seen elsewhere.

Elevation: 1,500–2,100m (4,900–6,900ft)
Harvest: October–January
Varieties: JARC varieties (bred by the Jimma Agricultural Research Centre), local landraces

JIMMA–LIMU

This region, in the south-west, produces a large portion of Ethiopia's coffee. Coffees from Jimma–Limu have recently been a little eclipsed by those from other parts of the country but are definitely worth investigating. The name Jimma can also be written as Jimmah, Jimma or Djimmah.

While Jimma–Limu does not have the same reputation as Sidama and Yirgacheffe, it still produces some astonishing coffee, aided in part by the number of washing stations in the area. This region's producers are mostly smallholders, but there are some large government-owned coffee farms in the area.

Elevation: 1,500–2,200m (4,900–7,200ft)
Harvest: October–January

TEPI

This area is home to the Tepi Coffee Plantation, the second largest farm in Ethiopia that is also state run. Dense forest, with populations of wild Arabica, still remain in the area.

Elevation: 1,200–2,100m (3,900–6,900ft)
Harvest: October–January

KAFFA

As you might expect from the name, this area is often referred to as the home of coffee. In the middle of the area is the town of Bonga, and to its west is the town of Wushwush, whose name was given to a coffee variety (see page 25).

Elevation: 1,300–2,200m (4,300–7,200ft)
Harvest: October–January

BENCH MAJI

This area is home to the town of Gesha, whose wild coffee forests are a fascinating contrast to the intensely managed coffee farms in the region. Bebeka Coffee Farm is the largest single coffee farm in the country, covering 93sq. km (40sq. miles). Sadly, there are no longer official tours of the farm, as there used to be.

Elevation: 1,000–2,300m (3,300–7,500ft)
Harvest: October–January

RIFT

RIFT NORTH

Coffee production is somewhat fragmented and spread out across this area.

Elevation: 1,800–2,200m (5,900–7,200ft)
Harvest: October–January

RIFT SOUTH

This smaller producing area in the country is to the south and west of Lake Abaya.

Elevation: 1,700–2,200m (5,600–7,200ft)
Harvest: October–January

SOUTH-EAST

SIDAMA/SIDAMO

Sidama is one of the three regions in the south-west of the country (along with Harrar and Yirgacheffe) that the Ethiopian government trademarked in 2004 to bring wider recognition to their distinctive coffees. It is also one of the major producing regions for coffee in Ethiopia. It produces a mixture of washed and naturally processed coffees that are incredibly popular among those who enjoy a fruity and intensely aromatic cup. The region was named after the Sidama people, but it is often referred to in coffee as Sidamo. In recent years, there has been some movement to reject the name Sidamo. However, it is something of a brand and deeply embedded in the industry. For this reason, both Sidamo and Sidama are used to describe coffees from the region. This region grows some of the highest coffee in Ethiopia. In the very south of Sidama is Guji, a coffee-producing area that you will often see referenced on bags of coffee.

Elevation: 1,300–2,300m (4,300–7,500ft)
Harvest: October–January

YIRGACHEFFE/YIRGA CHEFFE

The coffees from Yirgacheffe, a sub-region of Sidamo, are, in many ways, truly unique. So many of the great washed coffees from this area are explosively aromatic, full of citrus and floral notes and have a light and elegant body, so this is undeniably one of the greatest and most interesting regions for growing coffee. The best coffees from Yirgacheffe fetch rightfully high premiums, and while they can remind some people more of a cup of Earl Grey tea than of a cup of coffee, they are worth seeking out.

BALE

Named for the Bale Mountains, this region has very high elevations where temperature is the limiting factor for coffee growing, rather than a lack of space. Forest coffee extends all the way up to 2,300m (7,500ft) but most coffee production is confined to areas at lower altitudes.

Elevation: 1,400–1,800m (4,600–5,900ft)
Harvest: October–January

CENTRAL EASTERN HIGHLANDS

This is a small coffee-producing region that sits between Bale, to the south, and Arsi in Harrar to the north. The small production is spread over a fairly large area and little of it is exported.

Elevation: 1,300–2,000m (4,300–6,600ft)
Harvest: October–January

HARRAR

This is one of the oldest producing regions, surrounding the small town of Harrar (often spelled Harar). Coffees from this region are quite distinctive and are often grown in environments requiring extra irrigation. Harrar has maintained a strong reputation for many years, although the naturally processed coffees can veer between an unclean, woody earthiness to a more explicit blueberry fruit flavour. The coffees are often so unusual that they are remembered fondly by those who work in the industry as the coffees that opened their eyes to the diversity of flavours possible within a cup.

ARSI

Elevation: 1,500–2,000m (4,900–6,600ft)
Harvest: October–January

WEST HARAGE

Elevation: 1,700–2,200m (5,600–7,200ft)
Harvest: October–January

EAST HARAGE

Elevation: 1,900–2,200m (6,200–7,200ft)
Harvest: October–January

Above: The dense forests in Ethiopia contain a host of different shade plants and offer ideal conditions for wild coffee to thrive. Many varieties grow here, but their yield is low compared to farm-grown trees.

Uganda

Uganda is one of the few countries in the world with indigenous coffee, with Robusta growing wild around Lake Victoria. Coffee is an enormous part of the Ugandan export economy, and the country is one of the largest producers of coffee in the world. However, as most of that coffee is Robusta, Uganda has struggled to achieve a reputation for quality.

Although the indigenous Robusta crops had been part of Ugandan culture for hundreds of years, coffee wasn't originally part of the country's agricultural industry. In the early 1900s Arabica was introduced, probably from Malawi and Ethiopia. This crop didn't do well and struggled against disease. However, around the same time there was an increase in the farming of Robusta and the more disease-resistant variety seemed to flourish.

In 1925, under British colonial rule, coffee made up only 1 per cent of the country's exports but was considered an important crop and well suited to the increasing number of smallholder farmers. In 1929 the Coffee Industry Board was established. Cooperative farming acted as a catalyst for the industry's growth, and in the 1940s coffee became the country's principal export. Following independence in 1962, the government passed a Coffee Act in 1969 that gave the Coffee Industry Board full control over pricing.

Coffee remained a strong industry through Idi Amin's regime, buoyed for a time by the global increase in prices caused by the frost in Brazil in 1975. In the 1980s it was still the strongest cash crop, and production grew. However, an increasing amount of coffee was smuggled over borders into neighbouring countries to be sold at a higher price than that mandated by the government.

In 1988 the Coffee Industry Board increased the prices it paid to farmers, but by the end of the year it was deeply in debt and had to be bailed out by the government. The collapse of the International Coffee Agreement in 1989 caused a dramatic drop in prices, and the government devalued the Ugandan shilling in an effort to make coffee exports more appealing

Below: This Ugandan coffee nursery produces thousands of new young plants each year.

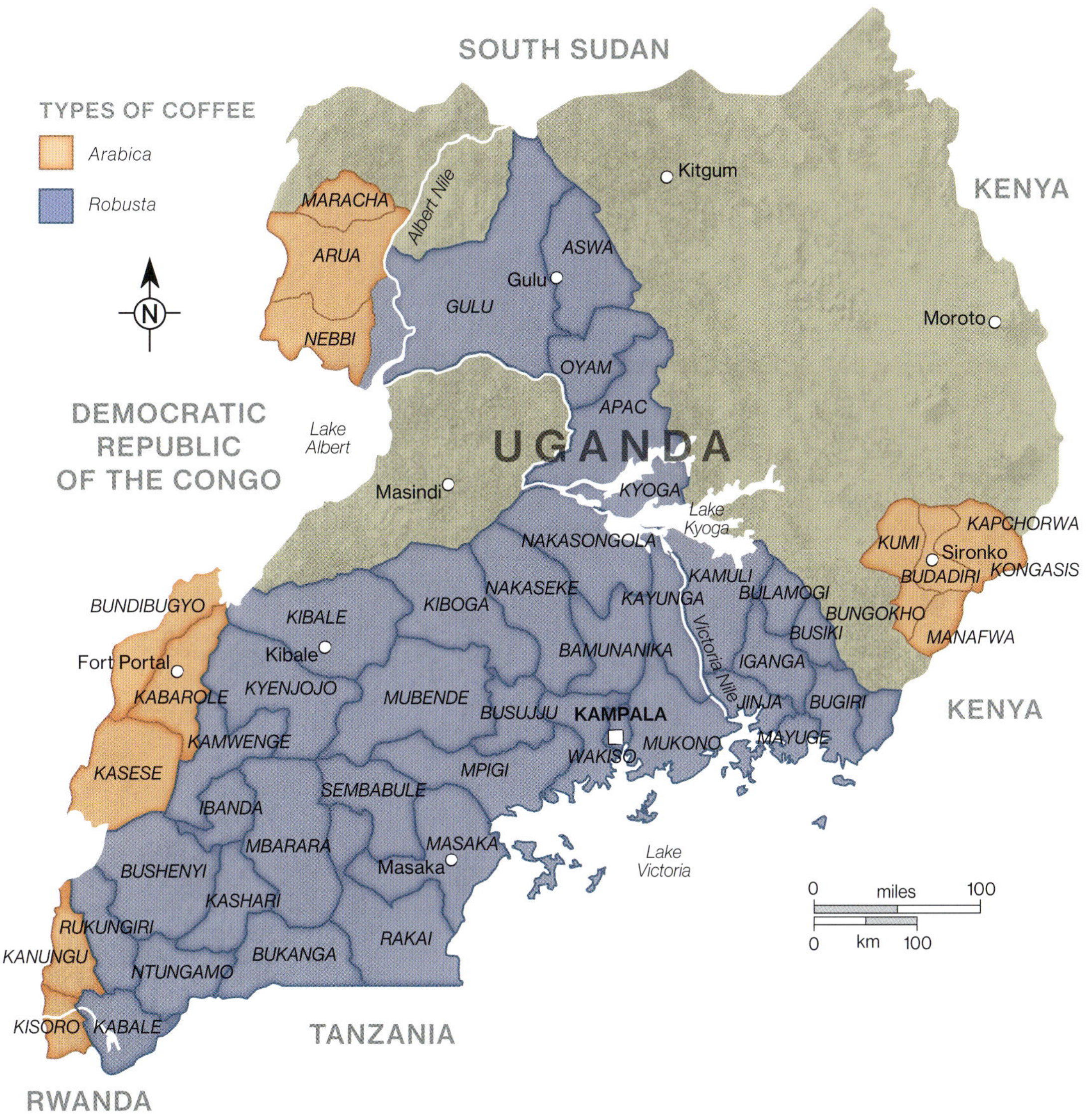
SOUTH SUDAN
TYPES OF COFFEE
Arabica
Robusta
KENYA
DEMOCRATIC REPUBLIC OF THE CONGO
UGANDA
TANZANIA
RWANDA
MARACHA
ARUA
NEBBI
Albert Nile
Kitgum
ASWA
Gulu
GULU
Moroto
OYAM
APAC
Lake Albert
Masindi
KYOGA
Lake Kyoga
NAKASONGOLA
KAPCHORWA
KUMI
Sironko
BUDADIRI
KONGASIS
BUNDIBUGYO
KIBALE
KIBOGA
NAKASEKE
KAMULI
KAYUNGA
BULAMOGI
BUNGOKHO
BUSIKI
MANAFWA
Kibale
Fort Portal
BAMUNANIKA
Victoria Nile
IGANGA
KABAROLE
KYENJOJO
MUBENDE
BUSUJJU
KAMPALA
JINJA
BUGIRI
KAMWENGE
WAKISO
MUKONO
MAYUGE
KASESE
MPIGI
SEMBABULE
IBANDA
MBARARA
MASAKA
Masaka
Lake Victoria
BUSHENYI
KASHARI
RUKUNGIRI
KANUNGU
NTUNGAMO
BUKANGA
RAKAI
KISORO
KABALE
0 miles 100
0 km 100

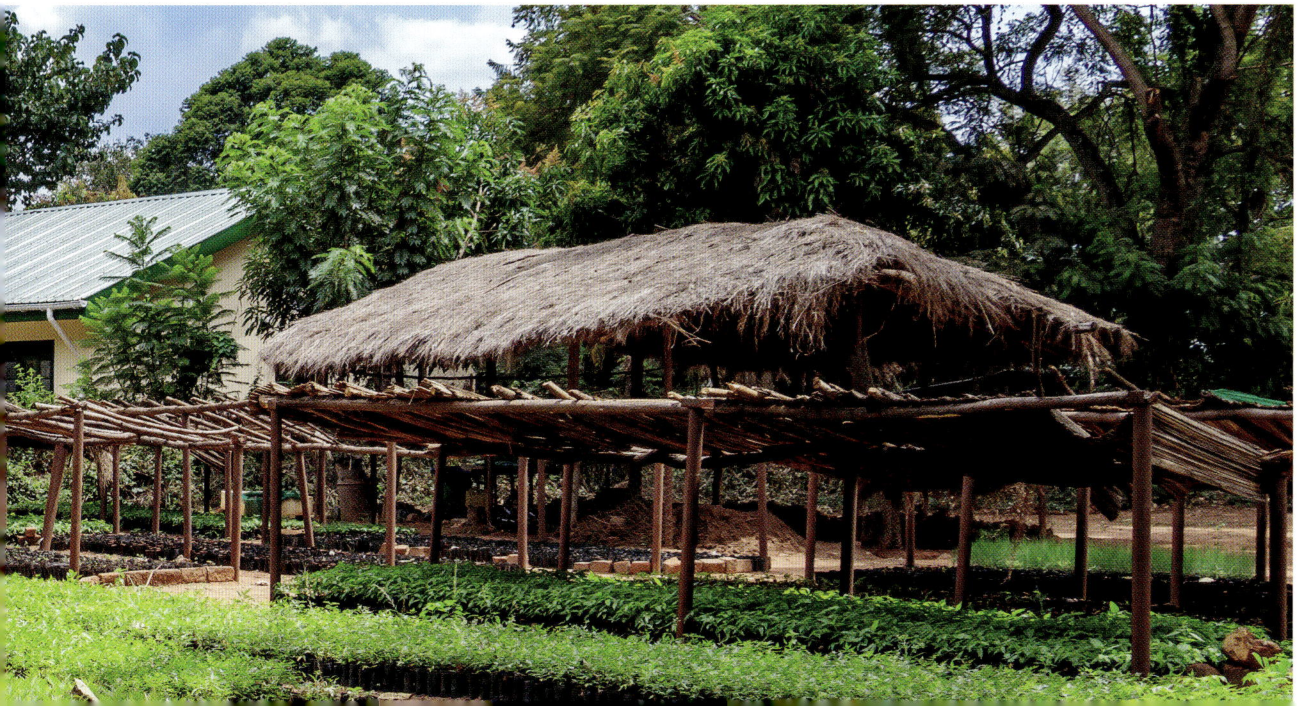

Above: Roasting coffee at the Good African Coffee company's factory in Kampala.

globally. In 1990 production dropped by 20 per cent, not only because of prices but also because of drought and a general shift away from coffee towards other subsistence crops.

In the early 1990s the industry became increasingly liberalized, with the government only playing a supporting role in marketing and development. From here we can draw a fairly straight line to today's coffee industry. The Ugandan Coffee Development Authority has continued to relax rules, allowing better traceability and easier access to Ugandan coffee. Producer groups are increasingly building their own brands and reputations.

Robusta remains the primary coffee export, and Uganda probably has the best reputation for cup quality for Robusta coffee worldwide, although there are plenty of quality-focused Robusta producers in other countries. Arabica production remains relatively small at about 15 per cent of total exports, but quality is increasing. Around 5 million people, in 1.7 million households, are involved in the production of coffee. About 85 per cent of the coffee exported comes from smallholders with fewer than 2.5 hectares of land.

Uganda is home to a number of native coffee species including *Coffea canephora*, *Coffea eugenioides*, *Coffea dewevrei* and *Coffea neoleroyi* (see page 12 for more on coffee species), and the forests of Uganda are also home to a great deal of genetic diversity in coffee. This is notable, as we look to address the impact of climate change on the coffee sector by locating the genetic resources to try to overcome the challenges the current coffee crop plants face from increases in global temperature.

Uganda's consumption of its own coffee is on the rise. In the last few years there has been an effort by the government to promote coffee consumption, and so there has been something of a boom of coffee shops and coffee carts in cities such as Kampala.

Traceability

The best coffees from Uganda generally come from producer groups or cooperatives. There are two terms unique to Ugandan coffees: Wugar (washed Ugandan Arabica) and Drugar (dried Ugandan Arabica). The country produces coffee nearly all year round, with most areas having a main crop and a second, smaller crop known as a 'fly crop'.

Taste Profile

Exceptional coffee from Uganda is still relatively rare, but the best cups are sweet and full of dark fruits and have a clean finish.

Growing Regions

Population: 49,300,000

Number of 60kg (132lb) bags in 2023: 6,500,000

Growing regions in Uganda are not always well or clearly defined and agreed upon.

BUGISU/MOUNT ELGON

This area has the best reputation for quality, in particular the area around Mount Elgon, close to the border with Kenya. Farms are on steep slopes here, and the lack of infrastructure can prove challenging. The area has the soil, elevation and climate to produce excellent coffee.

Elevation: 1,500–2,300m (4,900–7,500ft)
Harvest: October–March (main crop); April–July (fly crop)
Varieties: Kent, Typica, SL-14, SL-28

Opposite: Roasting coffee at the Good African Coffee company's factory in Kampala. The company was set up by a local businessman in 2003.

WEST NILE

More Arabica coffee grows in the north-west of the country, to the north of Lake Albert, up against the border with the Democratic Republic of Congo. Arabicas tend to grow closer to the lake, with more Robusta farther to the north.

Elevation: 1,300–1,800m (4,300–5,900ft)
Harvest: October–February (main crop); April–August (fly crop)
Varieties: Kent, Typica, SL-14, SL-28, native Robusta

RWENZORI

The highest coffee production is in the Rwenzori Mountains, bordering the Democratic Republic of Congo. It is common to see naturally processed coffees (drugar) produced in this region. This area also includes a pocket of coffee production in the very south-west of the country, around Mount Muhabura.

Elevation: 1,200–2,200m (3,900–7,200ft)
Harvest: April–July (main crop); October–January (fly crop)
Varieties: Kent, Typica, SL-14, SL-28, native Robusta

CENTRAL LOWLANDS

Robusta grows throughout much of the country, all the way down to the Lake Victoria Basin. Elevations are much lower, and crops are dependent on good rainfall. Tuzza is a modern Catimor variety grown in lower regions and is disease resistant.

Elevation: 1,200–1,500m (3,900–4,900ft)
Harvest: November–February (main crop); May–August (fly crop)
Varieties: native Robusta, some Tuzza

Below: A coffee farmer in the Kamuli region, where an NGO-run agricultural training programme helps people improve their livelihoods.

Kenya

Despite the fact that neighbouring Ethiopia is considered the home of coffee, Kenya did not start production until relatively late. The earliest documented import of coffee dates to 1893 when French missionaries brought coffee trees from Réunion. Most agree that the variety of coffee they brought was Bourbon. It yielded its first crop in 1896.

Initially, coffee was produced on large estates under British colonial rule, and the resulting crop was sold in London. In 1933 the Coffee Act was passed, establishing a Kenyan Coffee Board and moving the sale of coffee back to Kenya. In 1934 the auction system was established and is still in use today; a year later protocols were created for the grading of coffee to help improve quality.

Not long after the Mau Mau uprising in the early 1950s, an agricultural act was passed to create family holdings that combined subsistence farming with the production of cash crops for additional income. This act was known as the Swynnerton Plan, named after an official in the Department of Agriculture. This marked the start of the transfer of coffee production from the British to the Kenyans. The effect on the production of smallholdings was significant, with total income rising from £5.2 million in 1955 to £14 million in 1964. Notably, coffee production accounted for 55 per cent of this increase.

Kenya gained independence in 1963 and now consistently produces extremely high-quality coffees from a variety of sources. The research and development in Kenya is considered excellent, and many farmers are highly educated in coffee production. The Kenyan auction system should help to reward quality-focused producers with better prices, but while buyers are paying high prices for the excellent coffees, corruption within the system may sometimes prevent those premiums filtering back to the farmers. Roasters and importers are able to buy through what is called the 'Second Window', where they negotiate prices directly with the mills. The auction prices are often used as a reference point for these transactions.

Below: Kenyan women carry buckets of freshly picked ripe coffee cherries to be sorted and processed.

Grading

Kenya uses a grading system for all its exported coffee, regardless of whether the lot is traceable or not. As in many other countries, the grading system uses a combination of bean size and quality. The definitions clearly define size and, to some extent, also assume quality is linked to the size of the beans. While this is often true – the AA lots often being the superior coffees – I have recently seen harvests where the AB lots appeared to be more complex and of higher quality than many of the AA lots.

E – These are the elephant beans, the very largest size, so lots tend to be relatively small.
AA – This is a more common grade for the larger screen sizes, above screen size 18 (see page 44), or 7.22mm. Typically, these fetch the highest prices.
AB – This grade is a combination of A (screen size 16, or 6.80mm) and B (screen size 15, or 6.20mm). This grade accounts for around 30 per cent of Kenya's annual production.
PB – This is the grade for peaberries, where a single bean has grown inside the coffee cherry instead of the more usual two.
C – This is the grading size below the AB category. It is unusual to see this grade in a high-quality coffee.
TT – A smaller grade again, normally comprising the smaller beans removed from AA, AB and E grades. When sorted by density, the lightest beans are usually TT grade.
T – The smallest grade, often made up of chips and broken pieces.
MH/ML – These initials stand for Mbuni Heavy and Mbuni Light. Mbuni is the name used for naturally processed coffees. These are considered low quality, often containing underripe or overripe beans, and they sell for a very low price. They account for around 7 per cent of the annual production.

Traceability

Kenya's coffee is grown both on large estates and by smallholders who feed their coffee into their local washing station. Of the 110,000–112,000 hectares of land growing coffee, smallholder farms (where the farm is below 5 hectares) account for more than 75 per cent. There are approximately 700,000 smallholder

Kenyan Varieties

Two particular Kenyan varieties attract great interest from the speciality coffee industry. These are named SL-28 and SL-34 and are among the 40 experimental varieties produced as part of the research led by Guy Gibson at Scott Laboratories. These make up the majority of high-quality coffee from Kenya, but they are susceptible to leaf rust.

A lot of work has been done to produce rust-resistant varieties in Kenya. Ruiru 11 was the first to be considered a success by the Kenyan Coffee Board, although it was not warmly received by speciality coffee buyers. More recently, they have released a variety called Batian. There remains some scepticism towards its cup quality after the disappointment of Ruiru, although quality seems to be improving and there is more positivity around the potential of Batian to have great cup quality in the future.

coffee farmers in Kenya. The larger estates mean it is possible to get extremely traceable coffees from a single estate, but in recent years the higher-quality coffees have increasingly come from the smallholders. Typically, what one might find is a particular lot from a washing station that will still carry a size grading (such as AA), although that lot may have come from a group of several hundred farmers. These washing stations (or factories as they are known) play a role in the quality of the final product, so these coffees are definitely worth seeking out.

> **Taste Profile**
>
> Kenyan coffees are renowned for their bright, complex berry/fruit qualities as well as their sweetness and intense acidity.

Growing Regions

Population: 56,190,633

Number of 60kg (132lb) bags in 2022: 800,000

Kenya's counties are used as the geographic definition of coffee-growing areas. Coffee grows in around 33 of the 47 counties, but it is not evenly distributed. Central Kenya produces most of the nation's coffee, and the best Kenyan coffees come from this part of the country. There is growing interest in the coffees being produced in Western Kenya, in the Kisii, Trans-Nzoia, Keiyo and Marakwet regions. Below are the key growing regions you are likely to see in speciality coffee.

NYERI

The central region of Nyeri is home to the extinct volcano of Mount Kenya. The red soils here produce some of the best coffee in Kenya. Agriculture is hugely important to the area, and coffee is one of the main crops. Cooperatives of smallholder producers are common, rather than large estates. The coffee trees in Nyeri produce two crops a year and the main crop tends to produce higher-quality lots.

Elevation: 1,200–2,300m (3,900–7,500ft)
Harvest: October–December (main crop), June–August (fly crop)
Varieties: SL-28, SL-34, Ruiru 11, Batian

MURANG'A

Around 100,000 farmers produce coffee in the Murang'a region, within the Central Province. This inland region was one of the first to be settled by missionaries, who were prevented from settling around the coast by the Portuguese. This is another region that benefits from the volcanic soil and also has more smallholders than estates.

Elevation: 1,350–1,950m (4,400–6,400ft)
Harvest: October–December (main crop), June–August (fly crop)
Varieties: SL-28, SL-34, Ruiru 11, Batian

KIRINYAGA

The eastern neighbour of Nyeri, this county also benefits from volcanic soils. The coffee tends to be produced by smallholders, and the washing stations have been producing some very high-quality lots that are well worth trying.

Elevation: 1,300–1,900m (4,300–6,200ft)
Harvest: October–December (main crop), June–August (fly crop)
Varieties: SL-28, SL-34, Ruiru 11, Batian

EMBU

Near Mount Kenya, this region is named after the town of Embu. Approximately 70 per cent of the population are small-scale farmers, and the most popular cash crops are tea and coffee. Almost all the coffee comes from smallholders, and the region is a relatively small producer.

Elevation: 1,300–1,900m (4,300–6,200ft)
Harvest: October–December (main crop), June–August (fly crop)
Varieties: SL-28, SL-34, Ruiru 11, Batian, K7

MERU

Coffee is grown on the slopes of Mount Kenya and in the Nyambene Hills, mostly by smallholders. The name refers to both the region and the Meru people who inhabit it. In the 1930s these people were among the first Kenyans to produce coffee, as a result of the Devonshire White Paper of 1923, which asserted the importance of African interests in the country.

Elevation: 1,300–1,950m (4,300–6,400ft)
Harvest: October–December (main crop), June–August (fly crop)
Varieties: SL-28, SL-34, Ruiru 11, Batian, K7

KIAMBU

This central region's production is dominated by large estates. However, the spread of urbanization has seen the number of estates decline as owners have found it more profitable to sell their land for development. Coffees from the region are often named for places within it, such as Thika, Ruiru and Limuru. Many of the estates are owned by multinational companies, which means that farming practices are often mechanized with an eye towards higher yields rather than quality. There are a reasonable number of smallholders in the region, too.

Elevation: 1,500–2,200m (4,900–7,200ft)
Harvest: October–December (main crop), June–August (fly crop)
Varieties: SL-28, SL-34, Ruiru 11, Batian

MACHAKOS

This is a relatively small county in the centre of the country, named after the town of Machakos. Coffee production here is a mixture of estates and smallholders.

Elevation: 1,400–1,850m (4,600–6,050ft)
Harvest: October–December (main crop), June–August (fly crop)
Varieties: SL-28, SL-34

NAKURU

This region, in the centre of the country, has some of the highest-growing coffee in Kenya. However, some trees suffer from dieback at high elevations and stop producing. The region is named after the town of Nakuru. Coffee is produced by a mixture of estates and smallholders, although production is relatively low.

Elevation: 1,850–2,200m (6,050–7,200ft)
Harvest: October–December (main crop), June–August (fly crop)
Varieties: SL-28, SL-34, Ruiru 11, Batian

KISII

This region is in the south-west of the country, not far from Lake Victoria. It is a relatively small region, and most of the coffee comes from cooperatives of small producers.

Elevation: 1,450–1,800m (4,750–5,900ft)
Harvest: October–December (main crop), June–August (fly crop)
Varieties: SL-28, SL-34, Blue Mountain, K7

TRANS-NZOIA, KEIYO AND MARAKWET

This relatively small area of production in Western Kenya has seen some growth in recent years. The slopes of Mount Elgon provide some elevation, and most of the coffee comes from estates. Coffee is often planted to diversify farms that once focused on maize or dairy.

Elevation: 1,500–1,900m (4,900–6,200ft)
Harvest: October–December (main crop), June–August (fly crop)
Varieties: SL-28, SL-3, Ruiru 11, Batian

Above: A cooperative member sweeps freshly pulped coffee beans into fermentation tanks at Orinde Farmers' Cooperative Society in Rachuo South.

Tanzania

Oral histories tell of coffee coming to Tanzania from Ethiopia in the 16th century. Brought by the Haya people and known as 'Haya coffee', or *amwani*, this was probably a Robusta variety and has since become strongly entwined in Tanzanian culture. The ripe cherries would be boiled, then smoked for several days and chewed rather than brewed into a drink.

Coffee first became a cash crop for Tanzania (previously Tanganyika) under German colonial rule. In 1911 the colonists mandated the planting of Arabica coffee trees throughout the Bukoba region. Their methods were very different from the way the Haya people had traditionally dealt with coffee growing, and the Haya were reluctant to replace their food crops with coffee. However, the region did start to produce more and more coffee. Other parts of the country were less familiar with coffee and so provided less resistance to growing it. The Chagga people, living around Mount Kilimanjaro, switched completely to coffee production when Germany put an end to the slave trade.

After World War I, control of the region fell to the British. They launched a campaign to plant over 10 million seedlings in Bukoba but they, too, fell into conflict with the Haya, which often resulted in trees being uprooted. As a result, there was not a strong growth in production in the region, compared to that in the Chagga region. However, the first cooperative was formed in 1925, called the Kilimanjaro Native Planters' Association (KNPA). This was the first of several cooperatives, and the producers enjoyed their new-found ability to sell more directly to London and to achieve better prices for their crop.

After independence was granted in 1961, the Tanzanian government turned its attention to coffee, hoping to double production by 1970 – a goal they did not achieve. After struggling with low growth in industry, high levels of inflation and a declining economy, the government changed to a multiparty democracy.

During the early and mid-1990s reforms were implemented in the coffee industry to allow the more direct sale of coffee from producers to buyers, instead of driving everything through the State Coffee

Opposite: Overlooked by Mount Kilimanjaro, these recently planted coffee trees form part of a new coffee farm in Mwika, Tanzania.

Marketing Board. The coffee industry suffered a serious setback in the late 1990s when coffee wilt disease spread through the country and caused significant losses of coffee trees in the north, close to the border with Uganda. Today Tanzania's coffee production is about 61 per cent Arabica and 39 per cent Robusta. In the last decade there has been renewed efforts to increase coffee production in Tanzania, and as a result production has grown quite notably and is projected to grow further.

Traceability

Around 90 per cent of coffee in Tanzania is produced by its 450,000 smallholder farmers. The remaining 10 per cent comes from larger estates. It is possible to find coffees traceable back to a cooperative of growers and their washing station, or back to a single farm if it is an estate coffee.

Above: A worker sorts through dried, harvested beans at a factory near the Ngorongoro Crater, Tanzania. The coffee produced in this country is almost entirely harvested from smallholder farms.

Grading

Tanzania uses what is sometimes called the British nomenclature of grading, similar to that in Kenya. These grades include AA, A, B, PB, C, E, F, AF, TT, UG and TEX.

Taste Profile

Complex, with bright and lively acidity and often with berry and fruity flavours, Tanzanian coffees can be juicy, interesting and delicious.

Growing Regions

Population: 65,500,000

Number of 60kg (132lb) bags in 2023: 1,374,000

Tanzania produces a reasonable quantity of Robusta, although this production is focused in the north-west, near Lake Victoria. The other growing regions are, in some ways, defined by their high elevation.

KILIMANJARO

This is the oldest growing area in Tanzania for Arabica, so it is fair to say that it has had the most time to develop its recognition internationally and build its reputation. The long tradition of coffee production here means there is better infrastructure and facilities, although a lot of the trees are now very old and have comparatively low yields. Increasingly, coffee is facing competition from other crops in this region.

Elevation: 1,050–2,500m (3,500–8,100ft)
Harvest: June–September
Varieties: Kent, Bourbon, Typica, Typica/Nyara

ARUSHA

Arusha borders the region around Mount Kilimanjaro and in many ways is very similar. This region surrounds Mount Meru, an active volcano that has been quiet since 1910.

Elevation: 1,100–1,800m (3,600–5,900ft)
Harvest: June–September
Varieties: Kent, Bourbon, Typica, Typica/Nyara

RUVUMA

This region takes its name from the Ruvuma River and is in the extreme south of the country. The coffee tends to be centred around the Mbingo district and is considered to have great potential for high quality, although in the past it has been held back by a lack of access to finance.

Elevation: 1,200–1,800m (3,900–5,900ft)
Harvest: June–August
Varieties: Kent, Bourbon, Bourbon derivatives such as N5 and N39

MBEYA

Centred around the city of Mbeya in the south of the country, this region is a key producer of high-value export crops including coffee, tea, cacao and spices. The area has recently seen increased interest from certification groups and non-government organizations (NGOs) looking to improve the quality of the coffee produced, which traditionally has not always been very high.

Elevation: 1,200–2,000m (3,900–6,600ft)
Harvest: June–August
Varieties: Kent, Bourbon, Typica

TARIME

This is a small region in the far north of the country, bordering Kenya, with a limited international profile. It is starting to produce some higher-quality coffees and has the opportunity to expand its production. It has a relatively low production and limited infrastructure for coffee processing, but the increased attention it has seen recently has led to coffee production being tripled in the last ten years.

Elevation: 1,500–1,800m (4,900–5,900ft)
Harvest: July–November
Varieties: Kent, Bourbon, Typica, Robustas

KIGOMA

This region is named for the regional capital city of Kigoma and is situated on a plateau of gently rolling hills in the north-east of the country near the border with Burundi. The region has produced some stunning coffees, though the coffee industry there is still in its infancy compared to the rest of the country.

Elevation: 1,100–1,700m (3,600–5,600ft)
Harvest: May–August
Varieties: Kent, Bourbon, Typica

Rwanda

German missionaries first brought coffee to Rwanda in 1904, but the country did not produce enough to begin exports until 1917. After World War I, the League of Nations stripped Germany of its colonial rule over Rwanda and handed the country to the Belgians as a colonial mandate. This is why, historically, most of Rwanda's coffee has been exported to Belgium.

The first coffee trees were planted at the Mibirizi mission in Cyangugu Province, and the place gives its name to the first Rwandan coffee variety, a natural mutation of Bourbon. Gradually, coffee cultivation spread into the Kivu region and ultimately the rest of Rwanda. In the 1930s coffee became a compulsory crop for many producers around the country, mirroring the Belgian colonial approach in neighbouring Burundi.

The Belgians strictly controlled exports and enforced high taxes on the growers. This pushed Rwanda towards producing high volumes of low-quality coffee, which sold for low prices. However, the fact that Rwanda exported so little gave coffee an oversized impact and a sense of importance for the farmers. There was little infrastructure to allow the production of quality coffee, not even a single washing station.

By the 1990s coffee was Rwanda's most valuable export, but the events of the decade would decimate the coffee industry. In 1994 the widespread genocide in the country claimed nearly 1 million lives and had a massive impact on the coffee industry. This was compounded by worldwide coffee prices falling to a very low level.

Coffee's Role in Rwanda's Recovery

Coffee was to become a symbol of positivity as Rwanda got back on its feet following the genocide. As foreign aid and interest streamed into the country, there was a strong focus on the coffee sector. Washing stations were built, and there was a determined drive towards producing higher-quality coffee. The government took a more open approach to the coffee trade, and speciality coffee buyers from around the world have shown a strong interest in the country's coffees. Rwanda is the only African country to have hosted a Cup of Excellence competition, a project to find the very best lots and to bring them to market through an online auction system.

The first washing station was built in 2004 with assistance from the US Agency for International Development (USAID). Many more followed, and the number has grown dramatically in recent years with around three hundred in operation today. The PEARL project (Partnership for Enhancing Agriculture in Rwanda through Linkages) was successful in helping to spread knowledge and train young agronomists. It has since become the SPREAD project (Sustaining Partnerships to enhance Rural Enterprise and Agribusiness Development), and both projects have focused their efforts in the Butare region.

Rwanda is known as the 'land of a thousand hills' and this country certainly has the elevation and weather to grow great coffee. However, there is the problem of widespread soil depletion, and

Above: This coffee farm near Butare shows why Rwanda is known as the 'land of a thousand hills'. The elevation of the terrain makes it ideal for coffee growing.

transport still poses a challenge, often adding great expense to production costs.

When worldwide coffee prices increased around 2010, it was a challenge in Rwanda (and much of the rest of the world) to find suitable incentives to keep quality high. When the market pays high prices, there is little reason to spend money to increase quality, as even low-quality coffee is sufficiently profitable. However, recently the quality of Rwandan coffees has been excellent. Rwanda does grow and export a small amount of Robusta, but most of its output is fully washed Arabica. Around 400,000 families are currently involved in coffee production, and there are no larger estates operating.

Traceability

Coffees in Rwanda tend to be traceable back to washing stations and the numerous farmer groups and cooperatives that supply them. Each producer has on average just 183 trees, so it is not possible to find a coffee traceable to a single producer.

Taste Profile

Amazing Rwandan coffees often have a fruitiness and freshness reminiscent of red apples or red grapes. Berry fruit and floral qualities are also fairly common.

The Potato Defect

This is a particular and unusual defect found only in coffees from Burundi and Rwanda. It is caused by an unknown bacteria entering the cherry's skin and producing an unpleasant toxin. It is not harmful to health, but when afflicted beans are roasted and ground they release an unmistakeable and pungent aroma that is eerily similar to the smell of peeling a raw potato. This defect affects only specific beans, so finding it in your coffee does not mean the whole bag is spoiled, unless it has all been ground.

Eradication is tricky. It is undetectable once post-harvest processing is finished, so a coffee roaster cannot do anything to detect it before roasting. Even after roasting it is difficult to discover until a bean with the defect is ground. It is possible to do some work during processing to identify the cherries that have had their skins broken and are likely to be tainted. Work is being done both on the ground and at research level to eradicate this defect.

Growing Regions

Population: 13,780,000

Number of 60kg (132lb) bags in 2023: 327,900

Coffee is grown across the whole of Rwanda, and the country itself is relatively small. There isn't a great deal of coherence within speciality coffee regarding naming conventions. There are four provinces, and there are coffee-growing regions within each one. The most commonly found coffee-producing regions within each province are highlighted below.

Local Varieties

MIBIRIZI

This is the name of the mission in Rwanda that received some Bourbon trees from Guatemala. Mibirizi is a natural variant of Bourbon, which appeared at the mission. It was initially grown in Rwanda and later spread to Burundi in the 1930s.

JACKSON

This is another Bourbon variant that was initially grown in Rwanda and has since spread to Burundi. It was named for a coffee producer in Mysore, India, in the early 1900s who noticed his coffee plants were tolerant to leaf rust. Seeds were distributed to both Tanzania and Kenya in the 1920s. That tolerance to leaf rust has since been lost.

NORTHERN PROVINCE

The best-known region to the north is probably Virunga, named for the Virunga Mountains. The microclimate and volcanic soils are both well suited to speciality coffee. Coffee is also grown around Nyagatare.

Elevation: 1,500–2,100m (4,900–6,900ft)
Harvest: March–August
Varieties: Bourbon, Jackson, Caturra, Catuai, Mibirizi

EASTERN PROVINCE

The elevation in the east of the country is not as high as in other regions, but great coffees are being produced in Ngoma and in Nyagatare in the extreme north-east. In addition, the Muhazi region, named for Lake Muhazi, has a concentration of coffee production, too. Coffee is also produced around Akagera.

Elevation: 1,300–1,900m (4,300–6,200ft)
Harvest: March–August
Varieties: Bourbon, Jackson, Caturra, Catuai, Mibirizi

SOUTHERN PROVINCE

A number of notable coffee production areas are in the Southern Province. This includes areas around Mount Huye, as well as around Butare and Nyamagabe. There are some higher elevations here, capable of producing truly exceptional coffees.

Elevation: 1,700–2,200m (5,600–7,200ft)
Harvest: March–August
Varieties: Bourbon, Jackson, Caturra, Catuai, Mibirizi

WESTERN PROVINCE

To the west of the country are the growing regions around Lake Kivu, as well as down to the very south-western tip of the country.

Elevation: 1,500–1,800m (4,900–5,900ft)
Harvest: March–August
Varieties: Bourbon, Jackson, Caturra, Catuai, Mibirizi

Opposite: Workers spread the coffee out on drying tables, where it will dry out over a number of days in preparation for roasting or export.

Democratic Republic of the Congo

Coffee was introduced to the Democratic Republic of the Congo (DRC) in 1881 from Liberia, but it wasn't until Belgian colonists discovered a new variety growing there in 1898 that agricultural production began. Despite its tumultuous history, the DRC is now considered an up-and-coming producer of speciality coffees. Many have high hopes for its potential in the future, but significant challenges have yet to be faced.

The plant discovered in Belgian Congo in 1898 was a variety of *Coffea canephora*, which the colonists named 'Robusta' to promote its hardy nature (see page 12). Coffee production started to gain momentum on plantations under the brutal rule of the Belgian colonists. The vast majority of coffee was produced on these estates, rather than by smallholders, until independence in 1960. Until this point, agriculture, including coffee production, was well funded and supported, with 26 research stations in the country and 300 professionals working inside the Institut National Pour l'Étude Agronomique du Congo Belge (National Institute for Agricultural Studies in the Belgian Congo).

After independence in 1960, government funding was reduced, and in the 1970s the farms began to decline, in part due to the marginalization of non-nationals and in part due to a lack of infrastructure. By 1987 only 14 per cent of the coffee produced in the DRC came from estates, and by 1996 only 2 per cent. However, coffee production had boomed in the 1970s and 1980s as a result of the free market, and the government had tried to sustain the industry in the late 1980s by reducing tariffs on exports.

The 1990s was a brutal decade for the country and the coffee sector. The First and Second Congo Wars, spanning the period from 1996 to 2003, triggered a decline in production, which was further exacerbated by the spread of coffee wilt disease. The high production levels of the late 1980s and early 1990s dropped to less than half. Coffee wilt primarily affected only Robusta production, but this made up the vast majority of the coffee produced in the DRC.

Infrastructure in the country still poses a huge challenge. There are hopes that coffee can be a part of the economic revival of the DRC, as it struggles to move past the violence. Both the government and outside NGOs have invested heavily in the sector, and there is increasing interest in the country's potential for excellent coffee. The soil, elevation and climate of parts of the DRC lend themselves to the production of truly exceptional coffees, and they are worth seeking out and supporting.

In 2012 the government launched a $100 million

Right: A man sorts ripe coffee beans in Kivu. Coffee from the DRC disappeared from the international coffee market for many years, but attempts to revitalize production are starting to show success.

investment into the coffee sector. This was focused on increasing overall production of coffee in the country, with a particular focus on the provinces of South Kivu and Orientale, focusing on the production of Arabica and Robusta respectively.

Taste Profile

The very best coffees from the Democratic Republic of the Congo have a delightful fruitiness, are sweet and can be pleasingly full-bodied.

Traceability

Almost all coffee in the DRC is produced by groups of smallholders or cooperatives. It is extremely unlikely that you will find a single estate, and less likely still that they will produce excellent coffee.

Right: Workers at the Mutsora coffee-processing plant in Virunga National Park stack sacks of beans.

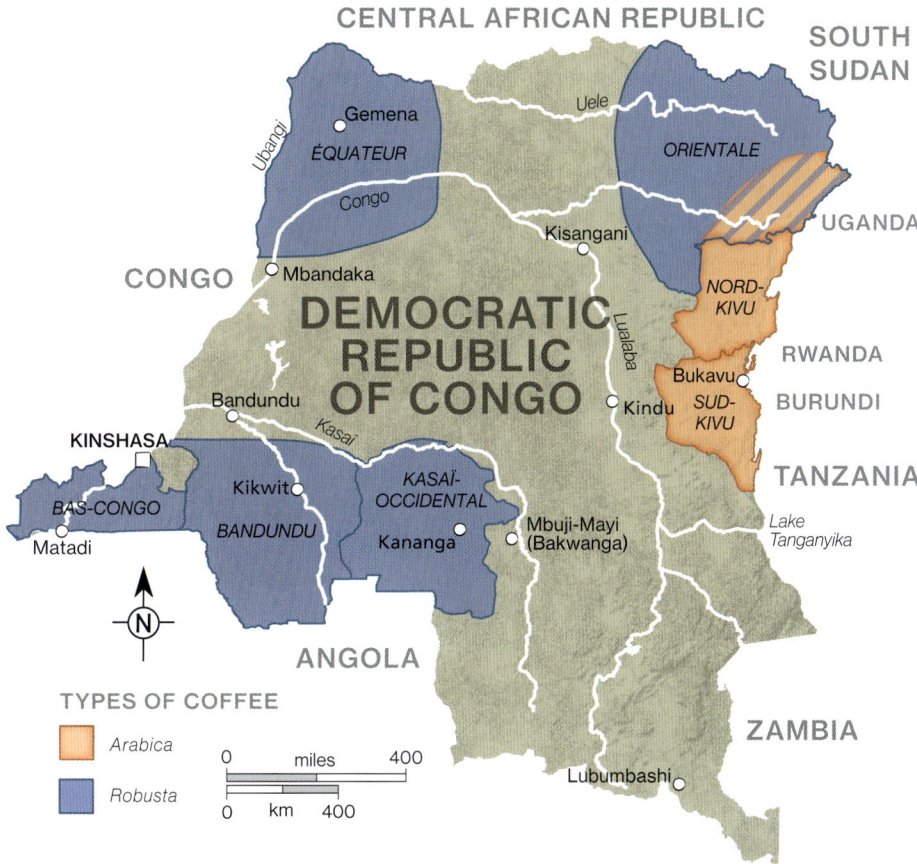

Growing Regions

Population: 99,010,000

Number of 60kg (132lb) bags in 2023: 340,000

Some regions of the DRC mostly grow Robusta, others mostly grow Arabica, and some grow a mixture of the two. It is difficult to get accurate figures for the production of the DRC because a great deal of coffee is smuggled across the borders into Uganda and Rwanda, to be sold as coffee grown there. This is in part because it may fetch higher prices, but also it is not subject to the same challenges of bureaucracy or corruption that can make exporting the coffee difficult.

KIVU

The Kivu region comprises four provinces: Ituri, North Kivu, South Kivu and Maniema, all surrounding Lake Kivu, after which the region is named. The higher elevation areas in Kivu grow the best coffee in the country, mainly Arabica, so these are worth seeking out.

Elevation: 1,500–2,000m (4,900–6,600ft)
Harvest: March–July (main crop); September–January (fly crop)
Varieties: Mostly Bourbon and Blue Mountain (a Typica variety)

ORIENTALE

A small amount of Arabica is also grown in this eastern region of the country, but it is mostly Robusta here.

Elevation: 1,400–2,200m (4,600–7,200ft)
Harvest: March–July (main crop); September–January (fly crop)
Varieties: Robusta and Bourbon

KONGO CENTRAL

Formerly Bas-Congo, this very westernmost corner of the country does produce some coffee, but it is all Robusta.

Harvest: March–July (main crop); September–January (fly crop)
Varieties: Robusta

EQUATEUR

This is another large producing area in the country, situated in the north-west. It is mostly Robusta here.

Harvest: March–July (main crop); September–January (fly crop)
Varieties: Robusta

Right: A woman on her way to work in a coffee farm near Kivu Lake. Arabica from the Highlands of Kivu was once renowned as some of the best coffee in the world.

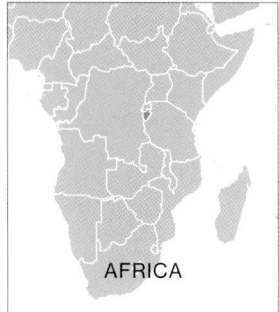

Burundi

Coffee came to Burundi in the 1920s under Belgian colonial rule, and from 1933 every peasant farmer had to cultivate at least 50 coffee trees. When Burundi gained its independence in 1962, coffee production went private. This changed in 1972, along with the political climate, but since 1991 coffee has slowly been returning to the private sector.

Coffee growing had been increasing steadily, but the civil war that broke out in 1993 (and which would last until 2005) caused a precipitous drop in production. Since the end of the war, efforts have been made to increase both production and the value of coffee in Burundi. Investment in the industry is seen as crucial, as Burundi's economy has been shattered by conflict. In 2011 Burundi had one of the lowest per capita incomes in the world with 90 per cent of the population relying on subsistence agriculture. Coffee and tea exports combined make up approximately 90 per cent of total foreign exchange earnings. Coffee production is recovering but has not yet reached the levels of the early 1980s, although in 2021 coffee was the second largest export for the country. There is hope for coffee in Burundi. With 650,000 families dependent on the crop – a significant portion of the country's total population – movements towards higher prices through improvement of quality can only be a good thing. However, the constant fear of political instability returning looms large – the unrest in 2015 being a good example of this.

Burundi's geography is well suited to coffee. Much of it is mountainous, providing the necessary elevations and climates. There are no coffee estates in Burundi; instead, coffee is produced by large numbers of smallholder farmers. Recently, these producers have become more organized, usually centring around one of the 160 washing stations in the country. Around two-thirds of these washing stations are under state ownership; the others are privately owned. Anything from several hundred up to two thousand producers feed their coffee into each washing station.

Within each region, these stations are grouped together into SOGESTALs (Sociétés de gestion des stations de lavage), which are effectively management organizations for groups of washing stations. Development of quality in recent years has been directed through these organizations, mainly through the provision of better infrastructure in their regions.

The best coffees from Burundi are fully washed and usually made up of the Bourbon variety, although other varieties are grown. In many ways there are similarities between Burundi and its neighbour Rwanda: the countries have similar elevations and coffee varieties, and both face the challenges of being landlocked, which can hinder the rapid export necessary for the raw coffee to arrive in the consuming countries in good condition. As in Rwanda, coffees in Burundi are also susceptible to the potato defect (see page 155).

Traceability

Until recently, the coffees from all the washing stations within each SOGESTAL were blended together. This meant that coffees exported from Burundi were only traceable back to their SOGESTAL, which is effectively their region of origin.

In 2008 Burundi began to embrace the speciality coffee sector, allowing more direct and traceable purchasing. In 2011 there was a coffee quality competition in Burundi called the Prestige Cup, a precursor to the more established Cup of Excellence. The lots from individual washing stations were kept separate and ranked on quality, then they were sold at auction with their traceability intact. This means that we are likely to see more unique and interesting coffees coming out of Burundi in the future, and there is great potential for quality.

Opposite: Until 1986, the state-owned Burundi Coffee Company had a monopoly on export, but deregulation has led to the creation of private export companies.

Taste Profile

Great coffees from Burundi can have complex berry fruit flavours and a pronounced juicy quality.

Growing Regions

Population: 12,890,000

Number of 60kg (132lb) bags in 2023: 215,000

Burundi is such a small country that it doesn't really have distinct growing areas. Coffee grows right across the country, wherever there is suitable land and elevation. The country is divided into provinces, and coffee farms are clustered around the washing stations (wet mills).

BUBANZA

This region is in the north-west of Burundi.

Elevation: 1,350m (4,400ft)
Harvest: April–July
Varieties: Bourbon, Jackson, Mibirizi, some SL varieties

BUJUMBURA RURAL

Located in western Burundi.

Elevation: 1,400m (4,600ft)
Harvest: April–July
Varieties: Bourbon, Jackson, Mibirizi, some SL varieties

BURURI

This south-western province contains three of Burundi's national parks.

Elevation: 1,550m (5,050ft)
Harvest: April–July
Varieties: Bourbon, Jackson, Mibirizi, some SL varieties

CIBITOKE

This province is in the very north-west of Burundi, close to the border with the Democratic Republic of Congo.

Elevation: 1,450m (4,750ft)
Harvest: April–July
Varieties: Bourbon, Jackson, Mibirizi, some SL varieties

GITEGA

This central region contains one of the two state-owned dry mills, used for the final stages of preparation and quality control before export.

Elevation: 1,450m (4,750ft)
Harvest: April–July
Varieties: Bourbon, Jackson, Mibirizi, some SL varieties

KARUZI

This region is slightly west of central Burundi

Elevation: 1,600m (5,200ft)
Harvest: April–July
Varieties: Bourbon, Jackson, Mibirizi, some SL varieties

Above: Coffee pickers bring their harvest to be washed in Kayanza, Burundi.

KAYANZA

This northern region, near the Rwandan border, has the second highest number of stations.

Elevation: 1,700–1,950m (5,600–6,400ft)
Harvest: April–July
Varieties: Bourbon, Jackson, Mibirizi, some SL varieties

KIRUNDO

This region is in the northernmost part of the country.

Elevation: 1,500m (4,900ft)
Harvest: April–July
Varieties: Bourbon, Jackson, Mibirizi, some SL varieties

MAKAMBA

One of the most southerly provinces in Burundi.

Elevation: 1,550m (5,050ft)
Harvest: April–July
Varieties: Bourbon, Jackson, Mibirizi, some SL varieties

MURAMVYA

A small region in the central part of the country.

Elevation: 1,800m (5,900ft)
Harvest: April–July
Varieties: Bourbon, Jackson, Mibirizi, some SL varieties

MUYINGA

This region borders Tanzania in the north-eastern part of the country.

Elevation: 1,600m (5,200ft)
Harvest: April–July
Varieties: Bourbon, Jackson, Mibirizi, some SL varieties

MWARO

Another small region in the middle of the country.

Elevation: 1,700m (5,600ft)
Harvest: April–July
Varieties: Bourbon, Jackson, Mibirizi, some SL varieties

NGOZI

The most concentrated region for coffee production, in the north of the country, with 25 per cent of the washing stations.

Elevation: 1,650m (5,400ft)
Harvest: April–July
Varieties: Bourbon, Jackson, Mibirizi, some SL varieties

RUTANA

This region is in southern Burundi, west of Mount Kiziki. It has one washing station.

Elevation: 1,550m (5,050ft)
Harvest: April–July
Varieties: Bourbon, Jackson, Mibirizi, some SL varieties

Zambia

Zambia has been, for quite some time, overlooked by much of the speciality coffee industry. One could argue that it is a chicken-and-egg situation, as historically little interest from speciality buyers has led to little investment in quality in the country, and little investment in quality has led to little interest from speciality buyers.

The first attempts at growing coffee in Zambia date back to just before World War 1. It was not a success, and the trees were removed in 1923. It would take another attempt in the 1930s for it to take hold in any meaningful way. However, the industry did not gear up production until the late 1970s and early 1980s with the assistance of funding from the World Bank. Problems with pests and diseases led growers to adopt the Catimor hybrid, which is considered less delicious than Bourbon. This was, in some ways, a temporary switch, and the government went back to recommending Bourbon, but there is still a fair amount of Catimor in the country. One challenge with coffee production in Zambia is that coffee requires irrigation, and there is only a single, distinct rainy season.

Zambia's coffee exports peaked in 2005/2006 at around 6,500 tonnes (7,150 tons) but have dropped dramatically since. Some attribute the drop to low prices and a crucial lack of long-term financing in the

Above: The Mubuyu coffee farm is located on the slopes of the blue Munali Hills at an altitude of 1,100m (3,600ft).

Right: Once ripened, coffee cherries are picked by hand on Zambia's coffee farms, most of which are large, well-run estates that have good access to modern equipment.

industry. In addition to this, the country's largest producer closed in 2008 after defaulting on its loans. The Northern Coffee Corp was producing one-third of the country's 6,000 tonnes (6,600 tons) at the time of closure. Total production dropped to just 180 tonnes (198 tons) in 2015 but this had recovered to around 2,000 tonnes (2,205 tons) by 2019. Most of the current production comes from a single large farm in the north of the country.

Most of Zambia's coffee comes from larger estates, although there has been some encouragement of smallholders, too. The estates are generally well run, have good access to modern equipment (because coffee production started relatively late here), and may be owned by multinationals. Smallholder farming has struggled to take hold, access to fertilizers and equipment has been difficult, and generally the quality has not been high. The lack of access to water and decent post-harvest processing has further hindered the production of clean, sweet coffees.

Taste Profile
The rare, excellent coffees are bright and floral, with a clean fruitlike complexity.

Traceability
The best coffees in Zambia tend to come from single estates, although you may have to look hard for them. Not only is overall production small in Zambia, but high-quality coffees are not commonplace. Frustratingly, the country has the undeniable potential to produce stellar coffees, from its seed stock to its geography.

Growing Regions

Population: 20,020,000

Number of 60kg (132lb) bags in 2023: 4,000

The regions in Zambia are not well defined and are typically just referred to as the Southern, Central, Copperbelt and Northern regions. Coffee is mainly grown in the Northern region around the Muchinga Mountains (an area that includes the regions of Isoka, Nakonde and Kasama) and around the country's capital city, Lusaka.

Elevation: 900–2,000m (3,000–6,600ft)
Harvest: April–September
Varieties: Bourbon, Catimor

Malawi

It seems that coffee was introduced to Malawi in the late 1800s. One claim states that a tree taken from the Edinburgh Botanical Gardens was brought to the country in 1878 by John Buchanan, a Scottish missionary and horticulturalist. It first took root in southern Malawi, in the Blantyre region, and by 1900 annual coffee production was at 1,000 tonnes (1,100 tons).

Despite its auspicious start, coffee production collapsed not long after due to a combination of poorly maintained soils, pests and diseases, and the competition from the increasingly dominant production of Brazil.

For most of the first part of the 20th century there was little African ownership of the large coffee farms, as the country was under British colonial rule. However, the cooperative movement started in 1946, and coffee production grew dramatically in the 1950s. While they looked like they might prove to be successful, all the cooperatives were dissolved in 1971 due to political interference. Coffee production in Malawi peaked in the 1990s at 7,000 tonnes (7,700 tons) and has since shrunk back to around 1,500 tonnes (1,650 tons) a year.

Even though it is landlocked, Malawi has built a strong agricultural export economy. In the case of coffee, some attribute its success to the lack of government interference in export, allowing direct relationships between sellers and buyers. However, for a long time quality was not a particular focus. Grading was a very simple system of Grade 1 and Grade 2, although in recent years there has been movement towards the AA-style grading system used throughout Africa (see page 147).

The coffee varieties grown in Malawi certainly cover the extremes of the spectrum. There has been quite a lot of Gesha variety planted, the same variety that has generated so much interest in Central America. However, there is also quite a lot of Catimor throughout the country, a disease-resistant variety that is generally of much lower quality.

Taste Profile

The coffees can be quite sweet and clean, though rarely as explosively fruity and complex as other coffees from East Africa.

Malawi's agricultural exports are a significant part of its economy, and up to 80 per cent of its population is involved in farming in some way. However, coffee has remained a small percentage of agricultural exports, currently somewhere around 3 per cent. Many feel that there is a lot of room to grow, and that there is five times more land suited to growing coffee than is currently being used. What will be a barrier to coffee's growth in Malawi is the price paid for coffee, and the fact that other crops are seen as being more lucrative to grow, such as macadamia nuts.

Traceability

Coffee in the south of Malawi is generally produced on large-scale, commercial estates and in the central and northern regions by smallholder farmers. Therefore, it is possible to trace coffees either back to a single farm or to a large group of producers. There has probably been more focus on quality and speciality coffee coming from the smallholder producers.

Growing Regions

Population: 21,240,689

Number of 60kg (132lb) bags in 2023: 25,000

Coffees from Malawi are rarely identified by their regions, and the regions themselves could be considered as defined pockets of coffee growing, rather than definable areas with distinct characteristics determined by the local terroir and microclimate.

CHITIPA DISTRICT

This area has a reputation for growing some of the best coffee in Malawi. It is close to the Songwe River, which provides a natural border between Malawi and Tanzania to the north. This area is home to the large Misuku Hills Cooperative.

Elevation: 1,700–2,000m (5,600–6,600ft)
Harvest: May–September
Varieties: Agaro, Gesha, Catimor, Mundo Novo, Caturra

RUMPHI DISTRICT

This area is located in the north of the country, close to Lake Malawi in the eastern part of the Nyika National Park. There are several areas here with clusters of producers, such as Chakak, Mphachi, Salawe, Junji and Vungu Vungu. The Phoka Hills and Viphya North cooperatives are located here.

Elevation: 1,200–2,500m (3,900–8,100ft)
Harvest: May–September
Varieties: Agaro, Gesha, Catimor, Mundo Novo, Caturra

NORTH VIPHYA

This region covers part of the northern Viphya Plateau, which is separated from Nkhata Bay Highlands by the Lizunkhumi River valley.

Elevation: 1,200–1,500m (3,900–4,900ft)
Harvest: May–September
Varieties: Agaro, Gesha, Catimor, Mundo Novo, Caturra

SOUTHEAST MZIMBA

This region is named for the city of Mzimba, and there are several valley and river systems running through it.

Elevation: 1,200–1,700m (3,900–5,600ft)
Harvest: May–September
Varieties: Agaro, Gesha, Catimor, Mundo Novo, Caturra

NKHATA BAY HIGHLANDS

This region is just to the east of the regional capital city of Mzuzu.

Elevation: 1,000–2,000m (3,300–6,600ft)
Harvest: May–September
Varieties: Agaro, Gesha, Catimor, Mundo Novo, Caturra

Below: Coffee farms in Malawi have a strong agricultural export economy and most coffee can be traced to a single farm.

Madagascar

Madagascar produces quite a lot of coffee, yet very little is exported. However, I believe it is worthy of inclusion here for its potential as well as for the genetic diversity in coffee on the island. While the crop species of Arabica and Robusta were introduced by French settlers in the early 19th century, Madagascar is also home to around half of the 130 wild species of coffee that have been discovered around the world.

The biodiversity in Madagascar is not confined to coffee by any stretch, but sadly, many of those wild species of coffee are considered under threat from climate change.

Madagascar primarily produces Robusta as a crop, and it makes up about 90 per cent of coffee grown on the island. The remaining 10 per cent is Arabica, and none of the other wild species have been commercialized. Most of the production comes from small farms, as many large farms were nationalized in the 1970s. Only around 6–7 per cent of the coffee production is exported, most being consumed domestically. Most of the export goes through French trading houses. There has been little traceable coffee from the island, although some are now working on making some of the Arabica grown there more widely available. Should you see a Madagascan coffee offered by a reputable roaster I would recommend trying it.

GROWING STATISTICS

Population: 30,300,000

Number of 60kg (132lb) bags produced in 2023: 285,000

Elevation: 1,000–1,200m (3,300–3,900ft) for Arabica; 100–300m (330–1,000ft) for Robusta
Harvest: April–July (Arabica)
Varieties: Robusta, Bourbon, Typica

Réunion

The island is a tiny producer of coffee, but it is still of great importance to coffee historically as well as being an increasing point of focus due to the particular variety of coffee that it grows. The island, once named Bourbon after the ruling house of France, gave its name to one of the most popular varieties of coffee to be spread around the world (see page 22).

The French first tried to bring coffee to the island in 1708, but that attempt failed. They tried again in 1715 and 1718, and eventually the plants took hold and would grow, adapt and evolve. Seeds would be taken from the island later and spread to much of the coffee-growing world as the variety that would bear the island's name. That variety is known as Bourbon Rond on the island.

Now a different variety called Bourbon Pointu locally, also known as Laurina (see page 26), has attracted fresh interest as it has about half the caffeine content of a typical Arabica variety. There is only a small amount of land on the island dedicated to coffee, and it produces only a few hundred kilos of beans each year.

GROWING STATISTICS

Population: 885,700

Number of 60kg (132lb) bags produced in 2023: unknown

Elevation: 800–1,500m (2,600–4,900ft)
Harvest: October–February
Varieties: Bourbon Pointu, Bourbon Rond

Côte d'Ivoire

The Côte d'Ivoire (Ivory Coast) is a large producer of Robusta, but when coffee was first introduced in the 19th century it was the *Coffea liberica* species (see page 14) that was first grown. It did not flourish, but once Robusta was introduced, production quickly grew. from 51 tonnes (56 tons) in 1925 to over 15,000 tonnes (16,500 tons) in 1939 to 112,500 tonnes (124,000 tons) in 1958, peaking in 2000 at 380,000 tonnes 419,000 tons).

In the 1960s the then president, Félix Houphouët-Boigny, encouraged the production of Arabusta – a hybrid of Arabica and Robusta. This was marketed as 'The Presidential Coffee' but did not hold lasting appeal, even though it was considered to taste better than Robusta, because it grew more slowly. However, there remains a market for Arabusta in Côte d'Ivoire, where it fetches higher prices than Robusta. The country consumes a good amount of the coffee it produces.

Most of the coffee is grown in the areas around the towns or cities of Abboisso, Abengourou and Divo. In many parts of the country coffee is intercropped with cacao, another important crop.

GROWING STATISTICS

Population: 28,160,000

Number of 60kg (132lb) bags produced in 2023: 1,350,000

Elevation: 100–400m (330–1,300ft)
Harvest: August–January
Varieties: Robusta, Arabusta

Togo

Coffee was introduced by French colonists in the 1920s, and the coffee they introduced was a Robusta variety known as Niaouli. This is still the most commonly grown variety of coffee in Togo today. Its production has varied over the years, and despite the importance of the crop from an export perspective, production is lower now than in the past.

The current area planted with coffee is about half of what it was in 2000. There are plans to reinvigorate the coffee sector, and the government aims to double production by 2030.

The north of the country is dry and arid, but it is different towards the coast. The coffee-growing area is to the south-west of the country, along the border with Ghana down to the ocean where there are higher elevations. Coffee tends to be grown in the same areas as cacao, also an important export for the country. Estimates put the total population involved in coffee at a little over 475,000 – a substantial percentage of the total population.

GROWING STATISTICS

Population: 8,849,000

Number of 60kg (132lb) bags produced in 2023: 455,000

Elevation: 200–800m (660–2,600ft)
Harvest: December–February
Varieties: Robusta (Niaouli)

Cameroon

Coffee production in Cameroon dates back to 1884, when it was introduced by German colonists. It was spread wider during the late 1920s and continued to flourish over the following decades. By 1990 Cameroon was producing 2.6 million 60kg (132lb) sacks of coffee and was the 12th largest producer in the world.

Over the next few decades production declined, with many blaming government policies for the drop. The country has always primarily produced Robusta, and today only about 8 per cent of its total coffee production is made up of Arabica varieties.

Coffee is grown in a number of regions in the country. Robusta is mostly produced in the southern regions, while Arabica grows in the western regions of the country, at surprisingly high altitudes. Very little traceable Arabica has made its way onto the market from Cameroon. However, if you see it carried by a roaster you trust and whose coffees you enjoy, then it is worth trying.

GROWING STATISTICS

Population: 27,910,000

Number of 60kg (132lb) bags in 2023: 285,000

Elevation: 1,000–1,900m (3,300–6,200ft) for Arabica; 200–1,200m (660–3,900ft) for Robusta

Harvest: October–December (Arabica); October–February (Robusta)

Varieties: Java (Arabica) – this variety was originally thought to be a Typica variety, but genetic testing has shown it to be related to an Ethiopian landrace population called Abyssinia

St Helena

This tiny, remote island has a long history with coffee – even though it only started exporting coffee in 1989. Coffee growing on the island dates to 1733, when coffee plants were introduced by the British via a ship of the East India Trading Company called the *Houghton*. The island would serve as Napoleon's home during his exile after his defeat at Waterloo.

The attraction of St Helena's coffee to many is that these plants are, genetically, pretty much unchanged from the plants that arrived nearly 300 years ago. The small amount of coffee exported, usually closer to 1,500kg (3,300lb), fetches high prices primarily for its story and its scarcity and will come from just one of two farms on the island.

GROWING STATISTICS

Number of 60kg (132lb) bags exported in 2023: approximately 40 bags

Elevation: 300–700m (1,000–2,300ft)
Harvest: October–February
Varieties: Green-tipped Bourbon

Opposite, top: A farmer tends to the coffee trees on a farm in Cameroon.

Opposite, bottom: Sacks of roasted St Helena coffee beans are stacked in the storeroom of a coffee grower's home in Jamestown, St Helena.

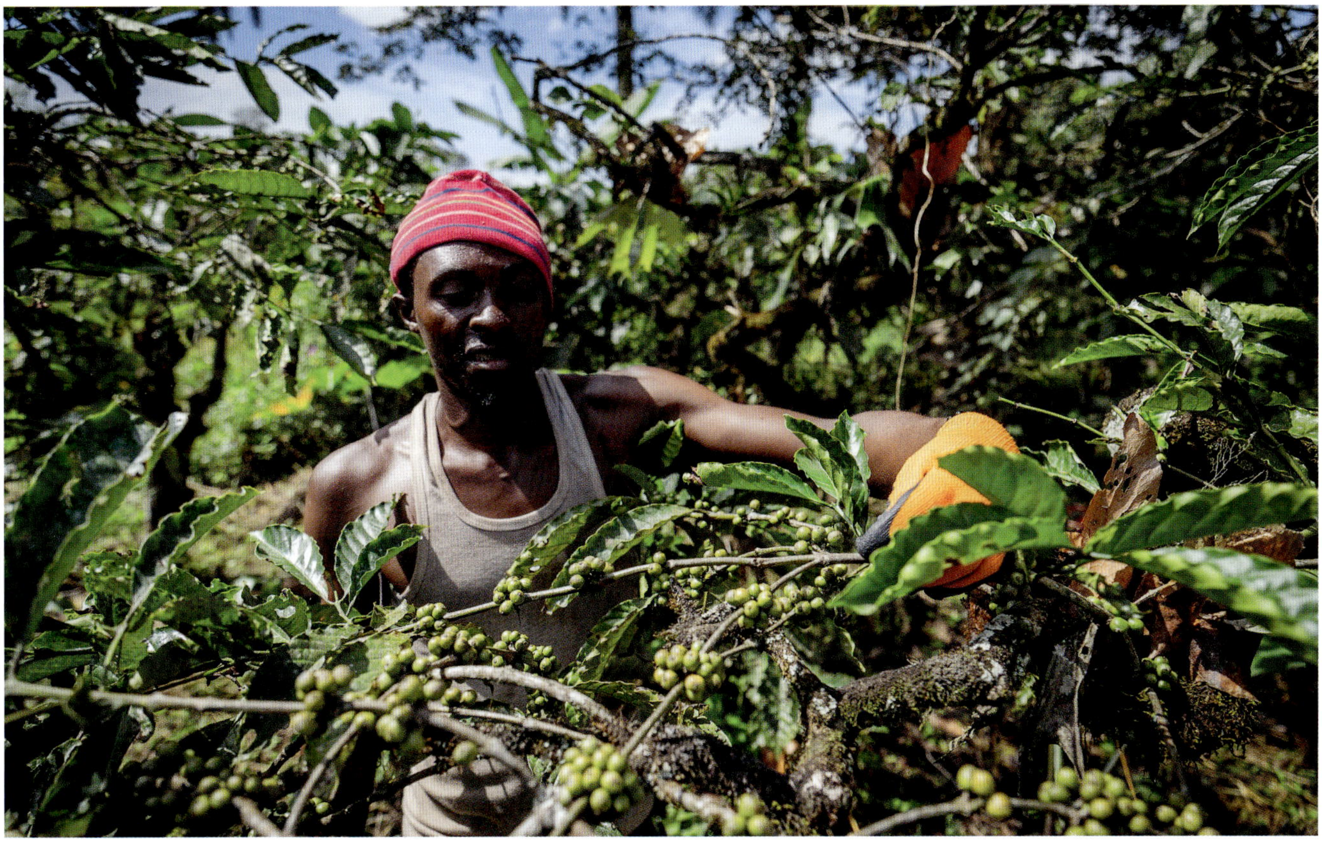

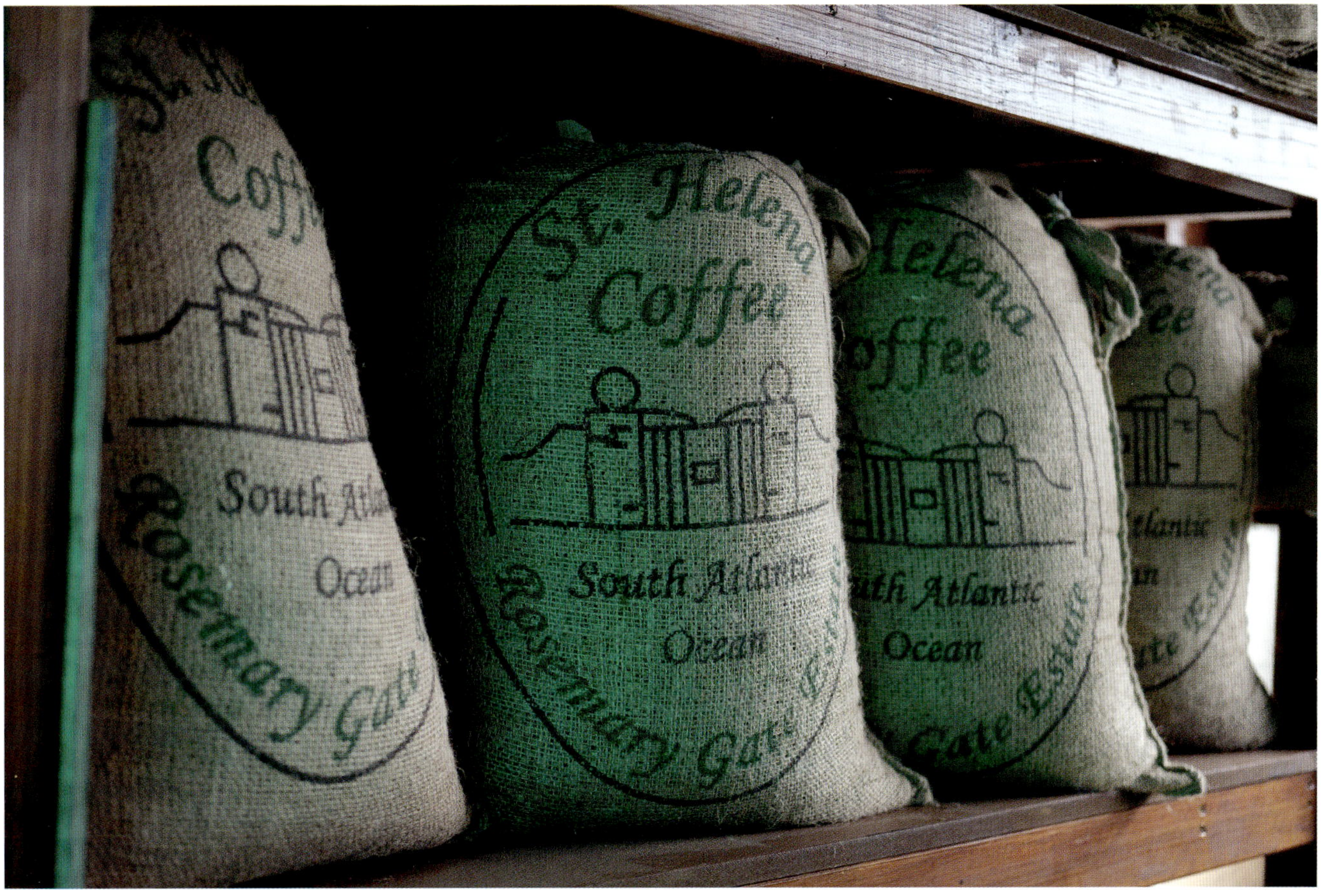
St. Helena
Coffee
South Atlantic
Ocean
Rosemary Gate

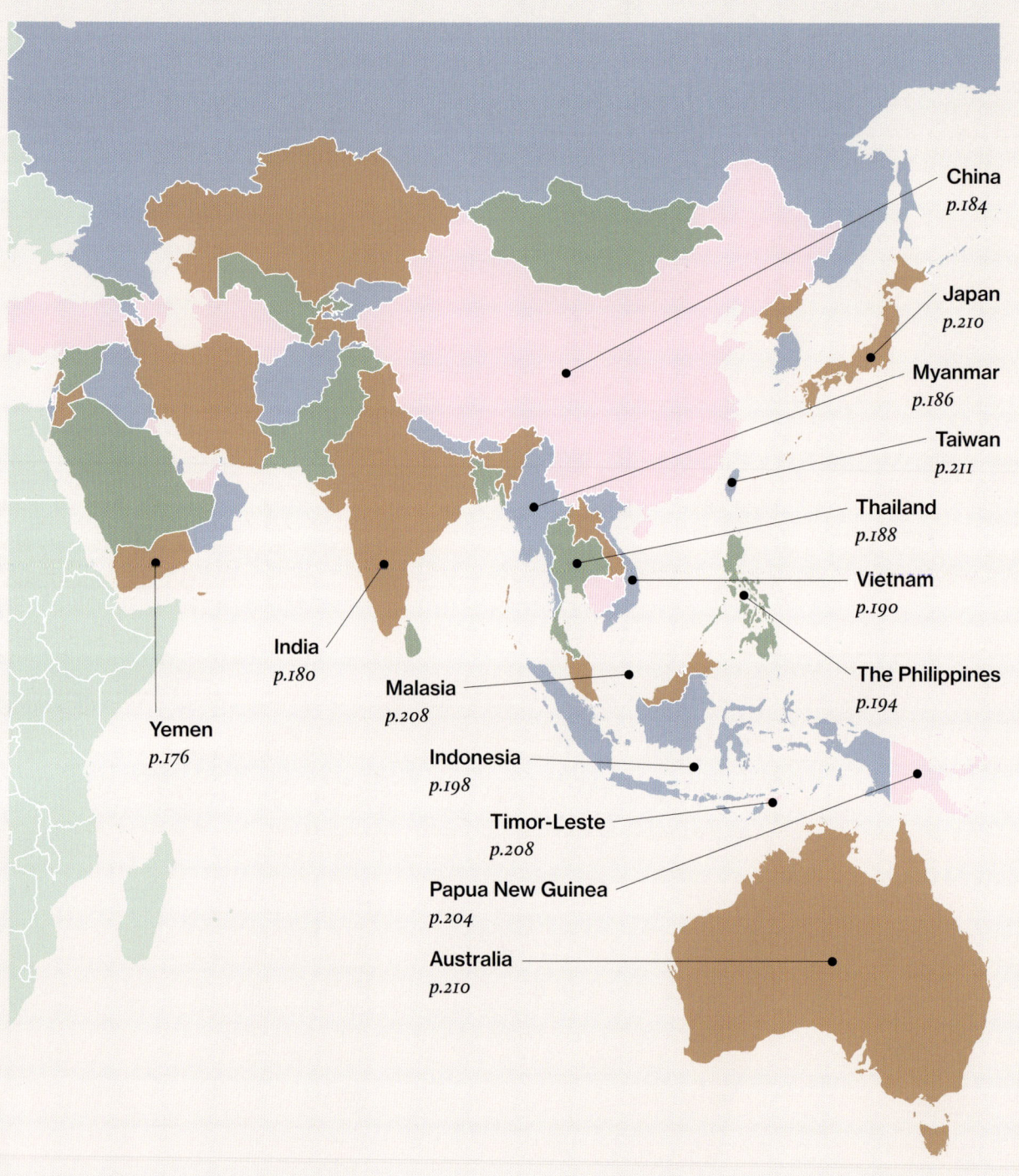

Asia and Oceania

Myth and history have shaped the inheritance of coffee cultivation in Asia. From Robusta beans smuggled into India by a pilgrim from Yemen to the lucrative export of Indonesian beans by the Dutch East India Company during the 16th century, Asia now supplies a significant percentage of commodity-grade coffee to the market. Yemen is perhaps the notable exception – its comparatively small export quantities of unique beans remain in strong demand across the world.

Oceania – the Earth's smallest, least populated and most dispersed continent – has minimal coffee production. Australia is the region's leading producer of speciality coffees, while Papua New Guinea's production traditions, while distinctive, are more like those of its South-East Asian neighbours.

Yemen

Yemen has been producing coffee on a commercial basis for longer than any other country, and its coffee is distinctive, perhaps challenging, and certainly unusual. Despite a strong demand for Yemeni coffee over the centuries, its trade has never commoditized. Yemen is unique, from its coffee varieties and its terraced farming to its processing and its trade.

Coffee came to Yemen from Ethiopia, either through trade or those making pilgrimages from Ethiopia to Mecca, and was well established in the country in the 15th and 16th centuries. Export of its coffee introduced the world to the port of Mocha, and I think it is fair to say that 'mocha' is probably the most confusing word in all of coffee's lexicon.

Only 3 per cent of the land in Yemen is suitable for farming, water being the major limiting factor. Coffee is grown on terraced land at high elevations and additional irrigation is required to keep the coffee trees healthy. Many farmers depend on non-renewable sources of deep underground water, and there is some concern over depleting stocks. Fertilization of the soil is not particularly common, so there is an additional problem of depleting soil nutrients. All these factors, coupled with the sheer remoteness of the coffee-growing regions, go some way to explaining the huge number and variation of heirloom varieties of Arabica found in the country, most of them peculiar to their growing regions.

Yemen's coffee is picked by hand, with pickers visiting a tree several times in a season. Despite this, selective picking is not particularly commonplace, with underripe and overripe cherries often being harvested. Whole cherries are usually dried in the sun after harvesting, often on the roofs of the farmers' homes. Rarely do these roofs provide enough space, so the cherries are often piled too deep to dry correctly, resulting in defects such as uneven drying, fermentation and mould.

Each producer may grow only a very small amount of coffee. Data from the 2000 census shows that around 99,000 households produced coffee and, based

on estimates of production, the average household produced just 113kg (249lb) of raw coffee that year.

There remains a strong global demand for Yemeni coffee, and about half of exports go to Saudi Arabia. Coupled with limited production and relatively high production costs, this makes it sell for high prices. Demand has not increased the traceability of the coffee, and it can travel through a network of intermediaries from the farmer through to the exporter. Coffees can also sit for quite some time (often years) at the point of export, as some exporters sell their oldest stocks first, and warehouse their newer crops in caverns underground.

Since the civil war began in 2015, coffee production in Yemen has been badly affected. The actual volumes produced have decreased only a little, but exports have fallen to a little over half of what they were before the war. Be aware that there has been an increase in the fraudulent mislabelling of Ethiopian coffees, with many being presented as Yemeni coffees to try to meet the existing demand and achieve a premium price.

Traceability

Trying to understand exactly where coffees come from in Yemen can be extremely confusing. Often the name of the coffee will include the term 'Mocha', indicating the port from which it has been exported. Usually,

The Term 'Mocha'

Originally, the word referred to the port in Yemen from where coffee was exported. This spelling soon changed to 'moka', and the term was used to describe the potent and pungent coffees produced in Yemen. Some naturally processed coffees from other countries are still described this way, such as Moka Harrar from Ethiopia.

The coffees from Yemen were often blended with coffees from Java, and the Mocha–Java blend was born. However, the name was not protected and thus became a kind of stylistic term used by many roasters to describe the flavour of a particular blend they created, rather than where the component coffees came from. The current use of the term 'mocha' to describe a mixture of hot chocolate and espresso serves only to further bewilder the consumer.

Qesher

Qesher, also q'shr or qishr, is a by-product of coffee production. It is the dried, but not roasted, husks removed from the coffee cherries. In Yemen, these husks are often brewed like tea as a way to consume a form of coffee. More recently, producers in Central America have been experimenting with the same product, there called cascara. This is usually just the dried fruit of the cherry, rather than both the husks and dried fruit.

coffees are only traceable back to a particular region within Yemen, rather than to the farm where they were produced. It is also common to see the local names for different coffee varieties used to describe the coffee, such as Mattari.

Having better levels of traceability doesn't necessarily guarantee better quality. Often, different coffees are blended together before export and then exported under the most valuable name. The high demand for Yemeni coffee is based on its unusual, wild and pungent flavours – and these come in part from defects in the process. Traceability has increased dramatically in the last few years, although this applies only to a small percentage of coffee exported from Yemen. If you want to buy highly traceable coffee, it is possible, although it will be expensive. There is a high demand for Yemeni coffee, particularly from Saudi Arabia, which creates a high price floor for coffee. This means that speciality lots, which are very traceable, can reach high prices. However, they can also be fascinating, unusual and delicious coffees.

Yemeni Varieties

As Yemen was the first country to grow coffee as an agricultural crop, taking seeds initially from Ethiopia, it is no surprise that there is a great deal of genetic diversity within coffee plants in the country. There are large numbers of cultivars with names distinct to Yemen. Recent studies have shown that there isn't a strong genetic link between different varieties for which Yemeni farmers use the same name, suggesting that they may not have been given accurate information about the crops they were planting or had

inherited. Another study showed that there is a group of varieties distinct to Yemen alone, and you will see these described on labels as 'Yemenia'. Confusingly, Yemenia is not a single variety but the name given to a mother population, a kind of umbrella term covering the group of undescribed, genetically distinct varieties. The local names remain in popular usage, too, and so are applied when talking about varieties within each area. Yemen remains full of huge genetic potential for the future of coffee, in particular in our search for coffee plants that can withstand higher temperatures but also produce good-tasting cups of coffee.

Taste Profile
Yemeni coffee is wild, complex and pungent, offering a completely distinctive coffee experience, different from other coffees around the world. For some the wild, slightly fermented fruit quality is off-putting, while others prize it highly. The more traceable lots tend to still have fermented fruit qualities but are sweet, relatively clean and very complex.

Growing Regions

Population: 33,700,000

Number of 60kg (132lb) bags in 2023: 330,000

Please note that Westernized spellings of place names in Yemen can vary quite dramatically. Each region described in Yemen is a governorate, rather than a geographically defined region. Yemen has 21 governorates, and 17 of these grow coffee, though fewer are key producing areas.

SANA'A
Many of the premium coffees exported from Yemen bear the names of the varieties grown in this region. Confusingly, Mattari can be used to describe a region (around Bani Matar), and the name of the variety is probably derived this way. The region is based around the city of Sana'a, one of the oldest continuously populated cities on earth, and at 2,200m (7,200ft) above sea level, also one of the highest. As a region, this is the largest producer of coffee in the country.

Elevation: 1,400–2,300m (4,600–7,500ft)
Harvest: September–March
Varieties: Heirloom varieties such as Mattari, Ismaili, Harazi, Dawairi, Dawarani, Sanani, Haimi

RAYMAH
This small governorate was established in 2004. It produces a reasonable amount of the country's coffee and has increasingly been the focus of water-management projects by non-government organizations to help increase coffee yields in the area.

Elevation: 1,400–1,700m (4,600–5,600ft)
Harvest: October–January
Varieties: Heirloom varieties such as Raymi, Dwairi, Bura'ae, Kubari, Tufahi, Udaini

MAHWIT
Located south of Sana'a, the city of At-Tawila rose to prominence between the 15th and 18th centuries as a hub for coffee-growing in the region. The city was a collection centre for coffee before it headed to ports for export.

Elevation: 1,400–2,150m (4,600–7,000ft)
Harvest: August–December
Varieties: Heirloom varieties such as Mahwaiti, Tufahi, Udaini, Kholani

SA'DAH
This governorate has unfortunately been plagued by civil war since 2004. Confusingly, *sada* is an Arabic term for black coffee, and is popular throughout the Middle East, often served with the addition of spices.

Elevation: 1,000–2,200m (3,300–7,200ft)
Harvest: October–January
Varieties: Heirloom varieties such as Dawairi, Tufahi, Udaini, Kholani

HAJJAH
This is another small producing region, centred around its capital city of the same name.

Elevation: 1,500–1,700m (4,900–5,600ft)
Harvest: October–December
Varieties: Heirloom varieties such as Shani, Safi, Masrahi, Shami, Bazi, Mathani, Jua'ari

Opposite: Only 3 per cent of Yemen is suitable for agriculture owing to the scarcity of water. This terraced farm in a traditional small fortress town is typical of Yemeni coffee-farming methods.

India

The origins of coffee production in Southern India are entwined with myth. The story goes that a pilgrim named Baba Budan passed through Yemen in 1670 while returning from Mecca and smuggled out seven coffee seeds, the export of which was strictly controlled. Because he took seven, a sacrosanct number in Islam, it was considered a religious act.

Baba Budan planted these first seeds in what is now known as the Chikmagalur district of the Karnataka region and there they thrived. The hills there now bear his name, Baba Budangiri, and this is still an important coffee-growing area.

It wasn't until the middle of the 19th century, under British colonial rule, that coffee plantations in Southern India began to flourish. This was short-lived, however, and coffee's popularity began to wane again. In the 1870s the industry suffered due to an increasing demand for tea, combined with an increasing incidence of leaf rust, which attacked the coffee plants. Many plantations switched to tea production, ironically the same plantations that had been successful exporting their coffee. Leaf rust did not drive coffee out of India, however, but instead encouraged research into rust-resistant varieties. This research was relatively successful, and some new varieties were bred, although this was before the flavour of the coffee was deemed to be very important.

In 1942 the Coffee Board of India was created, by way of a government act that began the regulation of the industry. Some argue that by pooling coffees from many producers, the government reduced incentives for producers to improve the quality of their coffee. However, production certainly grew, and in the 1990s India's output increased by an astonishing 30 per cent.

During the 1990s there was also a decrease in regulation governing how and where producers could sell their coffee. The domestic coffee market in India also grew rapidly. While India has a very low per capita consumption of coffee, tea being a far cheaper alternative, the population is so large that the total consumption is quite sizeable. The annual consumption per person is just 100g (3½oz), but this results in a total consumption of 2 million bags of coffee per year. Consumption is growing in India, with a speciality coffee culture starting to flourish in major cities. Many roasters are working directly with producers in the country, and many of the best lots may now be consumed internally rather than exported.

Robusta is, in many ways, better suited to India than Arabica. The lower elevations and climate make Robusta yields high. More care and attention are paid to the production of Robusta in India than in most other countries so it occupies the premium end of the market. Even the best Robustas still carry the distinctive woody flavours of the species, but the relative lack of unclean flavours in Indian Robustas makes them popular with roasters who still like Robusta in their espresso blends.

Left: Alongside the branding of the farmer or exporter, jute coffee bags have key information printed on them.

Monsooning

One of the better-known coffees from India is called Monsoon Malabar and is created by an unusual process called 'monsooning'. Monsooning is now a controlled process, but it began completely by accident. During its export from India to Europe at the time of the British Raj, coffee was transported in wooden boxes and was, therefore, subjected to the wet weather that came during the monsoon months. The raw coffee absorbed a great deal of moisture, which had a strong effect on the resulting cup of coffee.

As export practices improved, the demand for this unusual coffee remained, so the process was recreated in factories along the west coast. Monsooning is only done with naturally processed coffees; the raw coffee looks very pale afterwards and is somewhat brittle. Monsooned beans are difficult to roast evenly, and their brittle nature means that a bag of roasted coffee often contains lots of beans that have been damaged in the packing process. This is nothing to worry about, however, and is not the same thing as where packets of low-grade coffees contain broken pieces and

Grading

Indian coffees are graded in two different ways. The first is unique to India and classifies all washed coffees as 'Plantation Coffees', all naturally processed coffees as 'Cherry', and all washed Robusta coffees as 'Parchment Coffees'.

India also uses a size-based grading system, from AAA (the largest), down through AA, A and also PB (peaberry). As in many other countries that use a size system, the larger bean sizes are associated with higher quality, but this is not necessarily the case.

therefore should be avoided. During the monsooning process, coffee usually loses its acidity, but often gains pungent, wild flavours that make it somewhat divisive. Some people love the richness and intensity of the cup, while others believe the flavours are the result of defective processing and are very unpleasant.

Traceability
Because 98 per cent of the 250,000 coffee producers are small growers, it is often difficult to find coffees traceable to a single estate. However, these are often worth seeking out. Traceability may only be possible back to the point of processing or to a specific region.

> **Taste Profile**
> The best coffees from India tend to be heavy, creamy and low in acidity, but rarely particularly complex.

Growing Regions

Population: 1,370,695,000
Number of 60kg (132lb) bags in 2023: 5,600,000

Most of India's coffee is grown in four main states, each of which can be subdivided into several smaller geographic regions.

TAMIL NADU
Tamil Nadu (which translates simply as 'Land of the Tamils') is the southernmost of India's 28 states. The capital city is Chennai (formerly Madras), and the region is famous for its monumental Hindu temples.

PULNEY
This is the largest area of coffee production in the state. There are several challenges here for coffee growers, including a high incidence of leaf rust (which determines the choice of varieties to grow), labour shortages, absentee ownership, and a scarcity of water for post-harvest processing.

Elevation: 600–2,000m (2,000–6,600ft)
Harvest: October–February
Varieties: S795, Selection 5B, Selection 9, Selection 10, Cauvery

NILGIRI
Many growers in this mountainous region are tribal and have smallholdings with financial constraints. This region produces around twice as much Robusta as Arabica and struggles with high rainfall and many kinds of pests, including coffee berry borer. It is the westernmost of the growing regions, bordering Karnataka and Kerala.

Elevation: 900–1,400m (3,000–4,600ft)
Harvest: October–February
Varieties: S795, Kent, Cauvery, Robustas

SHEVAROY
This region produces almost exclusively Arabica. Most of the farmers in Shevaroy are smallholders, but the distribution of land is skewed in favour of larger farms, with only 5 per cent of the farms occupying around 75 per cent of the land under coffee. One of the problems with large farms in the area is the trend towards monocultures of trees used to shade the coffee, silver oak being extremely common here. Many consider that a diverse range of shade trees is important to maintain biodiversity and sustainable production.

Elevation: 900–1,500m (3,000–4,900ft)
Harvest: October–February
Varieties: S795, Cauvery, Selection 9

KARNATAKA
This state produces the majority of the nation's coffee. It used to be known as Mysore but was renamed Karnataka in 1973. The meaning of the name is not completely agreed, opinion divided between 'elevated lands' and 'the black region', the latter being a reference to the black cotton soil (vertisol) found in the area.

BABABUDANGIRI
This region is considered the home of Indian coffee, where Baba Budan first planted the seeds he smuggled into the country from Yemen.

Elevation: 1000–1,500m (3,300–4,900ft)
Harvest: October–February
Varieties: S795, Selection 9, Cauvery

CHIKMAGALUR
This is a larger region that encompasses Bababudangiri within it. It is centred around, and named for, the city of Chikmagalur. The region produces slightly more Robusta than it does Arabica.

Elevation: 700–1,200m (2,300–3,900ft)
Harvest: October–February
Varieties: S795, Selection 5B, Selection 9, Cauvery, Robustas

COORG

Many coffee farms in this region were started by the British in the 19th century, then sold to the locals when India gained independence in 1947. Nearly twice as much land here is used to grow Robusta as Arabica so, with its higher yield, nearly three times as much Robusta as Arabica is produced in the region.

Elevation: 750–1,100m (2,450–3,600ft)
Harvest: October–February
Varieties: S795, Selection 6, Selection 9, Robustas

MANJARABAD

This area is more focused on Arabica, although several of its estates have been recognized for the quality of their Robustas through competitions run by the Coffee Board of India.

Elevation: 900–1,100m (3,000–3,600ft)
Harvest: October–February
Varieties: S795, Selection 6, Selection 9, Cauvery

KERALA

This south-western state produces just under one-third of the total Indian coffee production. It is home to the Malabar coast, and therefore the Monsooned Malabar coffees, and organic coffee production has had greater success in this region than any other. The export of spices began here in the 1500s, which brought the first Portuguese to the region and established a trade route that would pave the way for the European colonization of India.

TRAVANCORE

This region grows mostly Robusta, although some Arabicas are produced at higher elevations.

Elevation: 400–1,600m (1,300–5,200ft)
Harvest: October–February
Varieties: S274, Robustas

WAYANAD

The low elevation in this part of India really only lends itself to Robusta production.

Elevation: 600–900m (2,000–3,000ft)
Harvest: October–February
Varieties: Robustas, S274

ANDHRA PRADESH

The Eastern Ghats mountain range runs along the east coast of India, providing the necessary elevation for coffee. Arabica production has grown in this region, and it is now the largest producer of Arabica in India outside of the Karnataka region.

Elevation: 900–1,100m (3,000–3,600ft)
Harvest: October–February
Varieties: S795, Selection 4, Selection 5, Cauvery

Above: Trees provide shade for coffee plants in Coorg, Karnataka state.

China

In many ways, the eyes of the coffee world are on China. As a consuming country, it has the potential to destabilize the global industry, but China is also starting to produce surprisingly large volumes of coffee. Growers are beginning to turn their attention to quality, pushing the boundaries of what is possible with the soil, climate and varieties found there.

Coffee was introduced to Yunnan province by a French missionary in 1892. The story is that he crossed the border from Vietnam, bringing with him coffee seeds, and then planted them near his church in the village of Zhukula. For almost a hundred years, very little happened in the way of coffee production – unsurprising in a region famous for the amount, and quality, of tea it grows. In 1988 coffee production was invigorated in Yunnan, as part of a joint venture with the United Nations Development Programme and the World Bank. Its success probably lies with the interest and support of Nestlé, which encouraged growth in the region.

Coffee production stayed relatively small until around 2009, when a significant jump occurred. This was probably due to a combination of lower tea prices and a brief spike in the global price of coffee. The coffee industry continues to grow in Yunnan, buoyed in particular by a growing market throughout China. Per capita consumption of coffee in China is still relatively low, but its enormous population means the Chinese market has the potential to have an enormous impact on the supply and demand of coffee production worldwide. In fact, we are now beginning to see the growth of coffee shops within China starting to impact the supply-and-demand relationship for coffee.

The rate of growth in coffee shops in China, particularly branded coffee shops, is unprecedented. There are now more branded coffee shops in China than in any country in the world, as it recently overtook the United States in that particular metric. Luckin Coffee, founded in 2017, already had 20,000 stores by 2024, and at that point Cotti Coffee had reached over 10,000 stores worldwide despite being founded only in 2022.

The best Chinese coffee I have tasted was only available in China. Quality-based auctions are increasingly popular, and prices being paid for locally grown coffee are very high. This makes China an unusual market, and certainly one to watch.

China is now exporting some excellent coffee, which is well worth seeking out. Many of the lots are still varieties chosen for disease resistance rather than taste, and there are still challenges to be overcome with the cultivation of more delicate varieties.

Traceability

The best lots from China can come from a single farm or from a group of producers. These are absolutely worth seeking out, despite the fact that China does not yet have the pedigree and expectation of quality that other producing countries have.

Taste Profile

The better coffees coming from China have a pleasant sweetness and fruitiness, although many still carry a little woodiness or earthiness, too. They are relatively low in acidity and often relatively full-bodied.

Growing Regions

Population: 1,412,000,000

Number of 60kg (132lb) bags in 2023: 1,700,000

While the growing regions in China cover a relatively small area of the country, they still cover vast amounts of land. Coffee has plenty of room to grow in China, both in terms of production and consumption.

Above: A coffee estate near Pu'er in south-west China's Yunnan Province.

Opposite: Workers in Pu'er harvest coffee by hand, using baskets to collect the cherries.

YUNNAN

The area where coffee was first grown in China remains the primary producing region for high-quality coffee in the country. The region is well known for Pu'er tea, and coffee production is now a key part of that same area. Coffee is concentrated around a few cities in the region: Pu'er, Baoshan, Dehong, Lincang, Wenshan and Xishuangbanna.

Elevation: 900–1,700m (3,000–5,600ft)
Harvest: October–March
Varieties: Catimor, with some Caturra and Bourbon

FUJIAN

This area is best known as a tea producer, home to Oolong and other teas. Coffee is a smaller industry in the region, and very little high-quality coffee is produced there.

Harvest: November–April
Varieties: Robusta

HAINAN

Coffee was brought to the island in 1908, probably from Malaysia. Robusta is grown here in the southernmost province of China, though there is no real reputation for quality in the region.

Harvest: November–April
Varieties: Robusta

Myanmar

Coffee was introduced to what was then Burma by the British in the late 1800s, but it was not a crop of much significance for quite some time. Interest in coffee was renewed in the 1980s, when the country was looking for an alternative crop to promote to combat poppy production.

However, the biggest change came after 2015, when speciality coffee-focused projects supported by Winrock International (which itself is almost entirely funded by the US government) along with the Coffee Quality Institute began work to improve quality and to help bring the coffees to market. There was a particular focus on improving post-harvest processing which, at the time, was the biggest barrier to better-tasting coffee in the region.

The timing could not have been better, as the speciality industry had become large and many roasters were seeking differentiation by sourcing coffee from previously unavailable countries. Consequently, there was a mini explosion in coffees

186 Coffee Origins

from Myanmar towards the end of the 2010s. The industry there continues to grow and develop, although it remains relatively small in the wider context of global coffee production.

One of the challenges the country faces regarding coffee production is the lack of infrastructure. More roads are needed to speed up the movement of coffee from farms to mills, and there will need to be more investment in the milling and post-harvest infrastructure too. Myanmar produces mostly Arabica, but some Robusta is also produced in the country.

Traceability

Traceability of speciality coffee is generally very good, going back to a single farm or to a producer group.

Taste Profile

The better lots of coffee from Myanmar have a pleasant sweetness and mouthfeel, though rarely a particularly notable acidity. Often post-harvest processing can be used to bring some additional complexity to the coffee.

Below: Coffee cherries laid out to dry in the sun in Bagan, Myanmar.

Growing Regions

Population: 54,130,000
Number of 60kg (132lb) bags produced in 2023: 125,000

SHAN STATE/MANDALAY

Most of the production in Myanmar comes from Shan State and neighbouring Mandalay, where the largest mill is based. There is some additional production in Kayin and Chin States.

Elevation: 600–1,500m (2,000–4,900ft)
Harvest: December–March
Varieties: Catuai, Caturra, Catimor, Bourbon, Typica, S795, SL34

Thailand

One of the most credible stories of coffee's introduction to Thailand relates how, in 1904, a Muslim pilgrim, returning home from Mecca, passed through Indonesia on his way back to Thailand and brought with him a Robusta plant, which he planted in the south of the country. Another story describes an Italian immigrant bringing Arabica to the north of the country in the 1950s.

Whether either or both these stories are true, it wouldn't be until the 1970s that any economic importance was placed on coffee as a crop.

Between 1972 and 1979 the Thai government ran a pilot project to try to encourage farmers in the northern region to grow coffee instead of poppies destined for opium production. Coffee was considered sufficiently high value to be worth switching from opium production and the slash-and-burn style of agriculture that accompanied it. While this project did mark the beginning of a coffee industry in Thailand, coffee did not become a major crop until later.

Production peaked in the very early 1990s, but global price fluctuations have deterred producers so there have been substantial swings in production over the last two decades. As it is mostly Arabica grown in the north of the country and Robusta in the south, a large part of the fluctuation comes from the northern highlands where the price would have a bigger impact.

Accurate tracking of production in Thailand is difficult, as coffee is often smuggled across the borders from Laos and Myanmar.

Today Thailand is steadily building a reputation as an underdog among producers of great coffees. While most coffee produced in the country isn't particularly high quality, there are some farms and cooperatives working hard to produce an excellent product. The increasing domestic consumption of quality coffee is also helping growth in the industry. There has been a recent shift in production that has increased the percentage of Arabica grown in Thailand, with it now making up around 41 per cent, up from around 35 per cent.

Traceability

Coffees very, very rarely come from single estates. More common are producer groups or cooperatives among the more quality-focused producers.

Growing Regions

Population: 71,700,000
Number of 60kg (132lb) bags in 2023: 750,000

NORTHERN REGION

The northern mountainous area of Thailand is made up of coffee-growing provinces such as Chiang Mai, Chiang Rai, Lampang, Nan, Mae Hong Son and Tak. All the speciality coffee from Thailand comes from this area.

Harvest: November–March
Elevation: 1,000–1,600m (3,300–5,200ft)
Varieties: Caturra, Catimor, Catuai, Bourbon, Typica, Pacamara and Thai Gesha

SOUTHERN REGION

The south of the country grows Robusta only, and coffee is produced in the provinces of Surat Thani, Chumphon, Nakhon Si Thammarat, Phang Nga, Krabi and Ranong.

Harvest: December–January
Elevation: 800–1,200m (2,600–3,900ft)
Varieties: Robusta

Taste Profile

Better coffee from Thailand is sweet, quite clean, but relatively low in acidity. Some spice and chocolate often accompany a relatively full mouthfeel.

Above: Thailand's increasing domestic consumption of coffee is helping to drive up production in the country.

Opposite: Coffee beans spread out to dry in the sun in northern Thailand, where mostly Arabica is grown. The south of the country only produces Robusta.

Vietnam

Vietnam could be considered an unusual inclusion in a book that focuses on high-quality speciality coffee, as it produces predominantly Robusta. However, Vietnam is different because of the impact it has had on every coffee-producing country in the world, and therefore merits inclusion to give some understanding.

Coffee was brought to Vietnam by the French in 1857 and was initially cultivated under the plantation model. However, this did not gain any momentum as a commercial venture until around 1910. Cultivation in the area around the city of Buôn Ma Thuột, in the Central Highlands, was interrupted by the Vietnam War (1955–75). After the war the coffee industry became increasingly collectivized, reducing yields and production. At this point around 20,000 hectares (50,000 acres) of land produced around 5,000–7,000 tonnes (5,500–7,700 tons) of coffee. Over the next 25 years the amount of land under coffee would increase by a factor of 25 and the country's overall production by a factor of 100.

Much of the industry's growth was down to the Doi Moi reforms of 1986, which permitted privately owned enterprises in industries that produced commoditized crops. In the 1990s a huge number of new companies were formed in Vietnam, many focusing on the large-scale production of coffee. At this time, specifically in between 1994 and 1998, prices for coffee were relatively high, which provided strong incentives to increase coffee production. Between 1996 and 2000 Vietnam's coffee production doubled, and this would come to have a devastating effect on the global price of coffee.

Vietnam's massive increase in production, which made it the second-largest producer of coffee in the world, resulted in a state of global oversupply and this caused a massive price crash. Even though Vietnam was producing Robusta rather than Arabica, it still affected the price of Arabica because many of the largest purchasers needed a commodity product

Taste Profile

Very little high-quality coffee is available in Vietnam, and most of it tastes somewhat flat, lacking in sweetness or complexity.

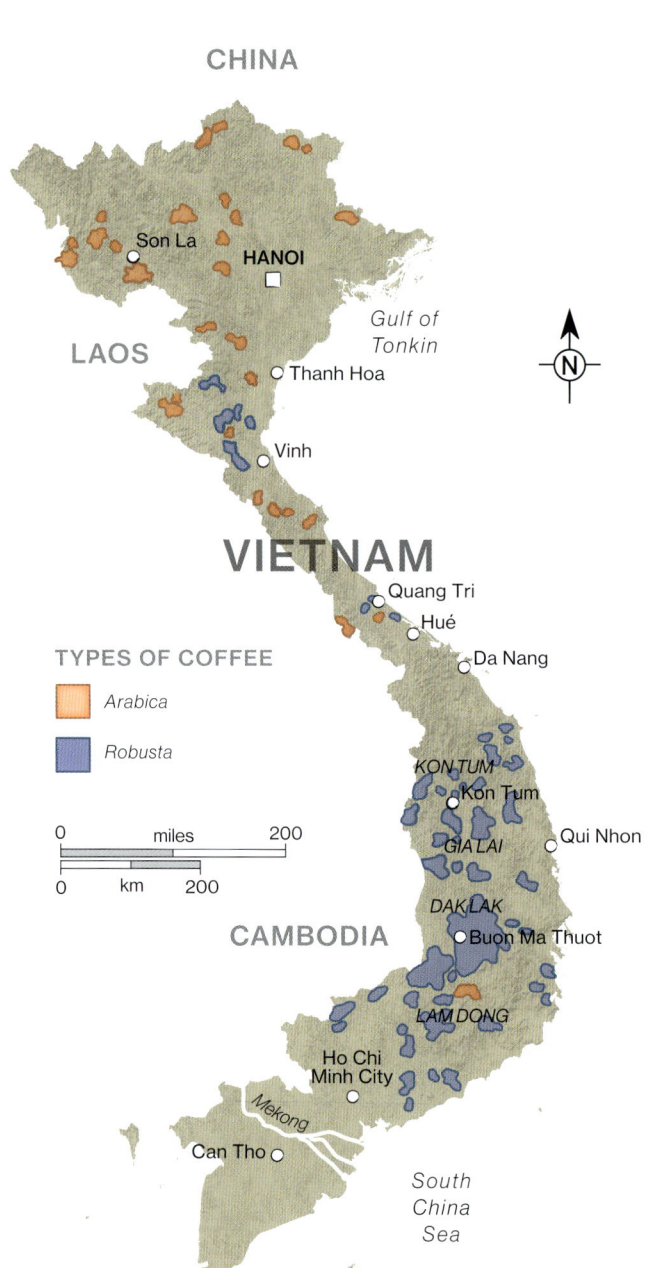

rather than a quality one. Thus, the oversupply of low-quality coffee worked in their favour.

From the high point of 900,000 tonnes (990,000 tons) of coffee in 2000, production declined sharply. However, as coffee prices recovered, so did Vietnam's production. The 2023 crop was around 1.7 million tonnes (1.9 million tons), and the country's production continues to have a large effect on the global industry. In recent years there has been a shift towards more Arabica, although the lack of elevation presents a challenge to achieving a high-quality product. Arabica makes up around 5 per cent of the total production, and while this might seem small it is still enough to fill 1 million 60kg (132lb) bags.

Traceability

There are several large estates in Vietnam, often controlled by multinational companies, so it is possible to see good levels of traceability. However, finding high-quality lots will prove extremely challenging.

Above: Robusta bushes in full bloom in the south of Vietnam. Here a lack of elevation makes the production of Arabica more difficult.

Growing Regions

Population: 98,190,000
Number of 60kg (132lb) bags in 2023: 29,100,000

Because there has been little demand for traceable coffee, there aren't strongly defined growing regions whose names are used by roasters.

CENTRAL HIGHLANDS

This region, a series of highland plateaus, contains the provinces of Đắk Lắk, Lâm Đồng, Gia Lai and Kon Tum and is primarily a producer of Robusta. The coffee industry is centred around Buôn Ma Thuột, the capital of the province. Đắk Lắk and Lâm Đồng are the primary producers, growing about 70 per cent of the country's Robusta crop between them. Arabica has been grown in the Central Highlands for about one hundred years, in the area around the city of Đà Lạt, in the Lâm Đồng province, but this makes up a very small part of the national production.

Elevation: 1,000–1,400m (3,300-4,600ft)
Harvest: November–March
Varieties: Robusta varieties, Catimor and some Arabica (Bourbon and Typica)

SOUTH VIETNAM

There is some production north-east of Ho Chi Minh City, in the province of Đông Nai. This is primarily Robusta and has attracted interest from large corporations such as Nestlé which is looking to improve its supply chain.

Elevation: 200–800m (660–2,600ft)
Harvest: November–March
Varieties: Robusta

NORTH VIETNAM

Arabica grows in the provinces of Sơn La, Thanh Hóa and Quảng Trị in the north of the country, near the city of Hanoi. There is sufficient elevation for Arabica to grow well, but it is rare to see high-quality coffees produced here. Despite Arabica making up only 3–5 per cent of Vietnam's total production, this is now enough to make it the fifteenth-largest producer of Arabica in the world.

Elevation: 800–1,600m (2,600–5,200ft)
Harvest: November–March
Varieties: Bourbon, Sparrow (or Se), Catimor, Robusta

In the southern province of Binh Dong, a worker moves one bag among hundreds in a warehouse owned by communist exporters. Most of the beans grown in South Vietnam are of the Robusta variety.

The Philippines

The history of coffee in the Philippines is another tale of the product going from being a bedrock of the economy to almost disappearing completely. The most common version of the story starts in 1740, when coffee was first planted by a Spanish monk in Lipa, in the Province of Batangas. It flourished under Spanish colonial rule and spread around the Philippines.

In 1828, as part of an effort to foster cultivation, the Spanish offered a prize to anyone who would plant and ripen 60,000sq. ft of coffee (equivalent to 6,000 coffee trees). One farmer transformed his property in Jala Jala, in the Province of Rizal, into a fertile plantation and won the prize of a thousand pesos. His success encouraged others to follow suit and increased the cultivation of coffee.

By the 1860s the Philippines were doing a healthy trade in coffee exports, with a large market being the United States through the gateway of San Francisco. The completion of the Suez Canal in 1869 opened up Europe as a potential market, too. By the 1880s the Philippines was the fourth largest coffee producer in the world, but in 1889 it would finally succumb to the leaf rust that had plagued so many other countries. A combination of leaf rust and insects took a particularly heavy toll in Batangas – still the dominant producing area – and two years later, in 1891, production was less than 20 per cent of what it had been. Some seedlings were transplanted north to Cavite, where they appeared to flourish. However, most farmers moved away from coffee to other crops and for at least 50 years the industry was relatively dormant.

In the 1950s the government attempted to resurrect the coffee industry. With assistance from the United States, it brought in disease-resistant varieties and Robusta as part of a five-year strategic plan. The strategy was reasonably successful and production increased, but it wouldn't be until 1962 or 1963 that the level was considered self-sufficient and coffee was no longer imported for local consumption. Part of the local demand came from the production of instant coffee in factories around the Philippines.

Coffee production has, in many ways, mirrored world prices, and there has been an ebb and flow in production according to whether there has been sufficient demand. The frost in Brazil in 1975 briefly gave the Philippines the chance to be an exporting country again.

Production is currently up once more, in comparison with recent years. Programmes remain in place to encourage production, although domestic consumption remains strong enough to mean that

Left: A farmer harvesting coffee on a farm in Mindanao in the south of the Philippines. Around 70 per cent of the country's coffee trees grow in this area.

very little coffee is exported from the Philippines. As so little coffee is exported, and so much of what is produced is Robusta, it is unlikely that any excellent coffees will be available in the immediate future.

However, the country does grow two other species of coffee, not commonly found elsewhere: *Coffea liberica* and *Coffea excelsa*. While neither is anything to get excited about from a taste perspective, they are undeniably interesting to try, should the opportunity present itself.

Traceability

Coffee comes from a mixture of cooperatives, estates and smallholder producers. The better coffees from the Philippines are usually more traceable, though very rare.

Taste Profile

Great coffee from the Philippines is a rarity, but better lots are quite full-bodied, with low acidity and with light florals or fruity qualities.

Opposite: Throughout the coffee-producing areas of the Philippines, farmers drying coffee by the side of the road are a common sight.

Growing Regions

Population: 115,600,000
Number of 60kg (132lb) bags in 2023: 450,000

The Philippines is made up of 7,641 islands (though only some 2,000 are inhabited). As such, growing regions are often collections of islands or groups of territories, rather than distinct topographical areas such as mountain ranges.

CORDILLERA ADMINISTRATIVE REGION

A mountainous region in northern Luzon which includes the Mountain, Benguet, Kalinga, Ifugao and Abra provinces, the Cordillera Administrative Region (CAR) is the only landlocked region in the country. This is the highest growing area in the Philippines, although Robusta is grown at lower elevations around the area of northern Luzon.

Elevation: 1,000–1,800m (3,300–5,900ft)
Harvest: October–March
Varieties: Red Bourbon, Yellow Bourbon, Typica, Mondo Novo, Caturra

CALABARZON

This administrative region is mostly lowlands, growing coffee species other than Arabica, around Manilla and to the south and east. The Liberica grown here is often called Batangas coffee, or Kapeng barako, and when consumed locally it is usually brewed and filtered with cloth and sweetened with muscovado sugar.

Elevation: 300–500m (1,000–1,60oft)
Harvest: October–March
Varieties: Robusta, Excelsa, Liberica

MIMAROPA

This region is a collection of islands in the south-west which make up the four provinces of Mindoro, Marinduque, Romblon and Palawan, its name made up of the first two letters of each. While the mountainous areas reach high elevations, coffee is mostly grown lower down.

Elevation: 300–900m (1,000–3,000ft)
Harvest: October–March
Varieties: Robusta, Excelsa

VISAYAS

This group of islands lies in the centre of the Philippines and includes Bohol, famous for its Chocolate Hills, which get their name from the cocoa brown colour they turn in the dry season. Negros Island's volcanic soil is well suited to coffee cultivation but lacks the elevation for better-tasting coffee.

Elevation: 500–1000m (1,600–3,300ft)
Harvest: October–March
Varieties: Catimor, Robusta

MINDANAO

The southernmost coffee-growing region in the Philippines is its most productive. Nearly 70 per cent of coffee trees in the Philippines are planted in this region.

Elevation: 700–1,200m (2,300–3,900ft)
Harvest: October–March
Varieties: Mysore, Typica, SV-2006, Catimor, Robusta, Excelsa

Indonesia

The first attempt to grow coffee on the Indonesian archipelago was a failure. In 1696 the governor of Jakarta (then Batavia) was sent a present of a few coffee seedlings by the Dutch governor of Malabar in India. These plants were destroyed during a flood in Jakarta, so a second shipment was sent in 1699. These plants flourished.

Exports of coffee began in 1711 and were controlled by the Dutch East India Company, usually referred to by its Dutch initials VOC (Vereenigde Oostindische Compagniey). Coffee arriving in Amsterdam sold for high prices, 1kg (2lb) costing nearly one per cent of the average annual income. The price slowly came down during the 18th century, but coffee was undeniably very profitable for the VOC. However, as Java was under colonial rule at the time, it was not at all profitable for the farmers who grew it. In 1860 a Dutch colonial official writing under the pen name Multatuli wrote a novel entitled *Max Havelaar; Or, The Coffee Auctions of the Dutch Trading Company*, which described the abuses of the colonial system. This book had a lasting impact on Dutch society, changing public opinion about the way coffee was traded and the colonial system in general. The name Max Havelaar is now used for an ethical certification within the industry.

Initially, Indonesia produced only Arabica, but coffee leaf rust wiped out much of the crop in 1876. There was some attempt to plant the Liberica species instead, but that also suffered at the hands of leaf rust, so production switched to the disease-resistant Robusta. Today Robusta still makes up a significant portion of the crop.

As leaf rust wiped out the crops, it led the Dutch to abandon the estates they had been farming, which were taken in small parcels by individual farmers. This is one of the reasons that there are so many smallholder coffee farmers in Indonesia today.

Giling Basah

One of the unique aspects of coffee production in Indonesia, and the source of Indonesian coffee's deeply divisive taste, is the traditional post-harvest process of *giling basah*. This hybrid process combines elements of the washed and natural processes and has a dramatic effect on the cup quality. It significantly reduces the acidity of the coffee and seems to increase

its body too, creating a softer, rounder, heavier-bodied cup of coffee. However, it also introduces a gamut of additional flavours, sometimes vegetal or herbal, sometimes woody or musty, sometimes earthy. This is not to say that all coffee processed this way is uniform in quality and has gone through some sort of flavour standardization.

There are huge variations in the quality of these coffees. The flavour of semi-washed coffees is particularly divisive within the coffee industry. If a coffee from Africa or Central America displayed the same flavours, regardless of how well the process was done, it would be considered defective and rejected immediately by any potential buyers. However, there are many people who find the intensity and heavy-bodied cups of coffee brewed from Indonesian semi-washed lots delicious, and so the industry continues to buy them.

Taste Profile

Semi-washed coffees tend to be very heavy-bodied, earthy, woody and spicy with very little acidity.

In recent years, speciality buyers have encouraged producers throughout Indonesia to experiment more with the washed process to allow some appreciation of the taste of the variety and the land rather than the dominant flavours of the process. We shall see whether demand for these coffees is strong enough to encourage widespread production of cleaner coffees, or whether the industry will see continued demand for semi-washed lots and simply continue to meet it.

Below: Workers sort organic Arabica beans for export to the US and Europe at a coffee warehouse in the highlands of Takengon, Aceh Province.

Kopi Luwak

In Indonesia, Kopi Luwak refers to coffees that are produced by collecting the droppings of civet cats that have eaten coffee cherries. This semi-digested coffee is separated from the faecal matter and then processed and dried. In the last decade it has come to be seen as an amusing novelty, with circumspect claims of excellent flavours, and it sells for spectacularly high prices. This has caused two main problems. First, the forgery of this coffee is quite commonplace. Several times more is sold than produced, and often low-grade Robusta is being passed off at high prices. Second, it has encouraged unscrupulous operators on the islands to trap and cage civet cats, force-feed them with coffee cherries and keep them in terrible conditions.

I find Kopi Luwak abhorrent on just about every level. If you are interested in delicious coffee, then it is a terrible waste of money. One-quarter of the money you might spend on a bag could instead buy you a stunning coffee from one of the very best producers in the world. I can only regard the practice as abusive and unethical, and I believe people should avoid all animal-processed coffees and not reward this despicable behaviour with their money.

Traceability

While it is possible to find coffees from individual farms on the islands, these are relatively rare. However, those that have been kept traceable and have been fully washed (rather than semi-washed) are worth trying. Most coffee is produced by smallholders with just 1–2 hectares (2¼–4½ acres) of land so usually a coffee is only traceable down to a specific washing station, or only a region. There is very wide variation in the quality of these regional coffees, and they can be something of a gamble.

Left: Workers rake Arabica beans spread out to dry in the sun at a coffee mill in Pangalengan, West Java.

Growing Regions

Population: 275,500,000

Number of 60kg (132lb) bags in 2022: 8,000,000

From its origins in Java, coffee slowly spread around the other islands in the region, first to Sulawesi in 1750. It did not reach Northern Sumatra until 1888, first being grown around Lake Toba, and eventually appeared in the Tawar region in Gayo in 1924.

SUMATRA

The island of Sumatra has three main growing regions: the province of Aceh in the north, the Lake Toba region a little to the south and, of more recent standing, the south of the island around Mangkuraja. It may be possible to trace coffees to smaller areas within these regions: Takengon or Bener Meriah in the Aceh region; and Lintong, Sidikalang, Dolok Sanggul or Seribu Dolok around Lake Toba. Traceability down to this level is relatively recent.

In the past it was common to see coffee sold under the name of 'Sumatra Mandheling'. There is no place called Mandheling; the name refers to an ethnic group from the island. Often Mandheling coffees were given a grade, either 1 or 2. The grading is apparently based on the cup quality rather than the green coffee, which is more usual, but I would be hesitant to recommend all Grade 1's because the awarding can occasionally seem somewhat random. It is unusual to separate different varieties into different lots, so most Sumatran coffee will probably be a mixture of unknown varieties. Coffees from Sumatra are shipped out of the port of Medan, but the hot, humid climate can have a negative effect on the coffee if it is left on the dockside too long before being shipped.

Elevation: Aceh 1,100–1,300m (3,600–4,300ft); Lake Toba 1,100–1,600m (3,600–5,200ft); Mangkuraja 1,100–1,300m (3,600–4,300ft)
Harvest: October–June
Varieties: Typica (including Bergandal, Sidikalang and Djember), TimTim, Ateng, Onan Ganjang

JAVA

It is more common to find large coffee estates here than anywhere else in Indonesia, due to the colonial history and practices of the Dutch. The four largest farms, previously government estates, cover over 4,000 hectares (8,800 acres) between them. For a long time the island enjoyed a stellar reputation for its coffee, although I am sure it was not long before other coffees came to substitute the real thing in the 'Mocha–Java' blend of a great many roasters. Javan coffees commanded huge premiums for a long time, although prices fell towards the end of the 20th century.

Much of the coffee is planted on the east side of Java, around the Ijen volcano, but there are producers on the west side of the island, too.

Elevation: 900–1,800m (3,000–5,900ft)
Harvest: July–September
Varieties: Typicas, Ateng, Timor Hybrid, Catimor

Old Brown Java

Some estates in Java choose to age their coffee before export, for anything up to five years. The raw coffee beans turn from the blue-green commonly associated with semi-washed coffee, through to a muddy shade of brown. Once roasted, there is no acidity left in the coffee whatsoever, and there is an intense pungency and woodiness that some enjoy. However, if you like your coffee sweet, clean and lively, you may well hate it.

Names

Variety names in Sumatra can be a little tricky. Most of the Arabica seed stock initially brought to the island would have been derived from the strain of Typica that was taken from Yemen. In Sumatra this is often called Djember Typica, but it should be noted that Djember also refers to a completely different variety (consider of lesser quality) found in Sulawesi.

It is common to see varieties that have, at some point, been crossbred with Robusta. The best-known hybrid is called the Hybrido de Timor, a parent of the more common Catimor variety. In Sumatra it is often called TimTim.

SULAWESI

Most of the coffee from Sulawesi is produced by smallholders, although there are seven large estates which make up about 5 per cent of the total production. Most of the Arabica on the island is grown high up around Tana Toraja. To the south is the city of Kalosi, which became a kind of brand name for coffees from the region. There are two other lesser-known coffee-growing regions: Mamasa to the west, and Gowa, south of Kalosi.

Some of the most interesting coffees from the island are fully washed and can be exceptionally enjoyable. I would recommend seeking them out if you get the opportunity. The semi-washed process is still common, though, and the island also produces a good amount of Robusta. Coffee production can be somewhat disorganized throughout the region, as many smallholders grow coffee for supplemental income, concentrating their efforts on other crops.

Elevation: Tana Toraja 1,100–1,800m (3,600–5,900ft); Mamasa 1300–1700m (4,300–5,600ft); Gowa average of 850m (2,800ft)
Harvest: May–November
Varieties: S795, Typicas, Ateng, Jember

FLORES

Flores is a small island about 320km (200 miles) to the east of Bali, and among the Indonesian islands it was a latecomer to both growing coffee and developing a strong reputation for it. In the past it was not uncommon for a large portion of the coffee from Flores to be sold internally or blended into other coffees rather than being exported as 'Flores coffee'. The island has a mixture of active and dormant volcanoes, which have had a positive effect on the soils. One of the key growing regions is Bajawa. There is now a good amount of washed coffee coming from the island.

Elevation: 1,200–1,700m (3,900–5,600ft)
Harvest: May–July
Varieties: Kartika, Yellow Caturra, Timor Hybrid

BALI

Coffee came to Bali fairly late, and it was initially grown on the highland plateau of Kintamani. Coffee production in Bali suffered a significant setback in 1963 when the Mount Agung volcano erupted, killing an estimated two thousand people and causing widespread devastation to the east of the island. By the late 1970s and early 1980s the government was doing more to promote coffee production, in part by handing out Arabica seedlings. One could argue that this had limited success, however, as today around 80 per cent of the island's production is Robusta.

While tourism provides the largest income for the island, agriculture is its biggest employer. In the past Japan bought a substantial portion, if not all, of the coffee crop.

Elevation: 1,250–1,700m (4,100–5,600ft)
Harvest: May–October
Varieties: Typica and Typica derivatives, Robusta

Above: Coffee grows on the hills around Lake Toba in the south of Sumatra.

Papua New Guinea

Many people would associate Papua New Guinea's coffees with those from Indonesia, but it would be unfair to do so. Papua New Guinea rightly stands apart, and the eastern half of New Guinea shares relatively little with neighbouring Papua when it comes to coffee.

The history of coffee production on the island is not long. While coffee was planted relatively early, in the 1890s, it was not treated as a commercial product at first. In 1926, however, 18 estates were established using seeds from Jamaica's Blue Mountain, and by 1928 coffee production had begun in earnest. The industry began a more structured growth in the 1950s, with the creation of infrastructure to help facilitate the movement of coffee around the island.

Further growth followed in the 1970s, perhaps spurred on by Brazil's drop-back in production. The government sponsored a series of programmes to encourage small farms to be run by cooperatives. At that time the industry was more focused on managed estates, but since the 1980s the industry has begun to change and decentralize. This is probably due to the drop in coffee prices, which has left many estates in financial trouble. Smallholders aren't at such risk from market forces and so have been able to continue to produce coffee.

Today 95 per cent of producers are smallholders, often subsistence farmers. They produce around 90 per cent of the country's coffee, which is almost entirely Arabica. This means a very large proportion of the population is involved in the production of coffee, especially in the highland regions. This has certainly

Opposite: Coffee thrives in the Eastern Highlands, here near Goroka. The Eastern Highlands make up part of the mountain chain running through the middle of the country.

Above: Although coffee production in Papua New Guinea only took hold in the 20th century, it is now an established crop. Arabica forms the majority of exports and is mostly grown in highland regions.

presented challenges when it comes to producing large quantities of high-quality coffee, as many producers lack access to proper post-harvest facilities, and a lack of traceability in the product prevents clear rewards for higher-quality coffee.

Grading

Exports are graded by quality, in descending order: AA, A, X, PSC and Y. The first three are awarded to estate coffees, while the last two are grades for smallholder coffees, PSC standing for Premium Smallholder Coffee.

Traceability

Several large estates still operate very successfully, so it is possible to find coffees from a single estate. There is not a long history of traceability, and in the past some farms were acquiring coffee from other producers to pass off as their own. The idea of coffee being sold by region is also relatively new. However, the elevation and soils in the country offer great potential for quality, so there has been renewed interest from the speciality market in the last few years. Look out for coffees traceable to a specific estate or a group of producers.

Taste Profile

Great coffees from Papua New Guinea are appreciated for their buttery quality, great sweetness and wonderful complexity.

Growing Regions

Population: 11,781,559

Number of 60kg (132lb) bags in 2023: 900,000

Most of Papua New Guinea's coffee is produced in the Highland regions, and the area shows great potential for producing some amazing coffees in the future. While some coffee is grown outside of these key regions, it is only a very small amount.

EASTERN HIGHLANDS

There is a single mountain chain that runs through the country, and the Eastern Highlands form part of it.

Elevation: 400–1,900m (1,300–6,200ft)
Harvest: April–September
Varieties: Bourbon, Typica, Arusha

WESTERN HIGHLANDS

This is the other key area of coffee production. Most of the coffee in this region grows around the regional capital of Mount Hagen, named for an old, inactive volcano. Coffee produced in this area is often milled in Goroka, so traceability of some coffees can be difficult. The combination of elevation and extremely fertile soil makes the potential for quality in this region very exciting indeed.

Elevation: 1,000–2,200m (3,300–7,200ft)
Harvest: April–September
Varieties: Bourbon, Typica, Arusha

SIMBU PROVINCE

Simbu (officially spelled as Chimbu) is the third-largest producing region, but its output is substantially lower than either of the Highlands provinces. The name is derived from the local dialect and the word *sipuu*, meaning 'thank you'. Most of the coffee here comes from the coffee gardens around the homes of smallholders. Nearly 90 per cent of the population is engaged in coffee production to some degree, and for many this is their only cash crop.

Elevation: 1,300–1,900m (4,300–6,200ft)
Harvest: April–September
Varieties: Bourbon, Typica, Arusha

Malaysia

Malaysia is an interesting coffee-producing country because it mostly produces Liberica coffee, alongside a little Robusta and a very small amount of Arabica. Arabica was introduced in 1779, but wasn't well suited to the elevation and conditions, and so Liberica was brought to the country in 1875 and continues to flourish there. Robusta was introduced a little later, after concerns that both Arabica and Liberica were susceptible to leaf rust.

Coffee consumption in Malaysia is growing much faster than current production. While Malaysia does export its coffee, it is still a net importer of coffee to cover domestic requirements. Production occurs in the states of Johor, Kedah, Sabah and Sarawak. With more interest in alternative coffee species, growing Liberica may continue to draw more attention to coffee from Malaysia, although to date there hasn't been a huge speciality focus there.

GROWING STATISTICS

Population: Population: 34,564,000
Number of 60kg (132lb) bags produced in 2023: 70,000
Elevation: 0–1,000m (0–3,300ft)
Harvest: April–July
Varieties: Liberica, Robusta, Arabica

Opposite, top: Much of Malaysia's coffee production is Liberica, as Arabica failed to thrive there.

Opposite, bottom: Workers collect up the washed beans after they have dried at a coffee factory in Emera County, Timor-Leste.

Timor-Leste

Timor-Leste may not be a significant producer of coffee, but coffee from this country has been hugely influential. The naturally occurring hybrid of Arabica and Robusta that was found growing there, called the Timor Hybrid, has been used extensively in plant breeding programmes around the world.

Coffee was brought to the country by the occupying Portuguese in the 1820s. They forced each household to grow 600 trees, and coffee became a part of the economy – albeit one designed for exploitation. Freedom from the Portuguese in 1975 was followed by occupation by Indonesia, which squeezed local coffee production by paying farmers low prices for their crop.

In the last 20 years, since Timor-Leste gained independence, there has been a growth in the coffee industry. Coffee is now the largest non-oil export and contributes to the livelihoods of around 35 per cent of the population. There has been investment to improve yields and move the production towards speciality coffee standards, with significant growth in both volume and value from better coffee production. While there is some Robusta produced in the country, the majority of the production is Arabica. Most of the coffee is wet-processed, rather than being wet-hulled as you would find in neighbouring Indonesia.

GROWING STATISTICS

Population: 1,341,000
Number of 60kg (132lb) bags produced in 2023: 200,000
Elevation: 750–1,900m (2,450–6,200ft)
Harvest: May–September
Varieties: Catimor, Typica, Timor Hybrid

Australia

Most people would be surprised to learn that coffee growing in Australia goes back around two hundred years. Initially, coffee produced there gained a good reputation for its quality, but it could not compete on price against the coffee-producing countries where colonial powers were exploiting local labour to keep costs low. In the 1980s interest flared up again, with mechanical harvesting making coffee financially viable in Australia.

Currently, production is small but growing – expected to increase by around 60 per cent between 2024 and 2029. Australia has been exporting coffee for some time now, although any Australian coffee you see in a supermarket is likely to have been grown on one of two farms in the country (Mountain Top or Skybury).

Production is centred on two regions: the Atherton Tablelands in North Queensland and in northern New South Wales. Despite the relatively low elevation of the farms here, the better coffees from Australia can have some nice acidity, sweetness and complexity. They often have the slightly higher body and mouthfeel associated with lower altitudes.

GROWING STATISTICS

Population: 27,100,000

Number of 60kg (132lb) bags in 2024: 5,400

Elevation: 200–400m (660–1,300ft)
Harvest: July–October
Varieties: Catuai, Mundo Novo, K7, SL6 and some African varieties including one thought to be a Typica variety, but genetic testing has shown it to be related to an Ethiopian landrace population called Abyssinia

Japan

Coffee grows mainly in the very south-west of Japan, in the Nagasaki, Miyazaki and Kagoshima Prefectures as well as on the Okinawa Islands. It was more of a hobby for many years, although that has changed in recent decades. In Okinawa Prefecture most of the coffee is grown in the Yanbaru region, and there are around 30 coffee farms on Okinawa Island itself.

It is hard to get good estimates of total production, as many farms produce small amounts – sometimes only 100kg (220lb) of raw coffee – and they will sell much of it directly to consumers who are tourists and visitors to those farms. Farms combine the experience of picking coffee with processing, roasting and drinking the coffee. Coffee consumption is very high in Japan, as the country is the third largest importer of coffee worldwide, and so there is inevitably interest in coffee grown within the country. As much of the production in Japan is certified organic, there is some accurate data there, but the total production is very much an estimate. Japan doesn't have the greatest geography for growing coffee, but what is grown there is often processed carefully and can be surprisingly interesting and complex considering the elevation at which it is grown.

GROWING STATISTICS

Population: 125,100,000

Number of 60kg (132lb) bags produced in 2023: 50–100

Elevation: 150–200m (500–700ft)
Harvest: October–May
Varieties: Red Bourbon, Yellow Bourbon, Yellow Mundo Novo, Typica

Taiwan

One of the earliest records of coffee-growing in Taiwan dates back to 1884, when a British merchant imported a hundred Arabica trees to the island from Manila. These were planted in Sanxia, to the south-west of Taipei. Formal experiments with coffee production began in 1917, and it was decided that Arabica was the species best suited for agricultural production in the country.

Coffee production in Taiwan gradually expanded up until 1942, by which point around 1,000 hectares (2,500 acres) of land were producing coffee. At the time, Taiwan was under Japanese colonial rule and most of the crop went to the Japanese market. After the Japanese withdrawal at the end of World War II, coffee was somewhat abandoned. There was a brief resurgence of interest in 1954, driven by high market prices, but that did not last. It wasn't until after the earthquake of 1999 that a renewed interest in coffee production took hold. It would take until 2016 for production to get back to previous levels, with coffee being grown on 1,000 hectares (2,500 acres) of land, and a couple of years later, the island was producing more than 1,000 tonnes (1,100 tons) of raw coffee a year.

Coffee is grown across most of Taiwan, but most of the production is found in Pingtung County, Nantou County, Taitung County and Chiayi County. These four counties account for approximately two-thirds of Taiwan's total production. Within these counties there are distinct coffee-growing regions. Owing to its higher altitudes, the region of Alishan in Chiayi County has a reputation for higher-quality coffees.

Coffee producers in Taiwan are a mixture of part-time and full-time farmers. Around 20 per cent of the production comes from dedicated coffee farmers, for whom coffee production is the main focus and livelihood. The rest of the production comes from private citizens who might be farming up to a hectare of land, and as such may produce up to 1,000kg (2,200lb) of coffee a year. Many of them make this profitable by roasting and even brewing the coffee they grow. Large-scale farms or cooperatives are not commonly found growing coffee on the island.

Most of the production is consumed in Taiwan, as coffee consumption has grown steadily over the past few decades. There is a thriving speciality coffee culture there too. Taiwanese coffee is relatively rarely seen outside the island, but if a roaster you trust and enjoy is offering a lot then it is worth trying. It is an origin I expect to see a little more frequently in the coming years.

Left: Coffee fruits ripening in Alishan Township in Chiayi County.

GROWING STATISTICS

Population: 23,894,000

Number of 60kg (132lb) bags produced in 2023: 17,000

Elevation: 200–1,400m (660–4,600ft)

Harvest: November–May

Varieties: SL-34, Typica, Catimor, Bourbon, Caturra, Catuai, Gesha

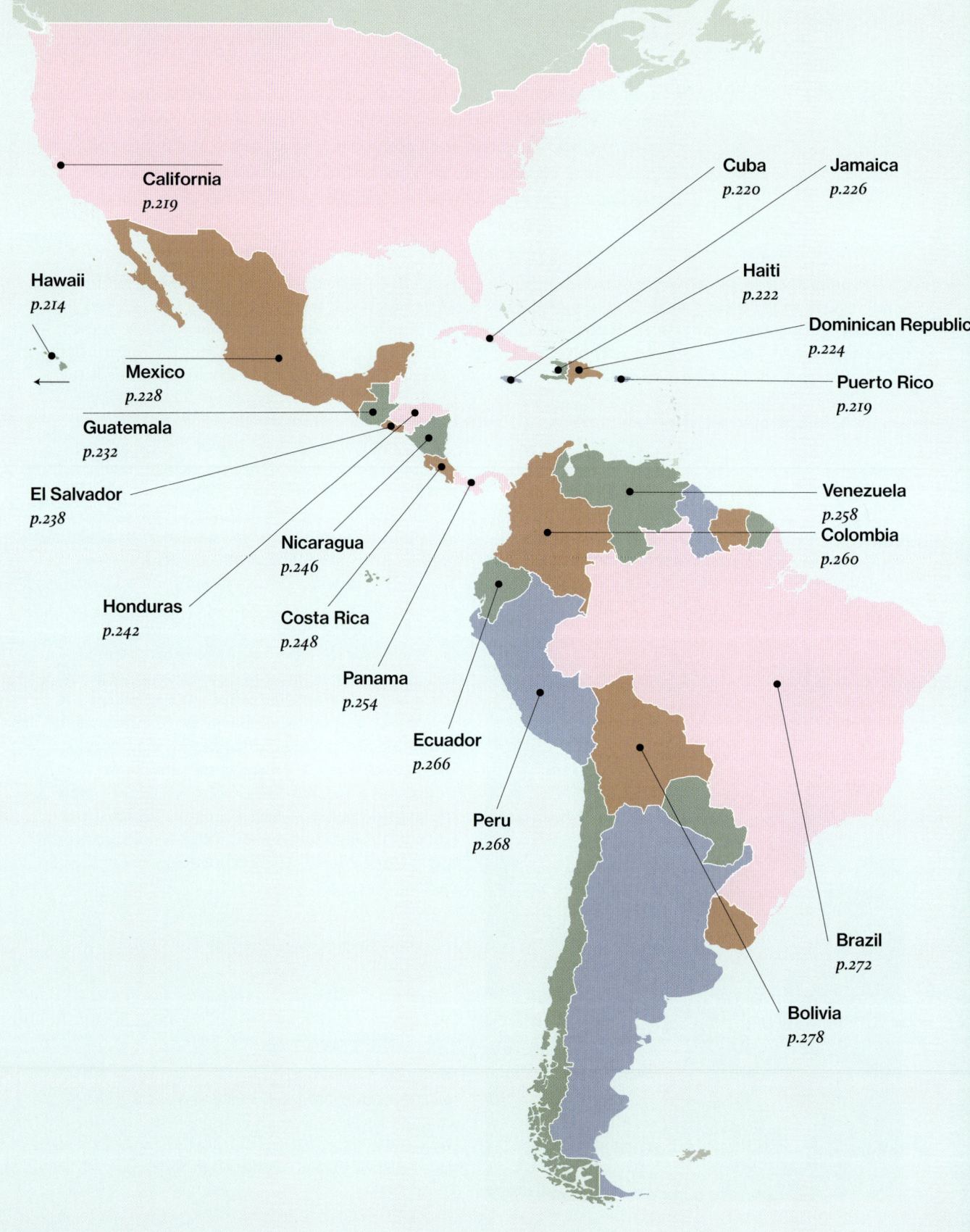

Americas

The Americas supply the majority of the world's coffee beans, but the range and quality of bean exports varies hugely. Though Brazilian harvests provide one-third of the international coffee market, there is increasing interest in unusual varieties from smaller growers, such as the Gesha variety produced in Panama. Ecotourism and awareness of sustainable and cooperative farming methods are changing the way coffee farms right across the Americas harvest and grow their crops.

United States: Hawaii

Hawaii is the only major coffee-producing region in the Global North (Californian coffee production is only very recent and very small – see page 219). This changes the economics, as well as the marketing, of the coffee. The producers here have been successful at engaging consumers directly – often entwining the coffee with a visit to the islands – but many coffee professionals feel that the quality of the coffee may not merit its price.

Coffee was first brought to Hawaii in 1817, although these initial plantings were unsuccessful. In 1825 the governor of the island of Oahu, Chief Boki, was *en voyage* from Europe and stopped off in Brazil where he picked up some coffee plants. These plants thrived in his native soils, and coffee production was soon widespread across the Hawaiian Islands.

The Bourbon variety was probably brought to the Big Island in 1828, and the first commercial plantation in Kauai began operation in 1836. However, plantations in the Hanalei Valley area of Kauai were destroyed by the coffee blight insect in 1858. The only region that continued to produce coffee from these initial plantings is the Kona region located on the Big Island (Hawaii).

In the late 1800s the industry attracted immigrants from China and then Japan, who came to work on the plantations. In the 1920s many Filipinos arrived to work on the coffee farms during harvest time and the sugar cane plantations in the spring.

However, coffee did not become hugely important to the island economy until the 1980s, when sugar production ceased to be sufficiently profitable. The event triggered a renewed interest in coffee right across the state.

Kona

The best-known growing region in Hawaii, and one of the best known in the world, is the Kona region on the Big Island. A long history of coffee production has helped cement the reputation of the region, although its success has led to its exploitation through the mislabelling of coffee. Legislation on the island now

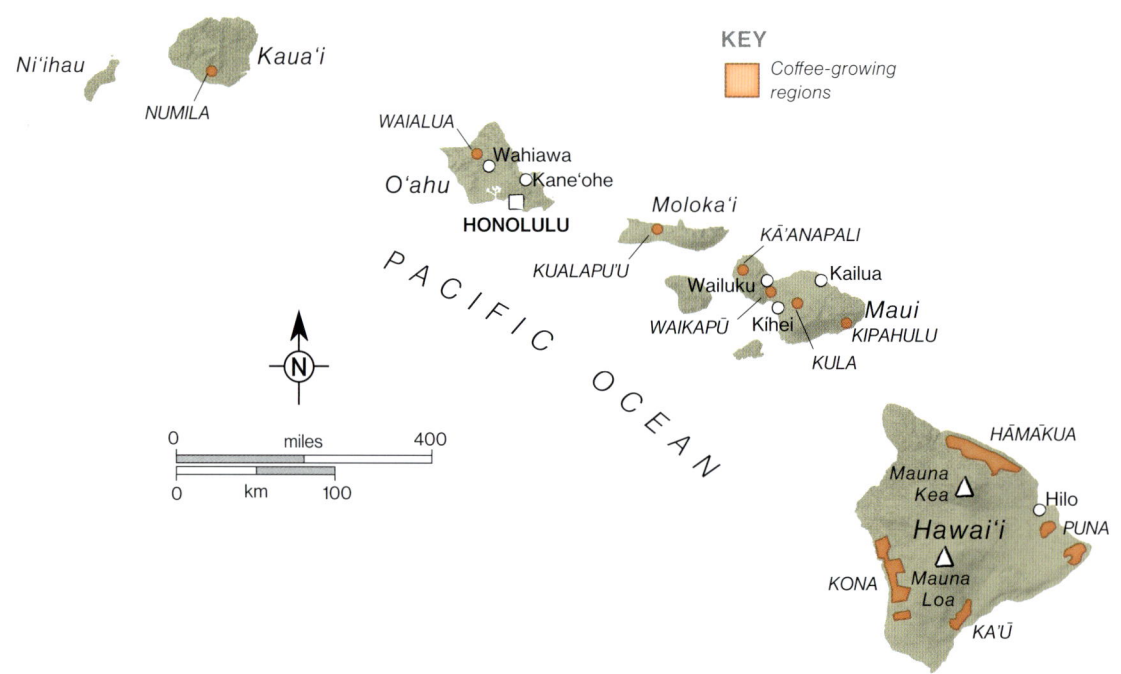

Above: Coffee beans dry on the roof of the Greenwell Coffee Farm in Kona, Hawaii.

means that any Kona blend must state the quantity of coffee from Kona on it, and the use of the '100% Kona' trademark is carefully controlled. A farm called Kona Kai in California had previously fought the awarding of any trademark or protection for the name, but in 1996 its executive was found guilty of filling his 'Kona Coffee' bags with beans from Costa Rica.

More recently, the region has been challenged by the problem of coffee berry borer. The island has introduced several measures to combat the blight, with some success, although there were fears that a reduction in yield would drive the already high price of Kona coffee even higher. The 2023 harvest was the lowest in perhaps a decade – owing to a combination of leaf rust and coffee berry borer, as well as the impact of the wildfires that destroyed agricultural land while also producing crop-damaging smoke.

Traceability

It will come as no surprise that in a higher-income country the expectations of traceability should be high. Coffees are usually traceable down to a specific farm. In many cases, the farms roast their own coffees to sell direct to consumers and tourists. Many also export some of their crop, predominantly to the mainland United States.

Kona Grading

Kona has its own grading system, mostly based on the size of the beans, but also divided into Type 1 and Type 2. Type 1 coffees are the standard coffee beans, with two beans per cherry, while Type 2 coffees are exclusively peaberries.

Within Type 1, Kona Extra Fancy are the largest beans, then they decrease in size through the following grades: Kona Fancy, Kona Number 1, Kona Select and Kona Prime.

Within Type 2 there are only two grades: Kona Number 1 Peaberry and the smaller Kona Peaberry Prime.

There are requirements for a maximum level of defects in most of the grades, but these are quite generous and not themselves a reliable indicator of quality.

Taste Profile

Hawaiian coffees are typically lower in acidity, with a little more body. They are approachable but rarely complex and fruited.

Growing Regions

Population: 1,440,000

Number of 60kg (132lb) bags produced in 2023: 30,000

Hawaii's reputation is dominated by a single region: Kona. The other islands are also worth exploring if you like a typical island coffee with relatively low acidity, a little more body and less fruitiness in the cup.

KAUAI ISLAND

This growing region is dominated by a single company running 1,250 hectares (3,100 acres) of coffee production. The Kauai Coffee Company started growing coffee to diversify away from sugarcane in the late 1980s. Due to its size, it is a heavily mechanized farm.

Elevation: 30–180m (100–600ft)
Harvest: October–December
Varieties: Yellow Catuai, Red Catuai, Typica, Blue Mountain, Mundo Novo

OAHU ISLAND

This is another island that is dominated by one estate, the Waialua Estate, which is around 60 hectares (155 acres) in size. This farm, which started production in the early 1990s, is fully mechanized in its production and also grows cacao.

Elevation: 180–210m (600–700ft)
Harvest: September–February
Varieties: Typica

MAUI ISLAND

Maui has one large commercial coffee farm, Ka'anapali, which has the unusual addition of a selection of small plots of land with houses and coffee trees for sale. Although the plots are owned by different people, the coffee production is done centrally. This large estate was a sugar plantation from 1860 to 1988, when production was turned over to coffee.

Elevation: 100–550m (330–1,800ft)
Harvest: September–January
Varieties: Red Catuai, Yellow Caturra, Typica, Mokka

KULA, MAUI ISLAND

This small region takes advantage of the slopes of the Haleakalā volcano to achieve some decent elevation for coffee growing. Coffee is relatively new to the area.

Elevation: 450–1,050m (1,500–3,500ft)
Harvest: September–January
Varieties: Typica, Red Catuai

WAIKAPŪ, MAUI ISLAND

This is the newest region of coffee production in Hawaii. A single farm operates here, held by a company based in the neighbouring island of Molokai, called Coffees of Hawaii.

Elevation: 500–750m (1,600–2,450ft)
Harvest: September–January
Varieties: Typica, Catuai

KĪPAHULU, MAUI ISLAND

This is a very low region on the south-east coast of Maui. Coffee is often grown on organic farms as part of a diverse set of crops.

Elevation: 90–180m (300–600ft)
Harvest: September–January
Varieties: Typica, Catuai

KUALAPUU, MOLOKAI ISLAND

This region is also dominated by a single coffee company, Coffees of Hawaii. The large farm is mechanized, often a requirement to reduce operational costs in an environment where labour is extremely expensive.

Elevation: 250m (800ft)
Harvest: September–January
Varieties: Red Catuai

KONA, BIG ISLAND

Unlike many other growing regions in Hawaii, there is a more diverse industry here, with over 630 farms producing coffee. Typically run by individual families, these farms are usually less than 2 hectares (5 acres). Yields here may well be the highest per area of anywhere in the world and as the farms are so much smaller than elsewhere in Hawaii, it is common to see manual harvesting of the trees.

Elevation: 150–900m (500–3,000ft)
Harvest: August–January
Varieties: Kona Typica

KAŪ, BIG ISLAND

Coffee production started in this region relatively recently, after the closure of the sugar mill in 1996. Until 2010 the farmers and cooperatives in the area had to travel to the neighbouring regions of Puna or Kona to have the coffee processed after harvest. However, a mill has now been constructed to alleviate the problem.

Elevation: 500–800m (1,600–2,600ft)
Harvest: August–January
Varieties: Typica

PUNA, BIG ISLAND

This region had around 2,400 hectares (6,000 acres) of land under coffee production at the end of the 19th century, but production ceased as sugar rose to prominence. However, the sugar mill closed in 1984, and some farmers are starting to grow coffee here again. Most farms in this area are relatively small – around 1.2 hectares (3 acres).

Elevation: 300–750m (1,000–2,450ft)
Harvest: August–January
Varieties: Red Catuai, Typica

HĀMĀKUA, BIG ISLAND

Coffee arrived here in 1852, and eight plantations were initially established. Like elsewhere in Hawaii, sugar soon became the favoured crop so coffee production declined. However, since the mid-1990s, some farms have started going back to coffee.

Elevation: 100–600m (350–2,000ft)
Harvest: August–January
Varieties: Typica

Above: The terrain on Maui lends itself in places to mechanization as much of it is relatively low lying, although volcanic slopes offer some better elevation for coffee growing.

Today, only a fraction of Puerto Rico's annual coffee crop is exported, with the majority being consumed on the island.

United States: California

The history of coffee growing in California is relatively short. After an experiment in 2002, farmer Jay Ruskey discovered that the land and climate in Southern California, near Santa Barbara, was viable for coffee production. Slowly, coffee growing has spread in the state and around 65 farms are currently growing coffee, although the amounts produced are as yet very small.

Unsurprisingly, coffee from the area is expensive. This is a combination of the scarcity of it, coupled with the higher costs that come from growing coffee in a higher-income country. The producers growing coffee are planting varieties of coffee like Gesha, Laurina, Caturra, Mundo Novo and more – all seemingly with an eye specifically on the speciality market and trying to produce something special to go with the higher price tag. All kinds of farming in the area are seeing challenges with climate change, wildfires and access to water – so it remains to be seen whether diversifying into coffee will be a financially sustainable challenge. I would recommend trying them should the opportunity arise, as the combination of interesting variety and careful process may trump the lower elevations and still produce an interesting and memorable cup.

GROWING STATISTICS

Population: 38,970,000
Number of 60kg (132lb) bags produced in 2023: 30
Elevation: 30–300m (100–1,000ft)
Harvest: May to September
Varieties: Gesha, Laurina, Caturra Rojo, Catuai Rojo, Mundo Novo and Pacamara

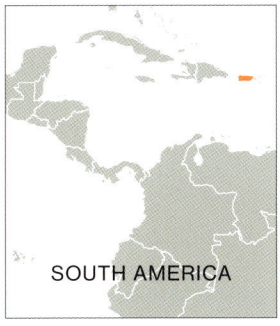

Puerto Rico

The island of Puerto Rico has been producing coffee for hundreds of years. First introduced in the 1730s, when the island was under Spanish colonial rule, coffee slowly took root as an export crop over the following decades. By the late 19th century Puerto Rico had become a significant producer on the global market.

In 1898, following the brief Spanish–American War, Spain ceded Puerto Rico to the United States. The combination of a hurricane destroying the majority of the island's crop and the occupying Americans being more interested in sugar production then led to a decrease in coffee production.

Today Puerto Rico is a net coffee importer. Almost all the coffee it produces is consumed on the island, but that makes up a minority of the coffee consumed in Puerto Rico, with larger volumes being brought in from Mexico and the Dominican Republic. A tiny fraction of the annual crop is exported, and it is generally very difficult to find as a traceable coffee.

The local coffee industry suffered further blows from the hurricanes in 2017 and 2020, which wiped out a huge amount of the crop. Production has returned in the last few years to almost pre-hurricane levels but remains very small.

GROWING STATISTICS

Population: 3,222,000
Number of 60kg (132lb) bags produced in 2023: 23,300
Elevation: 1,000–1,200m (3,300–3,900ft)
Harvest: August–March
Varieties: Bourbon, Typica, Pacas and Catimor

Cuba

Coffee came to Cuba from the island of Hispaniola in 1748, but there was little coffee industry to speak of until the influx of French settlers in 1791, fleeing the Haitian Revolution. By 1827 there were around two thousand coffee farms on the island and coffee became a major export, generating more money than sugar.

Castro's revolution, from 1953 to 1961, brought with it the nationalization of coffee farms and production dropped almost immediately. Those who volunteered to farm coffee had no experience, and those who had previously worked the land had fled the country in the wake of the revolution. Coffee production struggled on the island, and little in the way of incentives or encouragement from the government did much to bolster the industry, although production did peak in the 1970s at around 30,000 tonnes (33,000 tons) of coffee. As Cuba's coffee industry was faltering, many Central American countries continued to enjoy greater exports and success in international markets.

The dissolution of the Soviet Union in 1991 left Cuba increasingly isolated, and the trade embargo placed on Cuba by the United States removed a major potential market. Japan has been the major importer of Cuban coffee, although Europe remains a strong market. The best coffees are typically exported, usually around one-fifth of the total production, leaving the rest for domestic consumption. Cuba's own production does not cover domestic demand, and in 2013 the country spent nearly $40 million on imported coffee. The coffee being imported into Cuba is not of the highest quality, so it is relatively cheap, but high market prices have led to the reappearance of the habit of mixing in roasted peas to bulk out the coffee.

Cuban coffee production remains low at around 6,000–7,000 tonnes (6,600–7,700 tons) a year. Much of the equipment used is old, and many producers are still reliant on mules. Roads are often badly damaged by alternating rain and drought and are poorly maintained. Coffee is usually dried in the sun, though some mechanical drying takes place, and most of the coffees grown for export are washed. Cuba's climate and topography are well suited to coffee growing, and its scarcity may add much to its value, but there are many challenges facing those producers wishing to create high-quality coffees. Currently, Cuba produces both Arabica and Robusta, in a ratio of around 60:40 by volume.

Traceability

Cuban coffees are unlikely to be traceable down to a single farm and are often only traceable down to a particular region or sub-region of the country.

Opposite: Though the climate and topography suit the crop, Cuba's coffee industry suffers from poor infrastructure and aging equipment.

Cuban Coffee

A number of Cuban coffee preparations have spread around the world, including *cortadito*, *café con leche* and *café cubano*. The latter refers to an espresso that is sweetened as it is brewed, by adding sugar to the ground coffee.

In the United States especially, and in other places, it is not uncommon to see 'Cuban Coffee' advertised. Coffees, often from Brazil, are selected to represent the flavours one might expect from Cuba, but there are, of course, concerns about confusion among customers and mislabelling of goods.

Taste Profile

Cuban coffees have a typical island coffee profile: relatively low in acidity with a heavier body.

Growing Regions

Population: 10,055,000

Number of 60kg (132lb) bags in 2023: 100,000

Cuba is the largest island in the Caribbean. Much of it is relatively low-lying plains but there are some mountainous areas suitable for coffee.

SIERRA MAESTRA

This mountainous region runs the length of the southern coast and has a long history of guerrilla warfare, from the 1500s to the revolution in the 1950s. Almost all the coffee production on the island is located here. A lot of coffee in the region is certified organic.

Elevation: 1,000–1,200m (3,300–3,900ft)
Harvest: July–December
Varieties: Mostly Isla 6-14, Isla 6-11, Typica; some Bourbon, Caturra, Catuai, Catimor

SIERRA DEL ESCAMBRAY

A small amount of Cuba's coffee is grown in this mountain range in the middle of the island.

Elevation: 350–900m (1,100–3,000ft)
Harvest: July–December
Varieties: Mostly Isla 6-14, Isla 6-11, Typica; some Bourbon, Caturra, Catuai, Catimor

SIERRA DEL ROSARIO

Coffee farms have existed in this region since 1790, though relatively little of Cuba's coffee is grown here now. Instead, the mountains are home to Cuba's first Biosphere Reserve, and this is a protected area.

Elevation: 300–550m (1,000–1,800ft)
Harvest: July–December
Varieties: Mostly Isla 6-14, Isla 6-11, Typica; some Bourbon, Caturra, Catuai, Catimor

Haiti

Coffee probably came to Haiti from the island of Martinique, while it was a newly founded French colony in 1725. The first coffee was likely grown around Terroir Rouge in the north-east of the country; ten years later another coffee plantation appeared in the mountains in the north of Haiti. Coffee production rapidly increased on the island, and a number of sources claim that, between 1750 and 1788, Haiti produced 50–60 per cent of the world's coffee.

The industry would reach its peak in 1788, and the following years of revolution, ultimately leading to independence in 1804, would see coffee production rapidly decline. The ending of slavery on the island didn't just have an impact on the production of coffee, but also led to the country being ostracized in terms of international trade. However, the industry would slowly rebuild and see another peak in 1850 before receding again. Coffee production once again boomed in the 1940s, and in 1949 Haiti produced one-third of the world's coffee.

Coffee production, like many aspects of Haiti's economy, suffered under the Duvalier regimes between 1957 and 1986, and natural disasters would play a role in further hampering the industry. The collapse of the International Coffee Agreement led to reports in 1990 of farmers choosing to burn their coffee trees to make charcoal to sell instead.

In the mid-1990s an organization called the Fédération des Associations Caféières Natives (FACN) was created. It would buy dried parchment coffee then mill it, sort it and blend it. The coffee had been washed rather than dry-processed, and this was somewhat unusual. It created a brand name called Haitian Bleu, referencing the colour of the raw coffee caused by the washing process, and controlled its route to market. In doing so it was, for a while, able to lift prices paid to growers. While not traceable in the

Growing Statistics

Population: 11,580,000

Number of 60kg (132lb) bags produced in 2023: 100,000

The production of coffee in Haiti has dwindled to the point that it would not be accurate to describe it as having multiple growing regions.

Elevation: 300–2,000m (1,000–6,600ft)
Harvest: August–March
Varieties: Typica, Caturra, Bourbon

Right: Bags of coffee are hoisted aboard the SS Prins Frederik Hendrik in the port of Les Cayes in Haiti, 1912.

Opposite: Brewing coffee in Rivière Froide, in Haiti's Ouest department.

way we expect speciality coffee to be today, it did create a premium around provenance and story. However, mismanagement of the organization led to declining volumes, and not meeting contracts with roasters led to the eventual decline and bankruptcy of the FACN.

The earthquake in 2010 that devastated the island also devastated the coffee industry, which had already been in steady decline. Worth $7 million in 2000, by 2010 it had dwindled in value to just $1 million. There was hope that coffee would play a role in the country's economic recovery, alongside mangoes, the other major crop. Between 2015 and 2017 production dropped so low that coffee needed to be imported to meet domestic consumption, and exports would not begin again until 2019. Exports have remained relatively low since.

Traceability

If you can find high-quality coffee from Haiti, then it is going to come, most likely, from a cooperative of growers. There are no single estates selling coffee in the country. Haiti consumes almost as much coffee as it produces, so very little is exported.

Taste Profile

Haitian coffee is relatively full-bodied, earthy and sometimes spicy, with a little acidity – a typical 'island coffee' taste profile. Better lots have a soft sweetness.

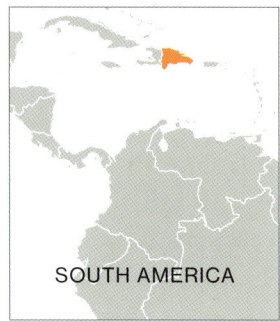

Dominican Republic

Coffee came to the Spanish-controlled portion of the island of Hispaniola – what is now the Dominican Republic – in 1735. The first plantings were probably on a hill in Bahoruco Panzo, near Neyba. By the end of the 18th century coffee had become the second most important crop after sugar, although both relied heavily on slavery until the revolution of 1791.

Coffee production really took root between 1822 and 1844, particularly in the region of Valdesia in the southern mountains. This region contains several coffee-growing areas and became the primary production area in the country by 1880.

By 1956 the country had started to export coffees from specific regions, predominantly Baní, (San José de) Ocoa and Valdesia. In the 1960s the farmers in these regions became more organized, and a mill was opened in 1967 with 155 members.

As in many coffee-producing countries, the turmoil and unpredictability of prices at the end of the 20th century led to a decreased dependence on coffee as an export product. Many producers diversified into beans or avocados, though a good number of them retained a small amount of coffee in case prices recover. Although Valdesia is not one of the main government-designated growing regions, they have sought to protect its origin name with the launch, in 2010, of the Café de Valdesia brand.

Export Versus Domestic Consumption

Interestingly, it seems that since the late 1970s the quantity of coffee produced in the Dominican Republic has varied little, but exports have dropped dramatically. Currently, only about 20 per cent of the coffee harvested is sold for export. This is because domestic coffee consumption is relatively high at approximately 3kg (6½lb) per person per year, more than the United Kingdom. In 2007 around half of exports were shipped via Puerto Rico, although this acts as a gateway to the United States. The rest of the coffee was destined for Europe and Japan. Since 2001 more and more of the coffee destined for export has been organically grown and certified, adding value and revenue to the industry. But while organic production is overall a good thing, it should be reiterated that it does not necessarily make a better cup of coffee.

Some argue that the high domestic consumption of coffee in the Dominican Republic has resulted in lower quality overall, as the coffee is not competing with other exporting countries for this particular market. Nonetheless, there are still great coffees to be found in the Dominican Republic.

Traceability

While it is possible to get some extremely traceable coffees from the Dominican Republic, usually down to a particular farm, much of what is exported is not particularly traceable past the growing region. These coffees are often graded by bean size, with designations such as 'Supremo', which may carry a premium but not one that is based on cup quality.

> **Taste Profile**
>
> Typical of coffees grown on islands, the better lots tend to be quite mild, low to middling in acidity and relatively clean.

Growing Regions

Population: 11,434,000

Number of 60kg (132lb) bags in 2023: 125,000

The climate in the Dominican Republic is a little different from many other coffee-producing countries. It doesn't have clear seasons, in terms of neither temperature nor rainfall. This means that coffee production is often taking place, to some extent, throughout the year, although the main harvest tends to be from November to May. However, there is a bit of a split when it comes to altitude. Lower elevations harvest their crop between October and February, while higher elevations do so between December and May.

Below: Dominican workers on a coffee farm spreading coffee beans on a concrete patio to dry in the sun.

BARAHONA

This region is on the south-west side of the island, and the coffee here is grown in the Sierra Bahoruco. The area has established a reputation for high quality, compared to the island's other coffee-growing regions. Agriculture is the main industry here, and coffee the main product.

Elevation: 600–1,300m (2,000–4,300ft)
Harvest: October–February
Varieties: Typica, Caturra

CIBAO

Coffee is an important product in this region, along with rice and cacao. The Cibao is on the north side of the island, and its name in the indigenous language Taino means 'place where rocks abound'. The name refers specifically to the valley lying between the Central and Septentrional mountain ranges.

Elevation: 400–800m (1,300–2,600ft)
Harvest: September–December
Varieties: Typica, Caturra

CIBAO ALTURA

This region is defined as being the higher-elevation areas within the Cibao region.

Elevation: 600–1,500m (2,000–4,900ft)
Harvest: October–May
Varieties: Typica, Caturra

CENTRAL MOUNTAINS (CORDILLERA CENTRAL)

This mountain range is the highest in the Dominican Republic and is also known as the 'Dominican Alps'. The geology of the region is notably different from the surrounding areas, so the coffee here is the only coffee on the island that is grown on granite substrate, rather than calcium.

Elevation: 600–1,500m (2,000–4,900ft)
Harvest: November–May
Varieties: Typica, Caturra, Catuai

NEYBA

This region (also spelled Neiba) is named after the capital city of the Baoruco province and is in the south-west of the island. The region is quite flat and low and is primarily used for grapes, plantain and sugar, but coffee does grow higher up in the Sierra de Neyba.

Elevation: 700–1,400m (2,300–4,600ft)
Harvest: November–February
Varieties: Typica, Caturra

VALDESIA

This is probably the best known of the growing regions on the island and has been awarded a Denomination of Origin to protect the value of its exports. As it is well defined and protected, it has gained a good reputation, and a small premium associated with it.

Elevation: 500–1,100m (1,600–3,600ft)
Harvest: October–February
Varieties: Typica, Caturra

Jamaica

The story of coffee on the island begins in 1728, when the governor, Sir Nicholas Lawes, received a coffee plant from the governor of Martinique. Lawes had already experimented with several crops, and he planted the coffee in the St Andrew area. Initially, its production was relatively limited: in 1752 Jamaica exported only 27 tonnes (30 tons) of coffee.

The real boom started in the second half of the 18th century, with coffee spreading from the St Andrew area up to the Blue Mountains. In 1800, 686 coffee plantations were in operation, and by 1814 Jamaica's annual production was around 15,000 tonnes (16,500 tons) (although some estimates are considerably higher than this).

After this boom, the industry started to see a slow decline. The primary reason was probably the lack of labour, although other factors also played a role. The slave trade had been abolished in 1807, but the emancipation of enslaved workers on the island did not happen until 1838. While there had been some efforts to recruit the formerly enslaved as private labourers, coffee struggled to compete with other industries. And when combined with both poor soil management and the loss of the favourable trade conditions that Britain had previously extended to its colonies, it resulted in a steep decline for coffee. By 1850 there were only around 180 plantations left, and production had dropped dramatically to just 1,500 tonnes (1,650 tons) a year.

At the end of the 19th century Jamaica was producing around 4,500 tonnes (5,000 tons) of coffee, but serious issues with quality were starting to appear. In 1891 legislation had been passed to try to spread knowledge about coffee production in an effort to increase quality, and infrastructure was put in place for the centralized processing and grading of coffee. This programme had limited success, although a Central Coffee Clearing House was constructed in 1944 for all coffee to pass through before export, and in 1950 the Jamaican Coffee Board was formed.

From this point onwards coffees from the Blue Mountain region made slow and steady gains in reputation until they came to be considered among the finest coffees in the world. At that time, however, few well-processed coffees were available, and today Jamaica's coffees cannot really compete against the very best coffees from Central and South America or East Africa. Jamaican coffees tend to be clean, sweet and very mild. They lack the complexity or distinct characteristics that one often expects from speciality-grade coffees. However, they were consistently producing, and cleverly marketing, clean and sweet coffees long before other producers were, and this gave their coffees a distinct advantage for some time.

Left: Barrels of Blue Mountain coffee awaiting export.

Opposite: The provenance of Blue Mountain coffee is tightly controlled, based on the altitude of crops. Distinctive wooden barrels further emphasize the brand.

Taste Profile

Jamaican coffees are clean and sweet, though rarely complex or juicy and fruity.

Growing Regions

Population: 2,827,000

Number of 60kg (132lb) bags in 2023: 15,000

There is really only one growing region of note in Jamaica, and it is probably one of the most famous growing regions in the world.

BLUE MOUNTAIN

The subject of one of the most successful pieces of marketing in coffee's history, this region of Jamaica is clearly defined and well protected. Only coffees grown between 900 and 1,500m (3,000 and 4,900ft) in the parishes of Saint Andrew, Saint Thomas, Portland and Saint Mary can be referred to as 'Jamaica Blue Mountain'. Coffees grown between 450 and 900m (1,500 and 3,000ft) can be called 'Jamaica High Mountain', and anything below this may be called 'Jamaica Supreme' or 'Jamaica Low Mountain'.

The traceability of Blue Mountain coffees can be somewhat confusing, as most of the coffees are sold under the name of the mill in which they are processed. These mills may occasionally keep a large estate's coffee separate, but usually they buy from the myriad of smallholders who grow coffee in the region.

For a long time, the majority of Jamaica's Blue Mountain production was sold to Japan. It was exported in small wooden barrels rather than in jute bags. Also worth noting is that, due to its ability to achieve very high prices, there is usually a fair amount of coffee fraudulently mislabelled as Blue Mountain on the market.

Elevation: 900–1,500m (3,000–4,900ft)
Harvest: February–June
Varieties: Jamaica Blue Mountain (a Typica derivative), Typica, Bourbon

Mexico

The first coffee plants were probably brought to Mexico around 1785, most likely from Cuba or what is now the Dominican Republic. There are reports of plantations in the region of Veracruz in 1790. However, due to the wealth earned from Mexico's rich mineral deposits, for many years there was little drive to create and energize a coffee industry.

Only after the Mexican revolution ended in 1920 did coffee growing spread to small farms. In 1914 there had been a redistribution of land back to Indigenous people and to labourers and many of those trapped working on coffee plantations were freed and were able to return to their communities, taking their coffee-growing skills with them. This land redistribution broke up many of the larger haciendas, and this was the beginning of smallholder production in Mexico.

In 1973 the government formed the Mexican Coffee Institute (Instituto Mexicano del Café) referred to as INMECAFE. This was tasked with providing technical assistance and financial credit to producers, and with working within the International Coffee Agreement (see page 280) to meet and stay within the agreed production quotas. This investment in the industry led to a rapid expansion in both production and the land dedicated to coffee. In some rural areas, production increased by almost 900 per cent.

However, the 1980s saw the Mexican government change its policy towards coffee, in part due to its heavy borrowing and the drop in the price of oil that had led to it defaulting on its loans. Support of the industry slowly began to decline, and in 1989 INMECAFE collapsed completely and the government sold off its state-owned coffee-processing facilities. The effect on the industry was devastating. Credit had dried up, and many farmers struggled to find places to

Below: Fairtrade and organic certification are common in Mexico, but it is rare to find great Mexican coffees outside the United States, or Mexico itself.

sell their coffee. This led to an increase in predatory coffee brokers, known as coyotes, who would buy coffee from farmers very cheaply to resell at a profit.

The loss of INMECAFE, combined with the coffee price crisis caused by the breakdown of the 1989 International Coffee Agreement, had a strong effect on the quality of coffee being produced, too. With less income, huge numbers of producers ceased using fertilizers, stopped investing in pest protection, and spent less time and resources on weeding and farm management. In some cases, farmers simply stopped harvesting their coffee.

Interestingly, some producers (particularly in the states of Oaxaca, Chiapas and Veracruz) responded by forming collectives to take over many of the responsibilities previously held by INMECAFE, including the collective purchasing and running of coffee mills, technical assistance, political lobbying and even assistance in developing direct relationships with buyers.

Coffee producers in Mexico seem to have embraced coffee certifications; fair trade and organic in particular are quite common. Mexico sells a great deal of its coffee to the United States, so it is relatively rare to find excellent examples of Mexican coffee elsewhere in the world, but not impossible. There are some truly excellent coffees from Mexico that are worth seeking out.

Coffee consumption is growing in Mexico, and in cities – particularly Mexico City – there is a growing speciality coffee movement. If you happen to be visiting, these cafés are worth hunting out if you want to taste some of the best Mexican coffees.

Traceability

Most coffee in Mexico is produced by smallholders, rather than large estates. In fact, farms larger than 50 hectares (about 125 acres) make up only 0.06 per cent of all farms. Traceability should be possible down to a producer group, cooperative or occasionally down to a single farm.

Taste Profile

Mexico produces quite a range of coffees across its regions, from lighter-bodied, delicate coffees through to sweeter coffees with caramel, toffee or chocolate flavours in the cup.

Growing Regions

Population: 127,500,000

Number of 60kg (132lb) bags exported in 2023: 3,870,000

Coffee is also grown outside of the key growing regions listed below and should not be ignored if offered by a roaster or retailer you trust. Production from these regions is very small compared to the major areas.

CHIAPAS

This region borders Guatemala. The Sierra Madre mountain range offers both the necessary elevation, as well as the beneficial volcanic soils, for good coffee production. It is the largest producing region, accounting for around 40 per cent of the country's production.

Elevation: 1,000–1,750m (3,300–5,750ft)
Harvest: November–March
Varieties: Typica, Bourbon, Maragogype, Red Caturra, Mundo Novo, Garnica, Yellow Caturra

OAXACA

Most farmers in this region own less than 2 hectares (4½ acres) of land, and there are several large cooperatives operating here. There are also a few larger estates, although some are starting to diversify into tourism.

Elevation: 900–1,700m (3,000–5,600ft)
Harvest: December–March
Varieties: Typica, Bourbon, Maragogype, Red Caturra, Mundo Novo, Garnica, Yellow Caturra

PUEBLA

This was not a significant coffee-producing region until relatively recently, and it now accounts for around 15 per cent of total production. Production is in seven areas in the region: Xicotopec, Zacatlán, Huauchinango, Zapotitlán, Cuetzalan, Sierra Negra and Teziutlán.

Elevation: 900–1,900m (3,000–6,200ft)
Harvest: December–March
Varieties: Typica, Bourbon, Maragogype, Red Caturra, Mundo Novo, Garnica, Yellow Caturra

VERACRUZ

This is a large state in the east of the country along the coast of the Gulf of Mexico. This area contains some of the lowest coffee production in Mexico, but also some very high-elevation farms around Coatepec that produce better coffee.

Elevation: 800–1,700m (2,600–5,600ft)
Harvest: December–March
Varieties: Typica, Bourbon, Maragogype, Red Caturra, Mundo Novo, Garnica, Yellow Caturra

Right: The Sierra Madre mountains in Chiapas offer both elevation and good volcanic soils, making this the largest coffee-producing region in Mexico.

Guatemala

Many believe that coffee was first introduced to Guatemala by the Jesuits around 1750, although there are accounts of it being grown and served in the country in 1747. As in El Salvador, coffee only became an important crop in Guatemala after 1856, when the invention of chemical dyes reduced demand for indigo, which was at that time the main cash crop.

The government had already made some attempts to diversify away from indigo. In 1845 it formed the Commission for Coffee Cultivation and Promotion, which produced educational materials for coffee producers and also helped establish a price and levels of quality. In 1868 the government distributed around one million coffee seeds to farmers, in an effort to further stimulate the industry.

When Justo Rufino Barrios came to power in 1871, he made coffee the backbone of the economy. Unfortunately, his reforms resulted in the Indigenous people of Guatemala being further deprived of their land, as they led to the sale of around 400,000 hectares (990,000 acres) of what was considered public land. These became large coffee plantations. The efforts to stimulate coffee production certainly worked, however, and by 1880 coffee made up around 90 per cent of Guatemala's exports.

Coffee would again be involved in the country's politics following the global depression in 1930. Jorge Ubico had come to power as president and worked to lower the price of coffee to help stimulate export. He built extensive infrastructure but gave more power and land to the United Fruit Company (UFC), an American corporation that grew to be extremely powerful. Ubico ultimately resigned due to a general strike and protests against him.

There followed a period of democracy, and President Jacobo Árbenz proposed a land reform act in 1953 to expropriate land (largely that controlled by the UFC) to redistribute it for agricultural purposes. Both large coffee plantation owners and the UFC (supported by the US State Department) fought against the reforms. In 1954 a CIA coup overthrew the Árbenz government and the proposed land reforms never took place. This set the country down a path towards a civil war that lasted from 1960 to 1996. Many of the issues that provoked the war – poverty, land distribution, hunger, and racism towards Indigenous people – are still issues today.

Opposite: Washing coffee beans at Finca Vista Hermosa coffee farm, Agua Dulce, Guatemala.

> **Taste Profile**
>
> A wide range of flavours are present in Guatemala's coffees, from lighter, very sweet, fruity and complex coffees through to the heavier, richer and more chocolatey cups.

Guatemala's coffee production peaked at the turn of the millennium, as many producers moved away from coffee into macadamia nuts and avocados after the coffee crisis in 2001. Coffee leaf rust has also been an increasing problem for producers throughout the country, damaging a large portion of their production.

Traceability

Guatemalan coffees should be traceable down to farm level, or down to a cooperative or producer group. While some regions in Guatemala are now protected denominations of origin, the country has a long history of traceability and estates producing high-quality coffee because many farmers have their own wet mills and process their own coffee.

Growing Regions

Population: 17,360,000

Number of 60kg (132lb) bags in 2023: 3,260,000

Guatemala has been more successful than most other countries at defining its key regions and marketing the coffees from these regions as being quite different from each other. In my experience, there are some flavour characteristics more common in certain regions, but there are no hard-and-fast rules for this.

SAN MARCOS

San Marcos is both the warmest and the rainiest of the coffee-growing regions in Guatemala. The rains come earlier to the mountain slopes facing the Pacific, so flowering is generally earlier too. The rainfall can provide challenges to post-harvest drying, so some farms rely on a mixture of sun drying and mechanical drying. Agriculture is a large part of the economy in this department, which produces grain, fruit, meat and wool.

Elevation: 1,300–1,800m (4,300–5,900ft)
Harvest: December–March
Varieties: Bourbon, Caturra, Catuai

ACATENANGO

Coffee production in this region is centred around the Acatenango Valley, which is named after the volcano there. In the past many producers here sold their coffee to 'coyotes' who would ship the cherries over to the Antigua region and process it there. Antigua had a better reputation for coffee, and so it commanded a higher price. This practice is now less common, as coffees from Acatenango can be excellent and are becoming more widely recognized so it is more profitable to keep them properly traceable.

Elevation: 1,300–2,000m (4,300–6,600ft)
Harvest: December–March
Varieties: Bourbon, Caturra, Catuai

ATITLÁN

The coffee farms here are located around Lake Atitlán. Sitting at around 1,500m (4,900ft) above sea level, the lake has captured the minds of writers and travellers over many years because of its stunning beauty. In the late morning and early afternoon, a strong wind often blows here and is known locally as *xocomil*, 'the wind that carries away sin'.

There are a number of private nature reserves here, set up to preserve the biodiversity of the area and help prevent deforestation. Coffee production is under pressure due to increased labour costs and competition for the labour force. Urban sprawl is also increasing pressure on land use, and some farmers are finding it is more profitable to sell their land than continue to grow coffee.

Elevation: 1,500–1,700m (4,900–5,600ft)
Harvest: December–March
Varieties: Bourbon, Typica, Caturra, Catuai

COBÁN

This region is named after the town of Cobán, which grew and thrived due to the German coffee producers who held a great deal of power here until the end of World War II. The lush rainforest comes with a very wet climate, which proves something of a challenge to coffee drying. The region is also somewhat remote, making transport more difficult and expensive, but there are, nonetheless, stunning coffees coming from here.

Elevation: 1,300–1,700m (4,300–5,600ft)
Harvest: December–March
Varieties: Bourbon, Maragogype, Catuai, Caturra, Pache

Elevation Grading

Similar to other Central American countries, Guatemala uses a version of elevation grading:

Prime: grown at 750–900m (2,500–3,000ft)

Extra Prime: grown at 900–1,050m (3,000–3,500ft)

Semi Hard Bean: grown at 1,050–1,220m (3,500–4,000ft)

Hard Bean (HB): grown at 1,220–1,300m (4,000–4,300ft)

Strictly Hard Bean (SHB): grown over 1,300m (4,300ft)

NUEVO ORIENTE

Unsurprisingly for a region whose name means 'New East', Nuevo Oriente is located in the east of the country by the border with Honduras. The climate is dryer here and most of the coffee is produced by smallholders. Coffee production arrived here quite late, beginning in the 1950s.

Elevation: 1,300–1,700m (4,300–5,600ft)
Harvest: December–March
Varieties: Bourbon, Catuai, Caturra, Pache

HUEHUETENANGO

This is one of the better-known regions of Guatemala, and the most enjoyable to pronounce. The name translates from Nahuatl as 'place of the ancients' or 'place of the ancestors'. This area has the highest non-volcanic mountains in Central America, and they are well suited to coffee growing. This region is probably the most dependent on coffee as an export and there are some truly astonishing coffees produced here.

Elevation: 1,500–2,000m (4,900–6,600ft)
Harvest: January–April
Varieties: Bourbon, Catuai, Caturra

FRAIJANES

This coffee-growing plateau surrounds the capital of Guatemala City. There is fairly regular volcanic activity in the area, which benefits the soil, but occasionally also endangers life and causes problems with infrastructure. Unfortunately, the amount of land under coffee continues to decrease as the city grows and land use changes.

Elevation: 1,400–1,800m (4,600–5,900ft)
Harvest: December–February
Varieties: Bourbon, Caturra, Catuai, Pache

Above: Guatemala's volcanic activity benefits the soil but can endanger life and infrastructure.

ANTIGUA

Antigua is probably the best-known coffee-producing region in Guatemala, and one of the best known in the world. The region is named after the city of Antigua, famous for its Spanish architecture and a UNESCO World Heritage Site. The region attained a Denomination of Origin in 2000 under the name 'Genuine Antigua Coffee', after the market had become devalued by coffee fraudulently labelled as Antigua. This has prevented coffee from other origins being sold as Antigua, but it has not stopped the fraudulent practice of bringing cherries in from other regions to be processed there. Nonetheless, it is possible to find clearly traceable coffees from Antigua, and while some are overpriced, others are of excellent quality and are worth seeking out.

Elevation: 1,500–1,700m (4,900–5,600ft)
Harvest: January–March
Varieties: Bourbon, Caturra, Catuai

Though changing land use and varying temperatures influence the amount of coffee produced and the way it is processed in Guatemala, much of the coffee is treated in the traditional way and dried by sun.

El Salvador

Coffee was first produced commercially in El Salvador in the 1850s. It soon became a favoured crop, with tax breaks for producers. Coffee production became an important part of the economy and the country's main export, and by 1880 El Salvador was the fourth-largest producer of coffee in the world, producing more than twice as much as it does today.

The growth of the coffee industry came about in part because El Salvador was moving away from its previous dominant crop, indigo, after the invention of chemical dyes in the mid-19th century. The land used to grow indigo had been controlled by a relatively small landed elite. Coffee production required a different type of land, so these landed families used their influence in government to pass laws to push the poor from their land so that it could be absorbed into the new coffee plantations. Compensation to the Indigenous people who lost their land was all but non-existent; sometimes they were simply offered the chance to work seasonally on the newly established coffee plantations.

By the early 20th century El Salvador would become one of the most progressive of the Central American nations, the first with paved highways and investment in ports, railroads and lavish public buildings. Coffee helped fund infrastructure and integrate Indigenous communities into the national economy, but it also served as a mechanism for the landed elite to maintain political and economic control over the country.

The aristocracy of the time exerted their power through the support of military rule from the 1930s, and this became a period of relative stability. The growth of the coffee industry in the decades that followed helped support the development of a cotton industry and light manufacturing. Up until the civil war of the 1980s, El Salvador had a reputation for quality and efficiency in its coffee production, with well-established relationships with importing

Above: El Salvador's unusually high percentage of heirloom coffee varieties and rich farmland mean exports for its sweet flavoured coffees have increasing potential.

countries. The civil war, however, would have a dramatic impact on this, as production fell and foreign markets looked elsewhere for their coffee.

Heirloom Varieties

Despite the drop in production and exports, the civil war had an unexpected benefit for the coffee industry. Throughout much of Central America at the time, coffee producers were replacing their heirloom varieties with newly developed high-yield varieties. The cup quality of these new varieties did not match that of the heirloom varieties, but yield was favoured over quality. El Salvador, however, never went through this process. The country still has an unusually high percentage of heirloom Bourbon trees, in total producing about 68 per cent of its coffee. Combined with its well-drained but mineral-rich volcanic soils, the country has the potential to produce some stunningly sweet coffees.

The Pacas Variety

In 1949 a mutation of the Bourbon variety was discovered by Don Alberto Pacas on one of his farms. It was named after him and was later crossed with Maragogype, a variety of coffee with very large beans, to create the Pacamara variety. Both desirable varieties remain in production in the region and in neighbouring countries.

This has been the focus of much of El Salvador's recent coffee marketing, and it has worked hard to regain its standing among the coffee-producing countries and re-establish old relationships with consuming nations. Large estates still exist in El

Salvador, but there are also a lot of small farms. It is a great country to explore, as there are many stunning coffees, full of sweetness and complexity. However, the varieties that make it appealing to speciality coffee also leave it exposed to diseases like leaf rust. In addition, labour shortages continue to be a challenge for the coffee sector. This isn't just the labour required for picking, but also for farming and plant care throughout the year. It might be worth noting, too, that there hasn't been much growth in domestic consumption either; in fact, what notable increase there has been has come from imports of instant coffee from neighbouring producing countries.

Traceability

The infrastructure in place means that it is relatively easy to retain the traceability on high-quality coffees right back to farm level, and many farms are able to create micro-lots based around process and variety.

Elevation Classifications

El Salvador still sometimes classifies coffee based on the elevation at which it was grown. These classifications have no relation to either quality or traceability.

Strictly High Grown (SHG): grown above 1,200m (3,900ft)
High Grown (HG): grown above 900m (3,000ft)
Central Standard: grown above 600m (2,000ft)

Taste Profile

The Bourbon variety coffees from El Salvador are famously sweet and well balanced, with a pleasing soft acidity to give balance in the cup.

Growing Regions

Population: 6,336,000
Number of 60kg (132lb) bags produced in 2023: 555,000

Most coffee roasters do not use the region names when describing coffees. While they are distinct, well-defined regions, some would argue that El Salvador itself is so small that it could be classified as a single region, with clearly defined pockets of coffee growing within it.

APANECA-ILAMATEPEC MOUNTAIN RANGE

With a reputation for great quality, this area produces many competition-winning coffees, despite the volcanic activity here. The Santa Ana volcano erupted as recently as 2005, having a massive impact on production for a couple of years. This is the largest-producing region of the country, and it was probably here that coffee was first cultivated in El Salvador.

Elevation: 500–2,300m (1,600–7,500ft)
Harvest: October–March
Varieties: Bourbon, Pacas and others

ALOTEPEC-METAPÁN MOUNTAIN RANGE

This mountain range is one of the wetter regions of El Salvador, with over one-third more rainfall than average. The region borders both Guatemala and Honduras, yet despite its proximity to those countries, the coffees here remain distinct.

Elevation: 1,000–2,000m (3,300–6,600ft)
Harvest: October–March
Varieties: Bourbon, Pacas and others

EL BÁLSAMO-QUEZALTEPEC MOUNTAIN RANGE

Some of the coffee farms in this region overlook the capital city of San Salvador, from high up on the sides of the Quetzaltepec volcano. This region was home to the pre-Hispanic Quetzalcotitán civilization, who worshipped the feathered serpent god Quetzalcoatl, still a common symbol in Salvadorian culture today. The mountain range also takes its name from the Peruvian balsam produced there, an aromatic resin used in perfumes, cosmetics and medicines.

Elevation: 500–1,950m (1,600–6,400ft)
Harvest: October–March
Varieties: Bourbon, Pacas and others

CHICHONTEPEC VOLCANO

Coffee was late coming to this region in the centre of the country, with barely 50 bags of coffee being produced here in 1880. However, the volcanic land is extremely fertile, and today the area is home to many coffee farms. The traditional practice of planting alternating rows of coffee and orange trees for shade is still common: some believe this imparts an orange blossom quality to the coffee, although others attribute this soft citrus element to the Bourbon variety that is grown here.

Elevation: 500–1,000m (1,600–3,300ft)
Harvest: October–February
Varieties: Bourbon, Pacas and others

TEPECA-CHINAMECA MOUNTAIN RANGE

This region is the third-largest producer of coffee in the country. Here they serve coffee with corn tortillas called tustacas, made with salt and dusted with sugar or made with a little panela (cane sugar).

Elevation: 500–2,150m (1,600–7,100ft)
Harvest: October–March
Varieties: Bourbon, Pacas and others

Above: In a sea of ripe coffee cherries at El Paste near Santa Ana, this worker shovels the harvest ready for processing. The Apaneca-Ilamatepec region is the biggest producer of coffee in El Salvador.

CACAHUATIQUE MOUNTAIN RANGE

Captain General Gerardo Barrios was the first Salvadorian president who, in the mid-19th century, saw the potential economic value of coffee, and it is rumoured that he was one of the first to cultivate coffee in El Salvador, on his property in this region, close to Villa de Cacahuatique, now Ciudad Barrios. This mountain range is known for its abundance of clay, used to make pottery. Farmers here often have to dig large holes in the clayey earth and fill them with rich soil, in which to plant their young coffee trees.

Elevation: 500–1,650m (1,600–5,400ft)
Harvest: October–March
Varieties: Bourbon, Pacas and others

Honduras

Given that it is now the largest producer of coffee in Central America, it is surprising how little is known about the introduction of coffee to Honduras. What is probably the earliest record, dated to 1804, discusses the quality of the coffee produced there. This dates the arrival of coffee to before 1799, as the plants would take a few years to produce a crop.

It has only really been since 2001 that Honduras's production of coffee has increased dramatically. While the coffee industry drove the growth and development of infrastructure in much of Central America during the 1800s, due to Honduras's late blossoming the infrastructure simply was not there. This has provided a challenge for quality and has meant that much of the coffee produced under this new expansion was destined for the commodity market. Only more recently have we begun to see excellent coffees coming out of Honduras.

The country's national coffee institute, the Instituto Hondureño del Café (IHCAFE), was established in 1970 and is working to improve quality: in each of the six regions it has defined, there is a coffee-tasting laboratory to assist local producers.

Honduras was producing just under 6 million bags of coffee a year by 2011, more than Costa Rica and Guatemala combined. Around 110,000 families are involved in the production of coffee across the country. As for its future, there are concerns about the impact of leaf rust. A state of national emergency was declared after harvests were badly damaged in 2012/13, with the effects of leaf rust usually lasting a few years. Leaf rust remains a challenge, but now labour shortages are also a growing pressure on producers and are creating something of a ceiling for overall production within the country.

Opposite: Coffee crops are well suited to the soil in Honduras but the country's high rainfall can make it difficult for farmers to dry beans.

> ### Taste Profile
> A range of different flavours are found in Honduran coffees, but the best often have a complex fruity quality and a lively, juicy acidity.

The Problem of Climate

While the land is well suited to growing great coffee, the weather poses a challenge. The high rainfall often makes it difficult to dry the beans after processing, so some producers use a combination of sun drying and mechanical drying. This has landed Honduras with a reputation for producing great coffees that can fade quite quickly, but much work is being done to address this problem. Much of the coffee is warehoused before shipping in extremely hot conditions near Puerto Cortez, which can further degrade it. There are obviously always exceptions to the rule, however, and the very best coffees from Honduras generally hold up better over time.

> ### Classification of Coffee
> Honduras uses a similar system to El Salvador and Guatemala, which describes and categorizes coffees by the elevation at which they were grown. Above 1,200m (3,900ft) a coffee can be described as Strictly High Grown (SHG), and above 1,000m (3,300ft) as High Grown (HG). While there is some correlation between elevation and quality, it is most common to see less traceable lots marketed this way, although more traceable coffees often carry the initials, too.

Traceability

It is possible to get high levels of traceability in Honduras, down to estate level or down to a specific cooperative or producer group.

Growing Regions

Population: 10,430,000

Number of 60kg (132lb) bags in 2023: 5,500,000

Although it is not described by IHCAFE as a coffee-growing region, many roasters label coffee as being from the Santa Barbara region of Honduras. Several coffee regions cross into the Santa Barbara department (a governmental division of the country). Some would argue that it requires its own description, but it seems more appropriate to stay within the official guidelines and use the growing regions listed below. There are some excellent Pacas variety lots coming from the Santa Barbara area. They have a distinctive and quite intense fruity quality when well produced and are worth seeking out.

Honduras holds the title for being highest coffee-producing country per capita in the world.

COPÁN

Copán is a department in the west of Honduras, named after the city of Copán, famous for its Mayan ruins. The region borders Guatemala, and areas like this remind me of the importance of focusing on exactly where a coffee is from rather than simply its country of origin. Geopolitical borders can be somewhat arbitrary, and consumer expectations of a coffee from Honduras and one from Guatemala are (unfortunately) quite a long way apart. Contained within Copán is the northern part of the Santa Barbara coffee region.

Elevation: 1,000–1,700m (3,300–5,600ft)
Harvest: November–March
Varieties: Bourbon, Caturra, Catuai, Pacas, Lempira, IHCAFE-90

MONTECILLOS

This region contains within it several sub-regions of note. The most notable are Marcala, now a protected name, and La Paz. Marcala is a municipality inside the department of La Paz. Roasters are more likely to use these names in order to be more accurate, instead of marking their coffee with the wider regional name of Montecillos.

Elevation: 1,200–1,700m (3,900–5,600ft)
Harvest: December–April
Varieties: Bourbon, Catuai, Pacas, Lempira

Left: Honduran coffee has a reputation for rapid fading, but much work is being done to rectify this.

AGALTA

This region stretches right across the north of Honduras. Much of it is protected forest, so ecotourism plays a significant role in the local economy.

Elevation: 1,000–1,700m (3,300–5,600ft)
Harvest: December–March
Varieties: Bourbon, Caturra, Typica, Lempira

OPALACA

Opalaca contains within it the southern part of the coffee-producing areas of Santa Barbara, as well as Intibucá and Lempira. It is named after the Opalaca mountain range, which stretches through the region.

Elevation: 1,100–1,700m (3,600–5,600ft)
Harvest: November–February
Varieties: Bourbon, Catuai, Lempira, Typica

COMAYAGUA

This region, in western central Honduras, is dense with tropical rainforest. The city of Comayagua in the region was once the capital city of Honduras.

Elevation: 1,200–1,700m (3,900–5,600ft)
Harvest: December–March
Varieties: Bourbon, Catuaí, Lempira, Typica

EL PARAISO

This is one of the oldest and also the largest growing region in Honduras, in the east of the country near the border with Nicaragua. Recently, the region has suffered badly with coffee leaf rust.

Elevation: 1,000–1,400m (3,300–4,600ft)
Harvest: December–March
Varieties: Catuai, Caturra, Pacas, Parainema, Lempira

Nicaragua

Coffee was first brought to Nicaragua by Catholic missionaries in 1790, and initially it was grown as something of a curiosity. It was not until around 1840 that it gained economic significance in response to an increasing global demand for coffee. The first commercial plantations appeared around Managua.

The hundred-year period between 1840 and 1940 is often referred to as the 'Coffee Boom' years in Nicaragua, and during this time coffee had a dramatic effect on the economy. As coffee gained importance and value, so it required the input of more and more resources and labour. By 1870 coffee was Nicaragua's principal export crop, and the government strove to make it easier for foreign companies to invest in the industry and to acquire land. Previously public land was sold to private individuals, and the government encouraged the creation of large farms with the Subsidy Laws in 1879 and 1889, which paid planters $0.05 for every tree they planted over 5,000 trees.

By the end of the 19th century Nicaragua came to resemble something of a banana republic, with most of the profit from coffee either leaving the country or going to a small number of local landowners.

The first growers' cooperative was formed in the early 20th century, and the idea of cooperatives was promoted again from time to time during the Somoza family dictatorship between 1936 and 1979. However, the overthrow of the Somoza family by the Sandinistas, and the ushering in of communism in 1979, was the beginning of a difficult time for the coffee industry. The Contras, rebel groups backed by the United States, especially the CIA, formed to oppose the new government and targeted the coffee industry as part of their campaign, attacking vehicles transporting coffee farm workers, as well as sabotaging coffee mills.

Despite these setbacks, in 1992 coffee was still Nicaragua's primary export. However, the crash in coffee prices between 1999 and 2003 massively damaged the coffee sector again. Three of the largest six banks in the country collapsed due to their level of exposure to coffee production. The effect of low prices was perhaps multiplied further after the devastation of Hurricane Mitch in 1998, and the drought at the turn of the millennium.

Things are now, however, looking up for Nicaraguan coffee, and more farmers are focusing on quality. In the past the traceability of coffee was poor, and most was sold as a mill brand or as being from a particular region. Now the levels of traceability are very high.

Interestingly, there has been a recent expansion of coffee-growing land focused on producing Robusta. This isn't in the traditional coffee-growing regions, but in the south of the country around the town of Nueva Guinea in the South Caribbean Coast Autonomous Region. Production is still relatively small at around 150,000 bags.

Traceability

You should be able to find coffees traceable down to single estates or to producer groups or cooperatives.

Taste Profile

A range of flavours are found in Nicaraguan coffees. They are typically quite complex and capable of pleasing fruit-like flavours and clean acidity.

Growing Regions

Population: 6,948,000

Number of 60kg (132lb) bags in 2023: 2,610,000

Nicaragua has several smaller growing regions, including Madriz, Managua, Boaca and Carazo, which are not listed below but do produce some excellent coffees. Despite the issues caused by leaf rust, producers in Nicaragua have not been as fast to adopt rust-resistant varieties as producers in neighbouring countries. This is, in part, down to a lack of access to them and the financial resources required to make the change.

Above: Nicaragua's favourable climate and fertile soil make perfect for growing quite complex Arabicas.

Opposite: More and more Nicaraguan farmers are working to improve the quality of their beans.

JINOTEGA

The name of the region, and its capital city, is derived from the Nahuatl word xinotencatl, although there is disagreement as to what this means. It is either 'city of old men' or 'neighbours of the Jiñocuabos', the latter probably being the accurate one. The region's economy has long been dependent on coffee, and it is still the primary producing region in Nicaragua, producing around 80 per cent of the country's coffee.

Elevation: 1,100–1,700m (3,600–5,600ft)
Harvest: December–March
Varieties: Caturra, Bourbon

MATAGALPA

Another region named after its capital city, a city with a museum dedicated to coffee. Coffee from this region is produced by a mixture of estates and cooperatives.

Elevation: 1,000–1,400m (3,300–4,600ft)
Harvest: December–February
Varieties: Caturra, Bourbon

NUEVA SEGOVIA

This region is on Nicaragua's northern border, and in recent years it has begun to distinguish itself for producing some of the very best coffees in the country, with a great deal of success in the country's Cup of Excellence competition.

Elevation: 1,100–1,650m (3,600–5,400ft)
Harvest: December–March
Varieties: Caturra, Bourbon

Costa Rica

Coffee has been grown in Costa Rica since the early 19th century. When the country's independence from Spain was declared in 1821, the municipal government gave away free coffee seeds to encourage production, and records show there were around 17,000 trees in Costa Rica at that point.

In 1825 the government continued its promotion of coffee by exempting it from certain taxes, and in 1831 the government decreed that, if anyone grew coffee on fallow land for five years, they could claim ownership of that land.

While a small amount of coffee had been exported to Panama in 1820, the first real exports began in 1832. Although this coffee was ultimately bound for England, it first passed through Chile where it was rebagged and renamed as 'Café Chileno de Valparaíso'.

Direct export to England followed in 1843, not long after the English became increasingly invested in Costa Rica. This ultimately led to the establishment of the Anglo-Costa Rican Bank in 1863, which provided finance to allow the industry to grow.

For nearly 50 years, between 1846 and 1890, coffee was the sole export of the country. Coffee drove infrastructure, such as the creation of the first railroads linking the country to the Atlantic, as well as

Below: Coffee farming has been strongly encouraged by Costa Rica's government, with land ownership being given to anyone willing to grow a crop.

funding the San Juan de Dios Hospital, the first post office and the first government printing office. It would have an impact on culture too, as the Teatro Nacional is a product of the early coffee economy, along with the first libraries in the country and Santo Tomás University.

Costa Rica's coffee infrastructure had long given it an advantage when it came to fetching a better price on the international market. The wet process had been introduced in 1830, and by 1905 there were two hundred wet mills in the country. Washed coffees achieved higher prices, and at this time processing coffee in this way added to its perceived quality.

The coffee industry continued to grow until it began to reach its geographical limits. The population was still spreading from San José to the rest of the country, and farmers were looking for new land upon which to grow crops. However, not all the land in the country was suitable for growing coffee, something that still checks the growth of the industry to date.

It is undeniable that Costa Rican coffee held a good reputation and achieved good prices for its coffees for a very long time, even though the coffees it was producing were typically clean and pleasant rather than interesting or unusual. There was a drive in the later part of the 20th century to move away from heirloom varieties, towards high-yielding varieties. While higher yields make economic sense, many in the speciality coffee industry felt that the cup quality decreased and became even less interesting.

The Government's Role

Right from the start, coffee production was strongly encouraged in Costa Rica, with land being given away to those who wished to grow the crop on it. In 1933 the government, under pressure from the coffee-growing community, created the rather bombastically titled Institute for the Defence of Coffee. Initially, the institute was to play a role in trying to prevent small coffee growers from being exploited by those who bought their coffee cherry cheaply, processed it and sold it for a much greater profit. They did this by setting a limit on the profits that could be made by larger processors.

In 1948 the government body for coffee became the Oficina del Café, though some of the responsibilities for coffee went to the Department of Agriculture. This organization became the Instuto del Café de Costa Rica (ICAFE), which still exists today. ICAFE has a wide-ranging involvement in the coffee industry, running experimental research farms and promoting the quality of Costa Rican coffee worldwide. It is funded by a 1.5 per cent tax on all exports of coffee from Costa Rica.

The Micro-Mill Revolution

Costa Rican coffee had a long-standing reputation for good quality and as such fetched a premium price in the commodity marketplace. What it lacked, as the speciality coffee market developed, was much in the way of traceable coffee. Typically, coffees exported from Costa Rica around the turn of the millennium carried marks that were essentially brands created by the large mills, or beneficios. These brands obscured exactly where the coffee had been grown and the unique terroir, or qualities, that it may possess. There was little in the processing chain to keep the individual lots distinct.

In the mid- to late 2000s, however, there was a dramatic increase in micro-mills. Farmers were investing in small-scale post-harvest equipment of their own and doing more of the processing themselves. This meant they were able to increase control over their coffee and the diversity of styles and coffees from all regions of Costa Rica dramatically increased. In the past a unique and unusual coffee would have been blended in with coffees of neighbouring farms, but not any longer.

This makes Costa Rican coffees exciting to explore, as it is now easier than ever to taste several different

Left: Costa Rica's rapidly growing tourist trade has encouraged tours of coffee farms. Some, like Finca Rosa Blanca Coffee Farm & Inn in Santa Bárbara de Heredia, are adopting organic farming methods.

Opposite: On many farms in Costa Rica, workers' profits depend on the percentage and size of ripe fruits picked.

coffees from a particular area side by side and begin to see the effect geography can have on taste. Recently, Costa Rican speciality coffees have become synonymous with the honey process (see page 39), as well as more unusual varieties such as Gesha or SL-28 starting to appear. The wider industry has struggled to grow its production, struggling with the challenges of weather patterns changing as well as labour shortages.

Coffee and Tourism

Costa Rica is the most developed, and is considered the safest, of the Central American countries. This makes it an incredibly popular tourist destination, especially with North Americans. Tourism has come not only to displace coffee as the primary source of income from abroad but also to collide and combine with it. Ecotourism is particularly popular in Costa Rica, and it is possible to visit and take tours of many coffee farms in the country. Typically, those offering tours are the larger farms, with less focus on absolute quality, but it is nonetheless interesting to have the opportunity to see how coffee farming works up close.

Traceability

Currently land ownership is extremely common in Costa Rica, with 90 per cent of coffee producers there owning small to medium-sized farms. As such it is possible to find coffees traceable to an individual farm or a particular cooperative.

Taste profile

Costa Rican coffees are typically very clean and sweet, though often very light bodied when washed, but many honey-processed coffees can be very fruity and a little fermented. Micro-mills are producing a wider range of flavours and styles.

Growing Regions

Population: 5,181,000

Number of 60kg (132lb) bags in 2023: 1,100,000

Costa Rica has been successful in the past in marketing its coffees under the names of the regions that produce them. However, there is a wide diversity of flavours within each region, so it is well worth exploring each of the different regions to see what they can produce.

CENTRAL VALLEY

With the Costa Rican capital city of San José located here, this is the most heavily populated region in the country, and the one that has been growing coffee for the longest. It is typically divided into the sub-regions of San José, Heredia and Alajuela. There are three key active volcanoes in the area – Irazú, Barva and Poás – which affect the topography and the soil.

Elevation: 800–1,600m (2,600–5,200ft)
Harvest: November–March

WEST VALLEY

The first farmers settled in the West Valley region during the 19th century and brought coffee with them. The region is divided into six sub-regions, centred around the cities of San Ramón, Palmares, Naranjo, Grecia, Sarchí and Atenas. The city of Sarchí lends its name to a specific coffee variety called Villa Sarchí. The highest elevations in the region are found around Naranjo, and some stunning coffees can be found in this area.

Elevation: 750–1,700m (2,500–5,600ft)
Harvest: November–February
Varieties: Caturra, Catuai.

Above: In the late 20th century, many farmers moved away from heirloom varieties, and those in the speciality coffee industry feel quality has decreased.

LOS SANTOS/TARRAZÚ

The region of Tarrazú has a long-standing reputation for quality, and for years the coffee from here could almost have been considered a high-quality grade. That coffee was probably just a mill grade collected from different farms and blended together to create a large lot. However, the brand of Tarrazú gained sufficient strength over the years that coffee from outside the region was being marketed as Tarrazú to increase its value. However, Costa Rica's coffee board – ICAFE – now uses the name Los Santos for the region. The highest coffee farms in the country are in this region and, like many of the other regions, it benefits from a distinct dry season during harvest.

Elevation: 800–1,900m (2,600–6,200ft)
Harvest: November–March
Varieties: Caturra, Catuai

TRES RÍOS

A small region just to the east of San José, Tres Ríos also benefits from the effects of the Irazú volcano. This area was considered relatively remote until recently, but now the greatest challenge to the coffee-growing industry is no longer gaining access to power or infrastructure, but the threat from urban development. More land is required for housing, and Tres Ríos is producing less and less coffee each year, as land is sold for property development.

Elevation: 1,200–1,650m (3,900–5,400ft)
Harvest: August–February

OROSI

Another small region but farther east from San José, Orosi has over a century of coffee production in its history. The region is essentially a long valley, compromising the three sub-regions of Orosi, Cachí and Paraíso.

Elevation: 1,000–1,400m (3,300–4,600ft)
Harvest: August–February; Cachí: October–February

BRUNCA

The region of Brunca is split into two cantons: Coto Brus, which borders Panama, and Pérez Zeledón. Of the two, Coto Brus depends more on coffee as an integral part of its economy. Italian settlers arrived here after World War II and, with Costa Ricans, started coffee farms in the area. Pérez Zeledón's coffee was first planted and produced by settlers from the Central Valley region of the country towards the end of the 19th century.

Elevation: 900–1,700m (3,000–5,600ft)
Harvest: September–February
Varieties: Caturra, Catuai

TURRIALBA

The harvest in this region is earlier than most, due to the weather and particularly the rainfall in the area. With less defined wet and dry seasons, it isn't unusual to see multiple flowerings on coffee trees here. The weather may present something of a challenge for coffee production, as coffees of very high quality are relatively scarce.

Elevation: 500–1,400m (1,600–4,600ft)
Harvest: June–February

GUANACASTE

This western region is large but there are only relatively small areas of it under coffee. The area is more dependent on beef ranching and rice than on coffee. There is still a sizeable production, though much of it is grown at lower elevations making stunning coffees less common here.

Elevation: 600–1,300m (2,000–4,300ft)
Harvest: July–February

Panama

Coffee plants probably arrived in Panama with the first European settlers in the early 19th century. In the past Panama did not have a very good reputation for its coffees, and its production was about one-tenth of that of its neighbour Costa Rica, but now there is increasing interest from the speciality coffee community in the high-quality coffees it can produce.

Panama's geography is such that there are several distinct microclimates in its coffee-growing regions, and there are some incredibly skilled and dedicated producers currently growing coffee. This means that there are some stellar coffees being produced, although these often come with relatively high asking prices.

These high prices are partly determined by the other major factor influencing the industry there: real estate. There is a high demand for land from North Americans wishing to buy a home in a stable, beautiful and relatively cheap country. Many farms that once produced coffee have now been sold as homes for ex-pats. Panama also has a higher standard of labour laws, so coffee pickers tend to be paid a higher wage here, a cost that is passed on to the consumer.

Hacienda La Esmeralda

When it comes to discussing the price of coffee, one farm in Panama merits a mention and it is hard to think of another single estate that has had such a strong influence on the coffee industry in Central America. That farm is Hacienda La Esmeralda, owned and operated by the Peterson family.

At a time when the commodity price of coffee was relatively low, the Speciality Coffee Association of Panama organized a competition called the Best of Panama: the best lots of coffee from different farms in

Opposite: The distinctive Gesha variety is commonly associated with crops from Panama. Its floral, citrusy flavour and efforts by local farmers to maintain high quality has created a growing demand.

254 Coffee Origins

Panama were ranked and then put up for an online auction. Hacienda La Esmeralda had been growing a distinct variety called Gesha (see page 25) for some years, but this competition brought their coffee to a wider audience. They won the competition for four successive years from 2004 to 2007, and then again in 2009 and 2010 as well as a category of the 2013 competition. From the outset this coffee broke records when it achieved a price of $21/lb in 2004, which incrementally crept up to $170/lb in 2010. A small lot of its naturally processed coffee sold for $350.25/lb in 2013, leaving no one in doubt that this was the most expensive single-estate coffee in the world.

Unlike some other very high-priced coffees (such as the appalling novelty-driven Kopi Luwak, or some of the Jamaica Blue Mountain coffees), this farm achieved its prices due to the genuinely high quality of its coffee, although high demand and great marketing undoubtedly played a role. This record-breaking coffee tastes quite unusual: extremely floral and citrusy though quite light and tea-like in body. These characteristics are attributed to the Gesha variety.

The impact of this farm can be seen in the number of farms in Panama, and in Central America, that have started planting Gesha. For many producers this variety seemed like a promise of higher prices, and to some extent this has proven to be true, as Gesha lots are usually sold for higher prices than other varieties.

Traceability

One should expect high levels of traceability from Panama. Coffees are often traceable down to a single estate, and it is not unusual to see distinct lots from one particular estate, such as a coffee produced by a distinctive post-harvest process or one from a specific variety of the coffee plant. Alongside Colombia, this is an origin that you can expect to find a wide array of experimental processes, and unusual varieties.

Taste Profile
The better coffees tend to be citrusy and floral, light-bodied, delicate and complex.

Growing Regions

Population: 4,409,000

Number of 60kg (132lb) bags in 2013: 75,000

Panama's regions have been defined more by how coffee has been sold than by geography. Previously, when coffee production was more widespread, the regions listed below could have been grouped as one entity, as they are small and closely clustered together. Much of the production is geographically around three volcanoes: Volcán Baru, El Valle and Le Yeguada. Coffee does grow in lower-elevation regions, too, where it harvests a little later, running from November to February.

BOQUETE

This is the best known of Panama's producing regions. Its mountainous topography produces various distinct microclimates. The fairly cool weather and frequent mists help slow the maturation of the coffee cherries, and some argue this mimics the effects of higher elevation.

Elevation: 600–2,300m (2,000–7,500ft)
Harvest: September–February
Varieties: Typica, Caturra, Catuai, Bourbon, Gesha, San Ramón

VOLCÁN-CANDELA

This region produces much of Panama's food, and some stunning coffees. Named after the Volcán Baru volcano and the city of Piedra Candela, the region borders Costa Rica.

Elevation: 1,200–1,600m (3,900–5,200ft)
Harvest: September–February
Varieties: Typica, Caturra, Catuai, Bourbon, Gesha, San Ramón

RENACIMIENTO

Another district within the Chiriquí Province, on the border with Costa Rica. The district itself is relatively small, so it is not a primary producer of Panama's speciality coffees.

Elevation: 1,100–1,500m (3,600–4,900ft)
Harvest: September–February
Varieties: Typica, Caturra, Catuai, Bourbon, Gesha, San Ramón

Left: The area around this coffee farm in Monte Lirio, near Piedra Candela, Chiriqí Province, produces much of Panama's food as well as some excellent coffees.

Venezuela

The introduction of coffee to Venezuela is generally credited to a Jesuit priest named José Gumilla in around 1730. Venezuela came to be known for its plantations of tobacco and cacao run on slave labour, and from around 1793 there is evidence of large coffee plantations, too.

From around 1800 coffee took an increasingly important role in the country's economy. During the Venezuelan War of Independence, from 1811 to 1823, cacao production began to drop but coffee production surged. The first boom in the country's coffee industry took place between 1830 and 1855, when Venezuela produced around one-third of the world's coffee. Coffee continued to grow in production, peaking in 1919 with a total export of 1.37 million bags. Together, coffee and cacao accounted for 75 per cent of the country's entire export revenue. Most of the coffee went to the United States.

In the 1920s Venezuela's economy became increasingly dependent on petroleum, although coffee remained a good source of revenue. Much of the revenue was spent on national infrastructure, until the prices dropped in the 1930s and the production and processing infrastructure suffered as a consequence. This period also saw a shift towards privatization in the coffee industry, stripping peasants of much of their power to grow their own coffee on public land.

Since this period the nation has been fundamentally dependent on petroleum products and other mineral exports. Coffee production and exports had remained relatively high, with Venezuela nearly matching the production of Colombia, but that changed under the government of Hugo Chávez. In 2003 the government introduced strict regulations on coffee production, which meant the country increasingly had to rely on imports for domestic consumption, mostly from Nicaragua and Brazil. Venezuela exported 479,000 bags of coffee in 1992/93, and this dropped again to 19,000 in 2009/10. Government-fixed sales prices have been considerably below the cost of production, which has inevitably damaged the industry. At the present time, production does not meet the demand for coffee in the country, and Venezuela is a net importer of coffee. Most of this is coming from Brazil and Colombia. There is a growing speciality coffee scene in the country, despite the challenges it faces, and this is likely where you can taste the best coffees produced in Venezuela.

Traceability

As so little coffee is exported from the country, coming across Venezuelan coffees of quality is rare. While some should be traceable down to single estates, it is more common to see coffees described by their region names. Generally speaking, the low elevation and lack of focus on cup quality means I would recommend trying Venezuelan coffees only if they are being provided by a roaster whose coffees you generally enjoy and whom you trust.

Taste Profile

The better coffees from Venezuela are quite sweet, a little low in acidity and relatively rich in terms of mouthfeel and texture.

Growing Regions

Population: 28,300,000

Number of 60kg (132lb) bags in 2023: 500,000

Coffees from Venezuela are currently quite rare to see as traceable lots, despite the relatively large production coming from the country. There are hopes that this may change in the future, but it seems unlikely in the short term.

WESTERN REGION

This region produces a large percentage of the country's coffee. It is easier to find export grades marked with the name of the state in which they were produced, such as Táchira, Mérida or Zulia, rather than the region. Some people make comparisons between coffees from this region and those from neighbouring Colombia.

Elevation: 1,000–1,200m (3,300–3,900ft)
Harvest: September–March
Varieties: Typica, Bourbon, Mundo Novo, Caturra

WEST CENTRAL REGION

This region contains the states of Portuguesa and Lara, some of the primary coffee-producing regions in the country, as well as Falcón and Yaracuy. The best coffees are considered to come from this region, relatively close to the Colombian border. These coffees are commonly referred to as Maracaibos, named for the port from which they are exported.

Elevation: 1,000–1,200m (3,300–3,900ft)
Harvest: September–March
Varieties: Typica, Bourbon, Mundo Novo, Caturra

Above: A farmer on his organic coffee farm in the coastal area of Caracaya on the outskirts of Caracas.

Opposite: Workers load coffee beans into hessian sacks in a coffee cooperative warehouse in Lara State.

NORTH CENTRAL REGION

A small amount of Venezuela's production comes from the states of Aragua, Carabobo, the Federal Dependencies, Miranda, Cojedes and Guárico in this region.

Elevation: 1,000–1,200m (3,300–3,900ft)
Harvest: September–March
Varieties: Typica, Bourbon, Mundo Novo, Caturra

EASTERN REGION

This region is home to the states of Sucre, Monagas, Anzoátegui and Bolívar. It is sometimes possible to find a type of coffee called Caracas produced in this region.

Elevation: 1,000–1,200m (3,300–3,900ft)
Harvest: September–March
Varieties: Typica, Bourbon, Mundo Novo, Caturra

Colombia

Coffee was probably first introduced to Colombia in 1723 by the Jesuits, although there are inevitably different accounts. It spread slowly as a commercial crop to various regions of the country, but its production did not become significant until the end of the 19th century. By 1912 coffee made up approximately 50 per cent of Colombia's total exports.

Colombia recognized the value of marketing and building its brand relatively early on. The creation in 1958 of Juan Valdez, the farmer who represents Colombian coffee, was perhaps their greatest success. Juan Valdez and his mule were created as the symbol of Colombian coffee and appeared on bags of coffee and also in various advertising campaigns, portrayed by three different actors over the years. Juan Valdez became a point of recognition, particularly in the United States, and added value to Colombian coffee. The character built on the success of early marketing phrases such as 'Mountain Grown Coffee', and the constant promotion of '100% Colombian Coffee' meant that Colombia would stand apart in the minds of consumers across the world.

This marketing was, and continues to be, undertaken by the Federación Nacional de Cafeteros (FNC). This organization, created in 1927, is particularly unusual in the coffee-producing world. While many countries have organizations involved in the export and promotion of their coffee, few are quite as large and complex as the FNC. It was created as a private non-profit organization to defend the interests of coffee producers and is funded through a special tax on all coffee exported. As Colombia is one of the largest coffee producers in the world, the FNC is well funded and has become something of a monstrous, bureaucratic organization. This bureaucracy is perhaps inevitable as the FNC is now technically owned and controlled by its 500,000 coffee-producing members. While the FNC is involved in the more obvious roles of marketing and production and in some financial matters, its reach goes deeper into coffee-growing communities, and it has a hand in the creation of both social and physical infrastructure including rural roads, schools and health centres. It has also invested in other industries besides coffee to help spur on regional development and wellbeing.

Colombia was badly impacted by the leaf rust epidemic that ran from 2008 until 2011. These years saw a drop in production of up to 30 per cent compared to 2007. This resulted in a big push to plant more resistant varieties, such as Castillo. This has now happened,

260   Coffee Origins

Above: Colombian coffee trees produce two harvests each year, the main harvest and the mitaca harvest. The resulting coffees cover a wide range of flavour profiles, from heavy and chocolatey to sweet and jammy.

with the vast majority of coffee planted in Colombia being an FNC-produced, resistant tree. One notable downside of these plants is their shorter lifespan, often up to a decade in length rather than the much longer lifespan of plants like Typica that can be productive for up to 30 years. This means more work on plant renewal on these farms.

Consumption inside Colombia has continued to grow, although Colombia tends to import coffee from neighbouring countries, rather than consume coffee that's purely locally grown – likely due to Colombian coffees being able to fetch a higher export price. There is a thriving speciality coffee scene in the cities in Colombia, serving coffee as good as you will get anywhere in the world.

The FNC and quality

There has been some friction between the FNC and the more quality-conscious section of the industry, as the FNC's perceived interests of the farmers may not always lead to the best possible quality in the coffee.

Taste profile

Colombian coffees have a huge range of flavours, from the heavier, chocolatier coffees through to jammy, sweet, fruity lots. A huge spectrum of flavours exists across the regions. A great many methods of experimental processing also seem to be coming out of Colombia, and these widen the spectrum of flavours quite dramatically.

The FNC has a research division called Cenicafé which breeds specific varieties, and many believe the promotion of varieties like Castillo has favoured quantity of yield above cup quality. It is possible to see both sides of the argument, and as global climate change has an increasing impact on the stability of Colombia's production, it is increasingly difficult to argue against varieties that ensure livelihoods for producers, even at the expense of losing some great cups of coffee.

Traceability

As part of the promotion of Colombian coffee, the FNC created the terms 'Supremo' and 'Excelso'. These terms relate only to the size of the bean, and it is important to understand that they have no relation to quality. Unfortunately, this classification obscures any traceability, as coffee marketed this way may come from many, many farms and be blended before being sieved mechanically to the necessary sizing grade. Essentially, this is generic coffee, and its naming offers no help when trying to buy quality. It is less commonly used than it once was, and the speciality coffee industry has been working to maintain traceability, so when looking for something incredibly enjoyable, make sure the beans come from a distinct place, rather than just being a certain size.

Growing regions

Population: 51,870,000

Number of 60kg (132lb) bags in 2023: 11,200,000

Colombia has well-defined growing regions, and they produce an impressive variety of coffees. Whether you want rounder, heavier coffees or something vibrant and fruity (or something in between), there is probably a coffee in Colombia that fits the bill. The regions are geographically defined, rather than politically, so it is not unusual to find that there are common traits to the coffees produced in each region. If you enjoy one coffee from a region, you will probably enjoy many of the others.

The coffee trees in Colombia yield two harvests each year, the main harvest and the second harvest, known locally as the mitaca harvest.

CAUCA

This area was perhaps the first to start growing coffee in Colombia. It is best known for its coffees grown around Inza and the city of Popayán. The Meseta de Popayán is a high plateau with attractive growing conditions provided by higher elevations, its proximity to the equator, and the surrounding mountains, which protect the coffee against the humidity of the Pacific and the trade winds from the south. The result is a very stable climate year-round, and the region has notable volcanic soil, too. Historically, there has been a predictable, single rainy season each year in October to December.

Elevation: 1,200–2,100m (3,900–6,900ft)
Harvest: March–June (main crop); November–December (mitaca crop)
Varieties: 79% resistant varieties (Castillo, Colombia); the remainder mostly Typica and Caturra

VALLE DEL CAUCA

The Cauca valley is one of the most fertile parts of the country, with the Cauca River running down between two large Andean mountain ranges. The area was one of the epicentres of the Colombian armed conflict that began in 1964. Typical of Colombia, most farms are pretty small, and the area has around 75,800 hectares (187,300 acres) under coffee production, split between 26,000 farms owned by 23,000 families.

Elevation: 1,450–2,000m (4,750–6,600ft)
Harvest: September–December (main crop); March–June (mitaca crop)
Varieties: 73% resistant varieties (Castillo, Colombia); the remainder mostly Typica and Caturra

TOLIMA

Tolima is now the third-largest producing region in Colombia. Quality coffees from this area tend to come from small farmers in very small micro-lots via cooperatives.

Elevation: 1,200–1,900m (3,900–6,200ft)
Harvest: March–June (main crop); October–December (mitaca crop)
Varieties: 74% resistant varieties (Castillo, Colombia); the remainder mostly Typica and Caturra

HUILA

The department of Huila has a combination of great soil and great geography for growing coffee, and some of the most complex, fruit-driven Colombian coffees I have tasted have come from here. The region has more than 70,000 coffee growers, covering more than 16,000 hectares (39,500 acres) of land. The mitaca crop is perhaps a little larger in this region, with a 60:40 ratio between main crop and the mitaca.

Elevation: 1,250–2,000m (4,100–6,600ft)
Harvest: October–December (main crop); May–July (mitaca crop)
Varieties: 65.5% resistant varieties (Castillo, Colombia); the remainder mostly Typica and Caturra

QUINDÍO

Quindío is a small region in the centre of the country, just to the west of Bogotá. Coffee is an incredibly important part of the economy here, as the region suffers high levels of unemployment. However, the risks involved in growing coffee, due to the effects of climate change and the increased incidences of diseases affecting coffee plants, has led many farmers to grow citrus fruits and macadamia nuts instead.

Quindío is home to the National Coffee Park, a theme park based around coffee and coffee production that was opened in 1995. At the end of June each year, the municipality of Calarcá has, since 1960, hosted the National Coffee Party. This is a day of celebration around coffee, including a national beauty contest of coffee. The ratio between the main and mitaca crops is 53:47, respectively.

Elevation: 1,400–2,000m (4,600–6,600ft)
Harvest: September–December (main crop); March–May (mitaca crop)
Varieties: 66% resistant varieties (Castillo, Colombia); the remainder mostly Typica and Caturra

RISARALDA

This is another well-established coffee-producing region, and here a large number of farmers belong to cooperatives. As a result, there has been some interest from ethical labelling organizations. Coffee plays an important social and economic role in the area, providing jobs and employment to many. While many people moved to the region in the 1920s, often to grow coffee, the recession at the turn of the millennium saw some wide-scale emigration back to other regions and other countries. The capital city is also a transport hub for the regions of Caldas and Quindío, and the interdepartmental road network is known as the Autopista del Café (Coffee Highway).

Elevation: 1,100–1,900m (3,600–6,200ft)
Harvest: September–December (main crop); March–May (mitaca crop)
Varieties: 82% resistant varieties (Castillo, Colombia); the remainder Caturra and Typica.

NARIÑO

Some of the highest coffees in Colombia are grown in Nariño, and they can also be some of the most stunning and complex. It is challenging to grow coffee at these high elevations in many areas, as the plants suffer from dieback. However, Nariño is close enough to the equator that the climate is sufficiently suitable for coffee plants.

The vast majority of Nariño's 40,000 producers are smallholders with fewer than 2 hectares (4.4 acres) each. Many have formed groups and institutions to provide each other with support and to interact with the FNC. In fact, the average farm size is less than 1 hectare (2.2 acres), and only 37 producers in the region own more than 5 hectares (11 acres) of land. Ninety per cent of the production comes from the main crop, with a very small second crop.

Elevation: 1,300–2,300m (4,300–7,500ft)
Harvest: March–May (main crop); September–December (mitaca crop)
Varieties: 77% resistant varieties (Castillo, Colombia); the remainder mostly Typica and Caturra

CALDAS

Along with Quindío and Risaralda, the state of Caldas is part of the Colombian Coffee-Growing Axis, or Coffee Triangle. Between them they grow a large portion of the nation's coffee. Historically, this was considered some of the best coffee in Colombia, but now other regions are more competitive on that front.

The region is also home to Cenicafé, the National Coffee Research Centre run by the FNC. It is considered to be one of the world's leading institutions for research into all aspects of coffee production, and it is here that a number of varieties unique to Colombia (such as the disease-resistant Colombia and Castillo varieties) have been created. It is also home to the Manuel Mejía Foundation, the academic arm of the FNC.

Elevation: 1,100–1,900m (3,600–6,200ft)
Harvest: September–December (main crop); March–May (mitaca crop)
Varieties: 83% resistant varieties (Castillo, Colombia); the remainder mostly Typica and Caturra

ANTIOQUIA

This department is the birthplace of both coffee in Colombia and the FNC. This is a key growing region with around 128,000 hectares (316,000 acres) of coffee, the most of any region. The coffee is produced by a mixture of large estates and cooperatives made up of small producers.

Elevation: 1,000–2,100m (3,300–6,000ft)
Harvest: September–December (main crop); April–May (mitaca crop)
Varieties: 89% resistant varieties (Castillo, Colombia); the remainder mostly Typica and Caturra

CUNDINAMARCA

This department surrounds the capital city of Bogotá, one of the highest capital cities in the world at 2,625m (8,612ft) above sea level, higher than coffee would grow. This was the second region in Colombia to produce coffee for export, with its production peaking just before World War II. At that time Cundinamarca produced about 10 per cent of the nation's coffee, but the percentage has since declined. In the past this region had some very large estates, some with over 1 million coffee trees.

Elevation: 1,100–1,900m (3,600–6,200ft)
Harvest (northern regions): September–December (main crop); April–May (mitaca crop)
Harvest (southern regions): March–June (main crop); October–November (mitaca crop)
Varieties: 78% resistant varieties (Castillo, Colombia); the remainder mostly Typica and Caturra

SANTANDER

This was one of the first regions in Colombia to produce coffee for export. The region has a little less elevation than some of the others, and this can often be detected in the coffees as they veer more towards round and sweet, rather than juicy and complex. A great deal of coffee from this region is certified by the Rainforest Alliance, and the biodiversity of the region is considered very important.

Elevation: 1,200–1,700m (3,900–5,600ft)
Harvest: September–December; some regions have a mitaca crop between April and June
Varieties: 95% resistant varieties (Castillo, Colombia); the remainder mostly Typica and Caturra

NORTH SANTANDER

In the north of the country, bordering Venezuela, this region was producing coffee very early on. Coffee's roots in Colombia may be traced back to a single Christian minister named Francisco Romero, born in 1810, who made the planting of coffee trees part of penance for his parishioners.

Elevation: 1,000–1,900m (3,300–6,200ft)
Harvest: September–December (main crop); March–May (mitaca crop)
Varieties: 70% resistant varieties (Castillo, Colombia); the remainder mostly Typica and Caturra

SIERRA NEVADA/MAGDALENA

This is another region at lower elevations, and again the coffees here tend to be heavier and rounder, rather than more elegant and lively. Coffee is grown on the Andean mountains in this area, and the incredibly steep hillsides (ranging from 50 to 80 degrees) offer a particular challenge to the farmers. Sierra Nevada, a geographic name found in many Spanish-speaking countries, translates as 'snow-topped mountains'.

Elevation: 800–1,600m (2,600–5,200ft)
Harvest: October–January
Varieties: 58% resistant varieties (Castillo, Colombia); the remainder mostly Typica and Caturra

Left: A worker harvests coffee at a farm in Ciudad Bolivar, Antioquia department, Colombia.

Ecuador

Coffee came relatively late to Ecuador, arriving in around 1860 in the province of Manabí. Coffee production spread throughout the country, and by around 1905 exports to Europe began from the port of Manta. Ecuador is one of the relatively few countries in the Americas to grow both Arabica and Robusta coffee.

After disease ravaged much of the cocoa crop in the 1920s, many farmers began to focus on coffee. Exports began to grow from 1935, and what was 220,000 bags then became around 1.8 million bags by 1985. The world coffee crisis of the 1990s caused an inevitable drop in production, but by 2011 production was back to around 1 million bags per year. Until the 1970s coffee had been Ecuador's main export crop, but it was later replaced by oil, shrimps and bananas.

Ecuadorians consume more soluble coffee than they do fresh, and, interestingly, the cost of coffee production in Ecuador is high enough that soluble coffee manufacturers there import coffee from Vietnam instead of buying it in Ecuador.

Ecuador does not hold a great reputation for quality coffee. In part this is because 40 per cent of its production is Robusta, but still most of Ecuador's exported coffee is relatively low quality. To keep production costs down, much of the crop is dried either on the tree before picking, or on patios, and the term to describe this natural process locally is *café en bola*. This coffee generally ends up in soluble coffee, and around 83 per cent of the country's export has been naturally processed. Colombia is one of the main importers because manufacturers of soluble coffee there will pay a better price than local ones. This is because Colombian coffee is expensive due to the strength of the national brand in foreign markets.

While coffee has been produced in Ecuador for a long time, there are those who feel that it is only now worth considering coffee from this country as a hidden gem full of potential. There is certainly the geography and climate to produce extraordinary coffees in the country, and it will be interesting to see whether investment from the speciality coffee industry results in some great new coffees hailing from Ecuador in the future.

Traceability

It is rare to find coffee traceable down to a single estate. It is more common to see a lot from a group of producers, or sometimes a lot can be put together by an exporter. Lots like this can come from a large number of farmers but may still be excellent.

Left: While much of the Ecuadorian harvest is processed naturally – a method known locally as *café en bola* – some coffee is mechanically depulped before being dried.

Taste profile

Coffees from Ecuador are beginning to live up to their potential for quality, with sweeter and more complex coffees becoming available. They are made more interesting by a pleasant acidity. The rise of the Sidra variety (see page 26) in particular has rightly brought some additional focus and interest to the coffees grown there.

Growing regions

Population: 17,483,326
Number of 60kg (132lb) bags in 2023: 354,000

Ecuadorean coffees are coming to increasing prominence within the speciality coffee industry, and while lower-lying regions are less likely to produce great coffees, the higher elevation areas hold great potential.

MANABI

Nearly 50 per cent of the Arabica in Ecuador is produced here. But with almost all the coffee in this region growing below 700m (2,300ft), this area does not have the necessary elevation to produce excellent coffees.

Elevation: 500–700m (1,600–2,300ft)
Harvest: April–October
Varieties: Typica, Caturra, Robusta

Above: The high altitudes of Ecuadorian Andes offer great potential for some interesting coffees in the years to come.

LOJA

Around 20 per cent of the Arabica in the country comes from this mountainous region in the south, and from a geographical perspective this region has the greatest potential for quality. Most of the focus from the speciality coffee sector is here. However, the area is susceptible to difficult weather which can, as happened in 2010, result in an increase in damage from coffee berry borer.

Elevation: up to 2,100m (6,900ft)
Harvest: June–September
Varieties: Caturra, Bourbon, Typica

EL ORO

This coastal region in the south-west of the country includes part of the Andes mountain chain and produces less than 10 per cent of Ecuador's annual coffee production. The main focus on coffee is around the town of Zaruma (not to be confused with the region of Zamora).

Elevation: 1,200m (3,900ft)
Harvest: May–August
Varieties: Typica, Caturra, Bourbon

ZAMORA CHINCHIPE

This province is just to the east of Loja and has sufficient elevation to produce great coffee, although only 4 per cent of the country's Arabica is produced here. Organic production is relatively common in this area.

Elevation: up to 1,900m (6,200ft)
Harvest: May–August
Varieties: Typica, Caturra, Bourbon

GALAPAGOS

A small amount of coffee is produced on the Galapagos Islands, and its proponents claim that the climate there mimics a much higher elevation, allowing higher-quality coffee to be grown. Coffees like this can be extremely expensive, and rarely does the quality in the cup match the price.

Elevation: 350m (1,100ft)
Harvest: June–September and December–February
Varieties: Bourbon

Peru

Coffee was first brought to Peru between 1740 and 1760, at a time when the Viceroyalty of Peru covered a larger area than the country does today. Although the climate was well suited to large-scale coffee production, all coffee grown in the first hundred years or so was consumed locally. The first exports of coffee, to Germany and England, did not begin until 1887.

In the 1900s the Peruvian government defaulted on a loan from the British government and ended up giving them 2 million hectares (5 million acres) of land in Central Peru as repayment. One-quarter of this land was turned over to plantations, growing crops, which included coffee. Migrant workers from the highlands came to work on these farms, and some ended up owning some land themselves. Others would later buy land from the British when they left Peru.

Unfortunately for the coffee industry, Juan Velasco's government brought in laws in the 1970s that would cripple growth. The International Coffee Agreement had guaranteed sales and prices, so there had been little incentive to create proper infrastructure. When state support was withdrawn, the coffee industry sunk into disarray. The quality of the coffee and Peru's market position further suffered at the hands of the Communist Party of Peru – known as the Shining Path – whose guerrilla activities destroyed crops and drove farmers from their land.

The vacuum left in Peru's coffee industry has recently been filled by non-government organizations such as Fairtrade International, and now a large quantity of coffee from Peru is Fair Trade certified. Peru is now the largest producer of organic-certified Arabica. More and more land is also being devoted to coffee: in 1980 there were 62,000 hectares (154,000 acres); today there are 375,000 hectares (680,00 acres) under coffee. Peru is now one of the largest producers of coffee in the world.

The infrastructure within Peru still stands in the way of the country producing extremely high-quality lots. Few mills are situated close to farms, which means that the coffee is often travelling longer than is desirable after harvest before processing starts. Some coffees end up being bought and blended with other coffees, then resold en route to the coast for export. Interestingly, around one-quarter of the 100,000 small producers in the country are now members of cooperatives, although it is important to remember that Fairtrade certification can only apply to coffee produced by a cooperative.

Due to the widespread cultivation of the Typica variety, leaf rust is increasingly a problem for Peruvian producers. From

2013 there have been several instances of severe leaf rust, as well as an issue with coffee berry borer in 2020, although this mostly impacted lower elevations of coffee farming. However, producers haven't moved to rust-resistant varieties, with 70 per cent of the coffee being Typica, and some 20 per cent Caturra.

Domestic consumption in the country is still very low, less than a kilo per capita, except for younger adults who drink a little more. Most of the coffee consumed in Peru is instant coffee, and that coffee is often imported from Brazil and Colombia.

> ### Taste profile
> Typically, Peruvian coffees have been clean, but a little soft and flat. They are sweet and relatively heavy bodied but not very complex. Increasingly, there are distinctive and juicier coffees becoming available.

Traceability
The best coffees should be traceable down to a producer group or down to a single estate.

Growing regions

Population: 34,050,000
Number of 60kg (132lb) bags in 2023: 4,000,000

Some coffee is grown outside the main regions listed below, but not in the same quantities and without the same level of recognition. Some might argue that Peru is well placed to deal with the increased temperatures that may come with climate change, as it has plenty of land at higher elevations that may become suitable for growing coffee in the future.

CAJAMARCA
Cajamarca is a state in the north of the country named for its capital city and covers the northern end of the Peruvian Andes. The region benefits from an equatorial climate and soils suitable for coffee. Most producers in the region are smallholders, although they are often well organized and belong to producers' organizations, which supply technical help, training, loans, community development and other support. One of these organizations in the region, CENFROCAFE, works with 1,900 families to promote coffee roasting and runs a local café to help the farmers diversify. Around half of the production from Peru comes from the Cajamarca region.

Elevation: 900–2,050m (3,000–6,750ft)
Harvest: March–September
Varieties: Bourbon, Typica, Caturra, Pache, Mondo Novo, Catuai, Catimor

JUNIN
This region produces 20–25 per cent of Peru's coffee, and here the coffee grows in among the rainforest. The area did suffer in the 1980s and 1990s as a result of guerrilla activity, and the neglect of the trees during this period allowed plant diseases to spread. The coffee industry had to be restarted from almost nothing in the late 1990s.

Elevation: 1,400–1,900m (4,600–6,200ft)
Harvest: March–September
Varieties: Bourbon, Typica, Caturra, Pache, Mondo Novo, Catuai, Catimor

CUSCO
Cusco is a region in the south of the country where coffee, in some ways, is the legal alternative to the other popular crop in this area: coca. Most of the coffee is grown by smallholders, rather than larger estates. The area thrives on tourism, and many visitors travel through the city of Cusco on their way to see the Inca citadel of Machu Picchu.

Elevation: 1,200–1,900m (3,900–6,200ft)
Harvest: March–September
Varieties: Bourbon, Typica, Caturra, Pache, Mondo Novo, Catuai, Catimor

SAN MARTÍN
This region is on the eastern side of the Andes, and many farmers produce coffee on plots 5–10 hectares (10–24 acres) in size. In the past this was the main area of coca production in Peru, although cooperatives in the region now promote the idea of diversification by growing other crops alongside coffee, such as cacao and honey. In recent years the level of poverty in the region has dropped dramatically, from 70 per cent down to 31 per cent of the population.

Elevation: 1,100–2,000m (3,600–6,600ft)
Harvest: March–September
Varieties: Bourbon, Typica, Caturra, Pache, Mondo Novo, Catuai, Catimor

Coffee farms around Villa Rica in Peru are environmentally friendly because the coffee plants are cultivated under the shade of forest trees that protect the soil and fauna of the region.

Brazil

Brazil has been the world's largest producer of coffee for more than 150 years. Currently, Brazil grows around one-third of the world's coffee, although in the past its market share was as high as 80 per cent. Coffee was introduced to Brazil from French Guiana in 1727, while Brazil was under Portuguese rule.

The first coffee in Brazil was planted by Francisco de Melo Palheta in the region of Para in the north of the country. According to legend, Palheta travelled to French Guiana on a diplomatic mission, seduced the wife of the governor there, and was given the seeds hidden in a bouquet from her on his departure. The coffee he planted on his return home was probably used just for domestic consumption, and it remained a relatively unimportant crop until it began to work its way south, being passed from garden to garden, as much as from farm to farm.

Commercial Production Begins

The commercial production of coffee initially began around the Paraiba River, relatively close to Rio de Janeiro. This area suited coffee, not just because the land was ideal, but also because its proximity to Rio de Janeiro facilitated export. In contrast to the smaller coffee farms that flourished in Central America, Brazil's first commercial farms were large, slave-driven plantations. This industrialized approach is still relatively uncommon in the rest of the world and fairly unique to Brazilian coffee production. The approach to production was aggressive: the most powerful, or forceful, would win disputes over poorly defined property boundaries and a single enslaved person looked after 4,000–7,000 plants. When the soil became depleted from the intensive farming, the farm would just move on to fresh land.

Coffee production boomed between 1820 and 1830, overtaking the demand of Brazilian coffee drinkers and beginning to feed the wider global market. Those who controlled coffee production became both incredibly wealthy and very powerful and were referred to as 'coffee barons'. Their needs would have a significant impact on the government's policies and its support of the coffee industry.

By 1830 Brazil produced 30 per cent of the world's coffee. This rose to 40 per cent by 1840, although the massive increase in supply resulted in a drop in the global price for coffee. Up until the middle of the 19th century, Brazil's coffee industry was reliant on slave labour. More than 1.5 million enslaved people had been brought to Brazil to work on the coffee plantations. When the British put a stop to Brazil's slave trade with Africa in 1850, Brazil turned to migrant labour or its internal slave trade. There were great fears that the abolition of slavery in Brazil in 1888 would endanger the coffee industry, but the harvest continued successfully that year and onwards.

A Second Boom

A second coffee boom ran from the 1880s through to the 1930s, a period named after the two most important products of the time. The huge influence of both coffee barons from São Paolo, and dairy producers in Minas Gerais, led to a political climate known as the café com leite (coffee with milk) period. This period also saw the Brazilian government start the practice of valorization, a protectionist practice designed to stabilize the price of coffee. The government would buy coffee from producers at an inflated price when the market was low and hold it until the market was high. This meant stable prices for coffee barons and prevented oversupply from lowering coffee prices.

By the 1920s Brazil was producing 80 per cent of the world's coffee, and coffee financed a huge amount of infrastructure in the country. This unabated production led to a massive surplus of coffee that only exacerbated the damage of the crash during the Great Depression in the 1930s. Brazil's government ended up burning around 78 million bags of stockpiled coffee in an effort to invigorate coffee prices, though in fact the practice had little effect.

During World War II there was growing concern in the United States that, with the European markets shut off, declining coffee prices could drive Central

and South American countries towards fascist or communist sympathies. In an attempt to stabilize the price of coffee, an international agreement was drawn up, based on a quota system. This agreement drove up the price of coffee until it stabilized in the mid-1950s and is considered a precursor to the much wider International Coffee Agreement (ICA) signed in 1962, which would come to encompass 42 producing countries. Quotas were fixed according to the indicator coffee price, determined by the International Coffee Organization (ICO). If prices dropped then quotas were reduced, and if prices climbed then quotas were increased.

This agreement lasted until 1989, when it broke down after Brazil refused to accept a reduction in its quota. Brazil believed that it was an extremely efficient producer and could prosper outside of the agreement. The result of the breakdown of the ICA was an unregulated market, and prices dropped dramatically over the following five years, resulting in the coffee crisis that would inspire the fair trade movement within coffee production.

Robusta Production

While not a focus of this book, it should be noted that Brazil is one of the world's primary producers of Robusta, along with Arabica. In Brazil, Robusta is usually called *conillon* and is produced in regions such as Rondônia.

On and Off Years

With Brazil being such a dominant supplier of the world's coffee, anything that affected production in Brazil had a knock-on effect on global pricing. One such factor was the alternating cycle of Brazil's annual crop. Over the years it became clear that Brazil's harvest would swing each year between a large and a small harvest. Some work has been done in recent years to try to mitigate this effect, creating less variation year to year and greater stability. The reason for this variation in crop is that a coffee tree will naturally have an alternating cycle of large and small crops, but this can be controlled by light pruning. Light pruning has not been a common practice in Brazil, with producers preferring to prune back hard so there is a notably smaller crop the following year.

In the past there have been dramatic incidents such as the Black Frost of 1975, which reduced the following year's crop by nearly 75 per cent. As a result of the frost, the global price of coffee almost doubled immediately. In 2000 and 2001 there were two off years in a row that resulted in a massive harvest in 2002, with a huge production of coffee. This coincided with another long period of low prices for coffee, caused by an excess of coffee on the global market. In recent years Brazil's production has continued to be one of the largest drivers of the C-market price for coffee.

Modern Coffee Production

Brazil is undeniably the most advanced and industrialized coffee-producing country in the world. With a focus on yield and production, it has not retained a great reputation for producing coffees of the highest quality. Most large farms employ relatively crude picking techniques, such as strip picking, where the entire branch is stripped of its cherries in one go. If the farms are large and flat (common in Brazil's larger coffee farms), they can use harvesting machines to shake the cherries loose from the branches. Neither method takes ripeness into consideration, and as a result there can be a large number of unripe cherries in the harvested coffee.

For a long time Brazil also processed a great deal of its coffee by sun-drying the whole cherries on patios. The introduction of the pulped natural process in the early 1990s did help to improve quality, but for years Brazil's speciality coffee producers – who may pick by hand, who may wash their coffee, and who may grow interesting varieties at higher elevations – have battled against the country's reputation for producing coffees with low acidity and increased body best suited to espresso blends.

However, while much of Brazil's coffee grows below the elevations best suited to quality, it is still possible to find some very interesting and delicious coffees there. Equally, the country produces some very clean and sweet coffees without much acidity that many people (quite rightly) find delicious and very approachable.

Domestic Consumption

Brazil has been actively trying to increase its internal coffee consumption, with increasing success. While giving children coffee at school from a young age may raise some eyebrows, the consumption in Brazil now rivals that of the United States. No raw coffee can be imported into Brazil, which means that a large percentage of the coffee grown in Brazil is consumed there, although generally the quality of coffee for domestic consumption is lower than that for export.

Coffee bars have appeared throughout the major cities, although the price of coffee in these places is similar to better coffee bars in the United States and Europe. The rise in speciality coffee consumption is often seen as evidence of a 'new middle class' in Brazil. Speciality coffee also seems to be the only sector in coffee consumption continuing to grow in Brazil, with more commercial consumption on a slight decline.

Traceability

High-quality Brazilian coffees are usually traceable down to a specific farm (fazenda), whereas the lower-quality coffees are bulk lots and not traceable. Coffees marked as 'Santos' have simply shipped from the port of Santos, and the name has nothing to do with where the coffee was grown. Brazil probably breaks the rule of thumb that traceability is linked to quality, as there are farms in Brazil producing more coffee than the whole of Bolivia. And while the coffee may be traceable due to the size of production, it will not necessarily be higher in quality as a result.

Opposite: Coffee production in Brazil is characterized by mechanization. Here a centre pivot sprinkler system irrigates a coffee farm.

Taste Profile

Better Brazilian coffees tend to be low in acidity, heavy in body and sweet, often with chocolate and nutty flavours. There is more variance in flavour in smaller-production, speciality-focused lots of coffee.

Growing Regions

Population: 203,080,756

Number of 60kg (132lb) bags in 2023: 66,400,000

There are many different coffee varieties grown across Brazil and many of them were developed in the country or evolved there, including Mundo Novo, Yellow Bourbon, Caturra and Catuai.

BAHIA

This large state in the east of Brazil is one of the northernmost coffee-growing areas in the country. In recent years there have been more and more interesting coffees from this region, and many people sat up and took notice when, in the 2009 Cup of Excellence competition, five out of the top ten lots came from Bahia.

CHAPADA DIAMANTINA

This beautiful area of Brazil, known for its national park, is named after its geology: *chapada* describes the steep cliffs in the region and *diamantina* the diamonds found there in the 19th century. A notable number of farms in the region are producing coffee biodynamically, an organic method of production originally developed by Rudolf Steiner.

Elevation: 1,000–1,200m (3,300–3,900ft)
Harvest: June–September

Below: Coffee cherries, from several different varieties of tree, are drying on mesh tables in state of São Paolo.

CERRADO DE BAHIA/WEST BAHIA

This region lends itself to large-scale, industrialized and irrigated coffee production. In the late 1970s and early 1980s this region was part of a government project to encourage agriculture, which provided cheap credit and incentives to around six hundred farmers who moved here. By 2006 around 1.5 million hectares (3.7 million acres) of land were being cultivated, although coffee made up a relatively small part of this. A stable, warm and sunny climate lends itself to higher yields, so it is a little harder to find something truly astonishing from this part of Brazil.

Elevation: 700–1,000m (2,300–3,300ft)
Harvest: May–September

PLANALTO DE BAHIA

This coffee region has more of a focus on small-scale production, taking advantage of the cooler temperatures and higher elevations to produce higher-quality coffees.

Elevation: 700–1,300m (2,300–4,300ft)
Harvest: May–September

MINAS GERAIS

In the south-east of the country, the state of Minas Gerais has some of the highest mountains in Brazil, providing good elevation for coffee.

CERRADO

The Cerrado refers to a vast ecoregion of tropical savannah that stretches through many states in Brazil, but when it comes to coffee the name usually refers to the Cerrado region in the west of Minas Gerais. This area is relatively new to coffee production and perhaps this explains why it is dominated by large, mechanized farms. In fact, over 90 per cent of the farms in the region are larger than 10 hectares (24 acres).

Elevation: 850–1,250m (2,800–4,100ft)
Harvest: May–September

SUL DE MINAS

Historically this is home to a great deal of Brazil's coffee production, and there have been many generations of smallholder farmers here. Perhaps for this reason there are many more cooperatives in the region. Despite the prevalence of small farms, it is still a well-industrialized area, with a lot of mechanical harvesting.

Certain areas within the region have attracted more attention recently, including Carmo de Minas. This municipality, around the village of Carmo, has a notable number of producers leveraging the soil and climate to grow better coffees.

Elevation: 700–1,350m (2,300–4,400ft)
Harvest: May–September

CHAPADA DE MINAS

This region is farther north, away from the other coffee-growing areas clustered together to the south. Coffee growing took hold here in the late 1970s. It is a relatively small area of production, with some producers taking advantage of the flat land to mechanize their farms.

Elevation: 800–1,100m (2,600–3,600ft)
Harvest: May–September

MATAS DE MINAS

This is a region where coffee took root early, and one that became rich on the back of coffee and dairy between 1850 and 1930. While the area has diversified a little in recent years, around 80 per cent of its agricultural income still comes from coffee.

The uneven land here, with steep hillsides, means that harvesting is commonly done by hand. Even though there are many smallholders in the region (almost 50 per cent of the farms are smaller than 10 hectares/24 acres) there is not the established reputation for quality one might expect. However, this is changing for the better, and there are plenty of farms producing great coffee here.

Elevation: 550–1,200m (1,800–3,900ft)
Harvest: May–September

SÃO PAOLO

The state of São Paolo contains one of the better-known coffee-growing areas of Brazil, Mogiana. The region was named after the Mogiana Railroad Company, which built the 'coffee railroad' in 1883, leading to better transport and a great expansion of coffee production here.

Elevation: 800–1,200m (2,600–3,900ft)
Harvest: May–September

MATO GROSSO AND MATO GROSSO DO SUL

This area produces only a small amount of Brazil's annual harvest. Its large, flat highlands are better suited to the vast number of cattle raised here and the extensive soybean production.

Elevation: average of 600m (2,000ft)
Harvest: May–September

ESPIRITO SANTO

While relatively small compared to other coffee-growing regions in Brazil, the second-largest chunk of the annual harvest is produced in the state of Espirito Santo, and the capital city, Vittoria, is a key port for export. However, nearly 80 per cent of the coffee it produces is conillon (Robusta). In the south of the region, the farmers tend towards Arabica production, and there can be some more interesting coffees there.

Elevation: 900–1,200m (3,000–3,900ft)
Harvest: May–September

PARANÁ

Some argue that this state is the most southern coffee-growing region in the world, and it is an important agricultural area for Brazil. Despite having just 2.5 per cent of the country's land, it produces nearly 25 per cent of its agricultural output. Coffee was once the biggest crop here, but after the damage caused by the Black Frost in 1975, many producers diversified. While the region once produced 22 million bags of coffee, now it produces closer to 2 million. The first colonists here settled close to the coast, but coffee was the reason many moved inland. The lack of elevation prevents very high-quality coffees being grown here, but the cooler temperatures do help slow down the maturation of the fruit.

Elevation: up to 950m (3,100ft)
Harvest: May–September

SOUTH AMERICA

Bolivia

Bolivia has the potential to produce truly great coffees and already does in very small quantities. The country's entire production is smaller than that of one of Brazil's larger coffee farms. Production is shrinking year on year, and coffee farms are disappearing at an alarming rate. We may soon see coffees from Bolivia (especially great ones) almost disappear.

This is all happening despite the quality of coffee coming from Bolivia being on the increase. The speciality industry remains very interested in sourcing Bolivian coffees, and some of these have been among the most memorable coffees of the last decade for me. If you haven't tried coffees from Bolivia, then I urge you to do so.

Frustratingly there is little information available about the introduction of coffee and the history of coffee growing in Bolivia; in fact, it is very difficult to find much concrete information about the coffee industry in the country as a whole. There are reports of substantial coffee production in the country going back to the 1880s, but not a great deal more. The country is large, about the same size as Ethiopia or Colombia. It is landlocked, which has traditionally posed something of a challenge to the export of coffee, adding both time and cost.

Bolivia is relatively unpopulated, with just 11.4 million inhabitants. The population is often characterized as being incredibly poor, with around 25 per cent categorized as living in extreme poverty. The country's economy is reliant on minerals and natural gas as well as agriculture, although coffee has never really featured prominently. It is impossible to ignore the impact on the economy, and on agriculture, of coca grown for the drug trade. Farmers are increasingly switching from coffee to coca, because coca provides greater security for producers because the price is subject to less variance.

The conditions for growing coffee in Bolivia are, in many ways, ideal. There is certainly the necessary elevation, and the climate has nicely defined wet and dry seasons. Most of the coffee grown here is old heirloom varieties, such as Typica and Caturra. Some excellent, clean and complex coffees have been coming out of Bolivia recently, although this wasn't always the case.

In the past producers picked and pulped the coffees they grew and then transported the pulp to a central processing station. There were two big problems: first, changes in temperature on the journey to the processing station could result in the coffee freezing and, second, the pulp still contained enough moisture to keep fermenting. Often, this resulted in a loss of quality or undesirable flavours creeping in. Quality-conscious producers are increasingly doing the post-harvest work on their own farms. The United States has funded the construction of a number of small coffee washing stations across the country as part of the anti-drugs programme. However, despite changes to help bolster quality, coffees from Bolivia still lack the reputation of those from neighbouring countries such as Colombia or Brazil.

Competitions such as the Cup of Excellence have helped shine a light on the best coffees in Bolivia. I would recommend seeking out and enjoying them

while they are still around. Even though speciality coffee does yield a greater return, even quality-conscious farmers are still giving up coffee production.

Traceability

Coffees in Bolivia are typically traceable down to a single farm or cooperative. Due to land reforms, large-scale landownership has reduced since 1991, and the 23,000 families that produce coffee in Bolivia do so from small farms, typically 1.2–8 hectares (3–20 acres). The export of Bolivia's output is handled by around 30 private exporting companies.

Taste Profile

The best Bolivian coffees tend to be very sweet and very clean, but relatively rarely are they particularly fruity in flavour.

Growing Regions

Population: 11,411,000

Number of 60kg (132lb) bags in 2022: 30,000

Coffee-growing regions in Bolivia have never been strongly defined and, as such, roasters will use different naming conventions to describe which part of the country the coffee comes from.

YUNGAS

Approximately 95 per cent of Bolivia's coffee is produced here. In the past this region held a reputation for quality in Europe, though less so recently. It can be defined as the region of forest stretching down the east side of the Andes, and which in fact crosses from Peru through Bolivia into Argentina. It produces some of the highest-elevation coffee in the world, and this is also where coffee has been grown the longest in Bolivia. In his 1935 book *All About Coffee*, William Harrison Ukers refers to coffee from here as 'Yunga'.

Yungas is to the north of La Paz, so many coffee buyers have to travel along the famous Yungas Road, nicknamed the 'Road of Death', to reach the coffee producers there. The road is often a winding single lane, dug into the sides of the mountains without any barrier to prevent vehicles dropping up to 600m (2,000ft) into the valleys below. As the region is so large, many coffee roasters describe coffees as being from a more specific area within the region such as Caranavi, Inquisivi or Coroico.

Elevation: 800–2,300m (2,600–7,500ft)
Harvest: May–November

SANTA CRUZ

This is the most easterly of the departments in Bolivia, and generally it lacks the elevation for high-quality coffees. There is some coffee production around Ichilo Province, although coffee is far less important as a crop compared to rice or timber. This region is hugely important to the country's economy because most of its natural gas is found here.

Elevation: 410m (1,340ft)
Harvest: July–November

BENI

This is a large and sparsely populated department in the north-east of the country. Technically, part of Beni falls within the geographical region of Yungas, but a small amount of coffee is grown in the department outside the Yungas region. Primarily this is a cattle ranching area, although many crops are grown here, from rice and cacao to tropical fruits.

Elevation: 155m (500ft)
Harvest: July–November

Above: An Aymara Indigenous woman pours coffee after a New Year ritual on the sacred mountain Apacheta Murmutani near Hampaturi, Bolivia.

Glossary

ARABICA: Short for *Coffea arabica*, the most widely grown species of the coffee plant. It is considered superior to Robusta, the other species commonly grown.

AROMATIC COMPOUND: A chemical compound within coffee that contributes to the aroma of the coffee when ground or brewed.

BLOOM: Pouring a small amount of water on to the coffee at the start of a pour-over brew in order to start the extraction process. It is called the 'bloom' because of the way the coffee swells when it gets wet.

BREW RATIO: The relationship between the amount of ground coffee used and the amount of water used to brew it.

BREW TIME: The total amount of time water is in contact with coffee when it is being brewed.

BURR GRINDER: A coffee grinder that has two sharp cutting discs, usually metal, that can be adjusted to grind coffee to the desired grind size.

C-PRICE: The price of commodity coffee traded on the stock market. This price is considered the base price for all types of coffee trading.

CHANNELLING: When making espresso, channelling occurs when water flows unevenly through the coffee puck, resulting in uneven extraction.

CHERRY: The fruit of the coffee tree is often called a cherry, or berry. The two flattened seeds found inside the cherry are the coffee beans.

COFFEE BERRY BORER: A pest that afflicts the coffee crop, burrowing into the fruit and consuming the beans.

COMMODITY COFFEE: Coffee that has no value linked to its quality, and whose traceability is neither important nor often available.

COOPERATIVE: A group of farmers working together for their mutual benefit.

CREMA: The layer of brown foam that appears on top of an espresso, caused by the drink being brewed under high pressure making the gases escape as bubbles.

CUP OF EXCELLENCE COMPETITION: A programme established to find, evaluate and rank fine-quality coffee from a particular country, and sell the winning coffees through an international online auction system.

CUP QUALITY: The combination of the positive taste and flavour attributes of a particular coffee.

CUPPING: The process of brewing, smelling and tasting coffee used by professional tasters in the coffee industry.

DARK ROAST: Coffee roasted for a longer time, until the bean is a very dark brown, with an oily surface.

DEFECT: A flaw in the coffee bean that contributes an unpleasant taste.

DIALLING IN: The process of adjusting an espresso grinder until the resulting coffee tastes good and is properly extracted.

DIEBACK: A progressive condition in shrubs and trees in which young shoots or larger branches are killed due to parasites, disease or unfavourable conditions.

DRY MILL: A facility that will hull, sort and grade parchment coffee, ready for export.

DRY PROCESS: A post-harvest process in which the whole coffee cherry is dried before being hulled to extract the green coffee inside.

EXTRACTION: The process of brewing coffee in which a percentage of the ground coffee is dissolved in the water.

FAIR TRADE MOVEMENT: A group of organizations looking to certify and reward cooperatives of coffee producers, with a guaranteed premium and minimum price for their coffee.

FAST ROAST: The commercial technique of roasting coffee very quickly, often in less than 5 minutes, as part of the process of making instant/soluble coffee.

FULLY WASHED: A post-harvest process in which the coffee beans are squeezed from the fruit, fermented and washed clean before being dried.

GILING BASAH: A post-harvest process common in Indonesia, in which the coffee is hulled from its parchment layer while still at high moisture levels and then dried. This contributes a particular earthy quality to the coffee's flavour. *See also* semi-washed process.

GREEN COFFEE: The coffee industry term for raw, unroasted coffee. This is the state in which coffee is traded internationally.

GRIND SIZE: The size of the particles of ground coffee. The finer and smaller the pieces, the easier it is to extract flavour from the coffee.

HEIRLOOM VARIETIES: A term used for varieties of coffee that have been traditionally grown for some time.

HONEY PROCESS: A post-harvest process, similar to the pulped natural process, in which the coffee bean is squeezed from the fruit but a variable amount of fruit flesh is left on during the drying phase.

IN REPOSO: Also known as 'resting', this describes the period of time when raw coffee is stored in parchment before it is hulled, graded and exported. This process is considered important in stabilizing the moisture content within the coffee bean.

INTERNATIONAL COFFEE AGREEMENT: First signed in 1962, this is a quota system in place between many coffee-producing countries and some importing countries in order to prevent supply and demand swings on the global market and stabilize pricing.

LATTE ART: The patterns created by carefully pouring foamed milk into espresso coffee.

LEAF RUST: An orange/brown fungus that attacks the leaves on a coffee tree, eventually causing the tree to die.

LIGHT ROAST: A coffee roasted in such a way as to preserve its acidity and fruitier flavours. The term refers to the coffee bean being a lighter shade of brown.

LOT: A distinct quantity of coffee, which has gone through some sort of selection process.

MICROFOAM: The tiny bubbles of foam created when milk is steamed properly.

MICRO-LOT: Typically ten bags (each weighing 60 or 69kg/132 or 152lb) or fewer of a particular selection from a farm or producer group.

MIEL PROCESS: *See* honey process.

MONSOONING: Along India's Malabar Coast, harvested coffee beans are exposed to the monsoon rain for 3–4 months, causing them to lose their acidity.

MOUTHFEEL: A term used to describe the texture and tactile attributes of the coffee when drinking it, ranging from very light and tea-like through to rich and creamy.

NATURAL PROCESS: A post-harvest process in which the coffee beans are picked and then carefully dried in the sun until the entire cherry is dry.

OVEREXTRACTION: This refers to extracting more of the soluble material than desired when brewing coffee, resulting in a cup that tastes bitter, harsh and unpleasant.

PARCHMENT: The protective papery layer surrounding the coffee bean, which is removed before the coffee is exported.

PARCHMENT COFFEE: Coffee that has been harvested and processed but still has its papery layer surrounding the bean. This protective layer prevents a decrease in quality before the coffee is exported.

PEABERRY: Term used to describe a single bean forming inside a coffee cherry instead of two.

POTATO DEFECT: A defect common in parts of East Africa, as a result of which a single bean will smell strongly of potato skins when ground and brewed.

PULPED NATURAL PROCESS: A post-harvest process in which the coffee beans are squeezed mechanically from the fruit before being dried on patios or raised beds.

RATIO (BREW): *See* brew ratio.

ROBUSTA: One of the two main commercially produced species of coffee, Robusta is considered lower in quality than Arabica but is easier to grow at lower elevations and more resistant to pests and disease.

RUST-RESISTANT VARIETIES: Varieties of Arabica and Robusta that are resistant to a fungus called leaf rust, or roya, which consumes the leaves on the tree, ultimately killing the plant.

SCREEN SIZE: Coffee beans are sorted by size using large screens with varying size holes in them. This is part of the grading process before a coffee is exported.

SEMI-WASHED PROCESS: *See* pulped natural process.

SILVERSKIN: A very fine, papery layer that clings to the coffee bean. It comes loose during roasting and is then referred to as 'chaff'.

SLOW ROAST: A slower, gentler roasting process, typically used by those looking to roast a coffee in such a way that it tastes as good as possible. Depending on the roasting machine and technique, the process can take between 10 and 20 minutes per roast.

SMALLHOLDER: A producer who owns a small amount of land on which to grow coffee.

SPECIALITY MARKET: The market for coffee traded on the basis of its quality and flavour. This term covers every aspect of the industry, including producers, exporters/importers, roasters, cafés and consumers.

STRENGTH OF COFFEE: A term to describe how much dissolved coffee a cup of coffee contains: typically, a cup of brewed coffee is 1.3–1.5 per cent dissolved coffee and the rest is water. With espresso, the ratio may be closer to 8–12 per cent dissolved coffee.

STRIP PICKING: A harvesting technique that involves pickers running their hands down a branch to remove all the cherries in one motion. While quick, this technique means unripe cherries are harvested along with ripe ones, and the cherries will need to be sorted later in the process.

TAMPING: When making espresso, this is the process of pushing the ground coffee down so that it forms an even, flat bed before it is brewed under very high pressure. This helps ensure the coffee brews evenly.

TERROIR: The combined effect of geography and climate on the way a coffee tastes.

TRACEABILITY: The transparency of the supply chain in coffee, and its preservation, so one can know exactly who produced a particular lot of coffee.

TYPICA: The oldest variety of Arabica that has been used in commercial coffee production.

UNDEREXTRACTION: In the process of brewing coffee this happens when we fail to dissolve all of the desired solubles in ground coffee, leaving us with a sour, often astringent cup of coffee as a result.

WASHED PROCESS: A post-harvest process where the coffee cherries are squeezed, forcing the beans out. These beans are then fermented to break down the sticky fruit flesh that is clinging to them. This is then washed off, and the coffee is then dried carefully and slowly.

WASHING STATION: A facility that receives coffee cherries and processes them until they are dry parchment coffee using a variety of post-harvest processes.

WET PROCESS: *See* washed process.

WET-HULLED PROCESS: *See* semi-washed process.

WET MILL: *See* washing station.

Index

Page numbers in *italics* refer to maps and illustration captions.

A

A grade 45, 152, 181, 206
AA grade 45, 147, 148, 152, 168, 181, 206
AAA grade 181
AB grade 45, 147
Abyssinia coffee 137
Acatenango, Guatemala 234
acids in coffee 65
Adler, Alan 98
aerobic and anaerobic fermentations 40
AeroPress 98, *98*
    inverted Aeropress method 99
    ratio and grind size 98
    traditional AeroPress method 99
AF grade 152
Africa *134*, 134–173
    Burundi 162–5
    Cameroon 172
    Côte d'Ivoire 171
    Democratic Republic of the Congo (DRC) 158–61
    Ethiopia 136–41
    Kenya 146–9
    Madagascar 170
    Malawi 168–9
    Réunion 170
    Rwanda 154–7
    size grades 45
    St Helena 172
    Tanzania 150–3
    Togo 171
    Uganda 142–5
    Zambia 166–7
Agalta, Honduras 245
Alotepec-Metapan, El Salvador 240
altitudes 15, 18, 141, 172, 210, 211, 225
    Blue Mountain coffee *226*
americano 127, *128*
Americas *212*, 212–279
    Bolivia 278–9
    Brazil 272–7
    Colombia 260–5
    Costa Rica 248–53
    Cuba 220–1
    Dominican Republic 224–5
    Ecuador 266–7
    El Salvador 238–41
    Guatemala 232–7
    Haiti 222–3
    Honduras 242–5
    Jamaica 226–7
    Mexico 228–31
    Nicaragua 246–7
    Panama 254–7
    Peru 268–71
    Puerto Rico 218
    United States 214, 219
    Venezuela 258
Amhara, Ethiopia 139
Amin, Idi 142
Andhra Pradesh, India 183
Anglo-Costa Rican Bank 248
Angola 135
animal cruelty 201
Antigua, Guatemala 235
Antioquia, Colombia 263
Apaneca-Ilamatepec mountains, El Salvador 240
Arabica 12
    Congo (DCR) 159, 160
    Ethiopia 139, 140
    genetics of coffee 12–14
    Indonesia 192, *199*
    Myanmar 187
    Papua New Guinea 205–6
    Rwanda 155
    Taiwan 211
    Tanzania 150, 152
    Thailand 188
    Uganda 142, 144
    wild Arabica varieties 27
Arabusta 171
Árbenz, Jacopo 233
aromatic compounds in coffee 65
Arsi, Ethiopia 141
Arusha, Tanzania 153
Asia *174*, 174–211
    China 184–5
    India 180–3
    Indonesia 198
    Japan 210
    Malaysia 208
    Myanmar 186–7
    Philippines 194–7
    Taiwan 211
    Thailand 188–9
    Timor-Leste 208
    Vietnam 190–3
    Yemen 176–9
Atitlán, Guatemala 234
auction coffees 50
    Cup of Excellence 50, 154, 162, 247, 276, 278
Australia 175, 210

B

B grade 152
Baba Budan 180
Bababudangiri, India 180, 182
bagging 41–4
Bahia, Brazil 276
Bale, Ethiopia 141
Bali, Indonesia 203
Barahona, Dominican Republic 225
Barrios, Justo Rufino 233
beans 19
    grinding 78–80
    parchment 19, 33, 39, 41, *44*
    sorting after harvest 30
Bench Maji, Ethiopia 140
Benishangul Gumuz, Ethiopia 139
Bentz, Melitta 90
Best of Panama Competition 254–6
Bialetti, Alfonso 102
bitterness 77
Black Frost, 1975 (Brazil) 142, 194, 274, 277
blade grinders 78–9
bloom 92
Blue Mountain, Jamaica 205, 227, 256
Bolivia 278, 278–9
    growing regions 279
    taste profile 279
    traceability 279
    varieties 279
Boquete, Panama 257
Bourbon 22–7
    Bourbon Pointu 26, 170
    Burundi 162
    Kenya 146
    Rwanda 154, 156
    St Helena 172
    Zambia 166
Brazil *213*, 272–7
    commercial production begins 272
    domestic consumption 274
    growing regions 276–7
    modern coffee production 274
    on and off years 273–4
    Robusta production 273
    second boom 272–3
    taste profile 274
    traceability 274
brewing 84
    AeroPress 98, 98–9
    electric filter machines 96
    espresso 106–11
    espresso method 112–17
    exact measurements 86
    filter brewing 90–5
    French press *88*, 88–9
    milk, cream and sugar 87
    pour-over brewing 90–5
    steep and release brewing 100–1
    stovetop moka pot 102–3
    strength 84–6
    vacuum pots 104–5
    water for brewing 81–3
broca del café (coffee drill) 18
Brunca, Costa Rica 253
Bubanza, Burundi 164
Buchanan, John 168
Bujumbura Rural, Burundi 164
burr grinders *78*, 79
Burundi 135, 162–5
    growing regions 164–5
    potato defect 155, 162
    taste profile 162
    traceability 162
Bururi, Burundi 164
buying coffee 68
    espresso roasts versus

filter coffee roasts 69–70
freezing coffee 71–2
freshness and resting 72
golden rules for fresh coffee 69
packaging 73
staling 72
storing coffee at home 70
strength guides 67
tasting notes 70–1
traceability 71
where to buy coffee 68

C

C grade 147, 152
Cacahuatique, El Salvador 241
café com leite period, Brazil 272
café con leche 220
café cubano 220
café en bola, Ecuador *266*, 266
cafés 6–9, *54*
cafetières 88–9
Caffe Florian, Venice *114*
caffe latte 126, *129*
caffeine 46–7
Cajamarca, Peru 269
Calabarzon, Philippines 196
Caldas, Colombia 263
California, USA 219
Calimani, Attilio 88
Cameroon 135, 172
cappuccino 126, *128*
  one cappuccino a day 126
caramelization 64, 65
carbon dioxide 47, 72, 92
  crema 106–7
carbonic maceration 40
Castillo 25–6
Castillo, Jaime 25
Castro, Fidel 220
Catimor 166, 168
Catuai 24
Caturra 24, 278
Cauca, Colombia 262
Cenicafé (National Coffee Research Centre, Colombia) 25
Central African Republic 135

Central America, size grades 45
Central Eastern Highlands, Ethiopia 141
Central Valley, Costa Rica 252
centrifugal roasters 67
Cerrado De Bahia / West Bahia, Brazil 276
Cerrado, Brazil 277
Chagga, Tanzania 150
Chapada de Minas, Brazil 277
Chapada Diamantina, Brazil 276
Chávez, Hugo 258
Chiapas, Mexico 230
Chichontepec Volcano, El Salvador 241
Chikmagalur, India 182
China 184–5
  growing regions 185
  taste profile 184
  traceability 184
Cibao Altura, Dominican Republic 225
Cibao, Dominican Republic 225
Cibitoke, Burundi 164
civet cats 201
Clever Dripper 101–2
cloth filters 95
co-fermentations 40–1
Cobán, Guatemala 234
coca growing 269, 278
Coffea species 12–14
  C. arabica 12, 17, 22, 27, 136
  C. canephora 12, 144
  C. dewevrei 144
  C. eugenoides 12, 14, 144
  C. excelsa 14
  C. liberica 14, 171, 208
  C. neoleroyi 144
  C. racemosa 14
  C. stenophylla 14–15
  C. zanguebariae 14
coffee 6–9
  coffee beans *see* beans
coffee berry borer (*Hypothenemus hampei*) 18
  Hawaii 215
  India 182

Peru 269
coffee berry disease (*Colletotrichum kahawae*) 18
coffee blight insect 214
Coffee Board of India 180
Coffee Development Authority, Uganda 144
coffee fruit (cherries) 19, *19*, 52
  seed (coffee beans) 19
  sweetness 19
coffee industry 6
  commodity coffee 6, 48–51
  speciality coffee 6, 50–1
Coffee Industry Board, Uganda 142
coffee roasters 66–7
coffee shops *54*, *57*, 68, 90, 104, 116, 120, 125
  China 184
  Uganda 144
coffee trees 17, 22
  blossom and fruit 18
  from seed to tree 17–18
  pests and diseases 18
  varieties 22–7
coffee wilt disease 152, 158
Colletotrichum kahawae (coffee berry disease) 18
Colombia 26, *260*, 260–5
  FNC and quality 261–2
  growing regions 262–5
  size grades 45
  taste profile 261
  traceability 261
Comayagua, Honduras 245
commodity coffee 6, 48–51
Congo, Democratic Republic of the (DRC) 158–61, *159*
  growing regions 160
  taste profile 159
  traceability 159
cooling 65
Coorg, India 183
Copán, Honduras 245
Cordillera Central, Dominican Republic 225
Cordillera, Philippines 196
cortadito 220

cortado 127
Costa Rica 248–53, *249*
  coffee and tourism 250
  government's role 249
  growing regions 252
  micro-mill revolution 250
  taste profile 250
  traceability 250
Côte d'Ivoire 135, 171
cream 87
crema 106–7
Cuba 220–1
  Cuban coffee 220
  growing regions 221
  taste profile 220
  traceability 220
cultivars 22
Cundinamarca, Colombia 263
Cup of Excellence 50, 154, 162, 247, 276, 278
Cusco, Peru 269

D

decaffeination 46
  carbon dioxide 47
  ethyl acetate 46–7
  natural versus synthetic caffeine 47
  Swiss water process 47
defect 33
  potato defect 155
Direct Trade coffee 50–1
diseases 14, 18, 152, 155, 158
Dominican Republic 224–5
  export versus domestic consumption 224
  growing regions 225
  taste profile 224
  traceability 224
drum roasters 66, 131
dry process 34–5, 36–7
  drying speed and storage potential 35
dual boiler machines 123
Dutch East India Company (VOC) 175, 198
Duvalier, Papa Doc 222

E

E grade 147, 152
East Harage, Ethiopia 141

Eastern Highlands, Papua New Guinea 207
Eastern Region, Venezuela 259
ecotourism 250
Ecuador 266–7
   growing regions 267
   taste profile 266
   traceability 266
El Bálsamo-Quezaltepec, El Salvador 240
El Oro, Ecuador 267
El Paraiso, Honduras 245
El Salvador *238*, 238–41
   elevation classifications 240
   growing regions 240–1
   heirloom varieties 239–40
   Pacas variety 239
   taste profile 240
   traceability 240
electric filter machines 96
elephant beans 147
Embu, Kenya 148
Equateur, Congo (DCR) 160
Espirito Santo, Brazil 277
espresso 106, *129*
   basic technique 107–8
   brew ratio 109
   crema 106–7
   evenness and channelling 109–10
   Ideale, La Pavoni *107*
   invention of espresso 106
   La Sardina, Gaggia Esportazione *108*
   pressure and resistance 108–9
   puck preparation 110
   tamping 110–11
espresso based drinks 125
   americano 127
   caffè latte 126
   cappuccino 126
   cortado 127
   espresso 115, 125
   flat white 127
   lungo 125
   macchiato 125
   ristretto 125
espresso equipment 122
   dual boiler machines 123

espresso grinders 122, 124
   heat-exchange machines 122
   lever machines 124
   temperature surfing 123
   thermoblock machines 122–3
espresso method 112
   brew pressure 115–16
   brew ratios and espresso style 115
   brew temperature 115
   changing the grind 115
   cleaning and maintaining machines 116–17
   coffees roasted for espresso 117
   judging the results 114
   steaming milk 120–1
Ethiopia *111*, 135, *136*, 136–41, 150
   ECX (Ethiopian Coffee Exchange) 138
   growing regions 139–41
   move towards democrac 138
   People's Revolutionary Democratic Front 138
   production systems 137
   taste profile 138
   traceability 138
European Coffee Brewing Centre 96
Excelso grade 45, 262

F
F grade 152
FACN (Fédération des associations caféières natives) 222–3
Fairly Traded coffee 51
Fairtrade 49–50
   Peru 268
farm gate pricing 51
fermentation 38, 40–1
filter brewing 90–2
   method 93–4
   troubleshooting 94
   types of filter 95
flat white 127, *128*
Flores, Indonesia 203
flotation tanks *30*

fluid bed roasters 66
FNC (Federación Nacional de Cafeteros) 260–1
forest coffees, Ethiopia 137
Fraijanes, Guatemala 235
free on board (FOB) pricing 51
freezing coffee 71–2
French press *88*, 88
   method 89
freshness 69, 72
Fujian, China 185

G
Gaggia, Achille 106
Galapagos Islands 267
garden coffees, Ethiopia 137
Gesha (Geisha) 25, 213, *254*, 256
Ghana 135
Gibson, Guy 147
giling basah 198–9
Gitega, Burundi 164
grading *38*, 44–5
   common size grades 45
   El Salvador 240
   elevation grading 235, 240, 244
   Guatemala 235
   India 181
   Kona 214–15
   Papua New Guinea 206
grinding coffee 78, 122, 124
   blade grinders 78–9
   burr grinders *78*, 79
   density and grind size 80
Guanacaste, Costa Rica 253
Guatemala *233*, 232–7, *236*
   elevation grading 235
   growing regions 234–5
   taste profile 234
   traceability 234
Guinea 135
Gumilla, José 258

H
Hacienda La Esmeralda, Panama 254–5
Haile Selassie of Ethiopia 137
Hainan, China 185
Haiti 222–3

   taste profile 223
   traceability 223
Hajjah, Yemen 179
Hāmākua, Big Island 217
handpicking 30, *30*
Hario 101
Harrar, Ethiopia 137, 141
harvesting 29
   fallen fruit 30
   handpicking 30, *30*
   labour problems 30
   machine harvesting 29, *30*
   sorting the beans 30
   strip picking 30
Hawaii, USA *214*, 214
   growing regions 216–17
   Kona 214–15
   taste profile 215
   traceability 215
Haya coffee 150
heat-exchange machines 122
Hemileia vastatrix (leaf rust fungus) 18
history of coffee drinking 54–6
   change through innovation 56–7
   coffee reaches Europe and beyond 56
   coffee today 57
home roasting 130
   drum roasters 131
   home-roasting machines 130–1
   hot-air roasters 131
   perfect roast 130
Honduras *242*, 242–5
   classification of coffee 244
   growing regions 245
   problem of climate 244
   taste profile 244
   traceability 244
honey (MIEL) process 39
hot-air roasters 131
Houphouët-Boigny, Félix 171
Huehuetenango, Guatemala 235
Huila, Colombia 262
hulling 41, *41*
Hurricane Mitch, 1998 246
hybrid processes 39

hybrid roasters 66
Hypothenemus hampei (coffee berry borer) 18

I
Illubabor, Ethiopia 139
India 180-3, *181*
　grading 181
　growing regions *181*, 182-3
　monsooning 180-2
　taste profile 182
　traceability 182
Indonesia *198*, 198
　giling basah 198-9
　growing regions 202-3
　Kopi Luwak 201
　taste profile 199
　traceability 201
　varieties 202
Instituto del Café de Costa Rica (ICAFE) 249, 252
Instituto Hondureño del Café (IHCAFE) 242
Instituto Mexicano del Café (INMECAFE) 228-9
International Coffee Agreement (ICA) 142, 222, 228-9, 273

J
Jackson 26, 156
Jamaica 226-7
　growing regions 227
　Jamaican Coffee Board 226
　taste profile 226
　traceability 227
Japan 210
Java, Indonesia 202
Jesuits 233, 258, 260
Jimma-Limu, Ethiopia 140
Jinotega, Nicaragua 247
Juan Valdez 260
Junin, Peru 269

K
Ka'ū, Big Island, Hawaii 216
Kaffa, Ethiopia 140
Kaffee Hag 47
Karnataka, India 182
Karuzi, Burundi 164
Kaua'i Island, Hawaii 216

Kayanza, Burundi 165
Keiyo, Kenya 149
Kent 27
Kenya 135, 146-9, *147*
　grading system 147
　growing regions 148-9
　Kenyan Coffee Board 148
　Kenyan varieties 147
　taste profile 148
　traceability 147-8
Kerala, India 183
Kiambu, Kenya 149
Kigoma, Tanzania 153
Kilimanjaro Native Planters' Association (KNPA) 150
Kilimanjaro, Tanzania 153
Kīpahulu, Maui Island, Hawaii 216
Kirinyaga, Kenya 148
Kirundo, Burundi 165
Kisii, Kenya 149
Kivu, Congo (DCR) 160
Kona, Big Island, Hawaii 214-15, 216
Kongo Central, Congo (DCR) 160
Kopi Luwak 201, 256
Kualapu'u, Moloka'i Island, Hawaii 216
Kula, Maui Island, Hawaii 216

L
labour problems 9, 30
lactic fermentations 40
Laurina 26, 170
Lawes, Sir Nicholas 226
leaf rust fungus (*Hemileia vastatrix*) 14, 18, 156, 208
　Guatemala 234
　Hawaii 215
　Honduras 242, 245
　India 180
　Indonesia 198
　Peru 268-9
　Philippines 194
Loja, Ecuador 267
Lollobrigida, Gina *118*
Los Santos, Costa Rica 252
lungo 115, 125, *129*

M
macchiato 115, 125, *129*
Machakos, Kenya 149
machine harvesting 29, *30*
Madagascar 170
Magdalena, Colombia 265
Mahwit, Yemen 179
Maillard reactions 64-5
Makamba, Burundi 165
Malawi 135, 168-9
　growing regions 169
　taste profile 168
　traceability 168
Malaysia 208
Manabi, Ecuador 267
Mandalay, Myanmar 187
Manjarabad, India 183
Maragogype 24, 239
Marakwet, Kenya 149
Matagalpa, Nicaragua 247
Matas de Minas, Brazil
Mato Grosso and Mato Grosso Do Sul, Brazil 277
Maui Island, Hawaii 216
Max Havelaar: Or the Coffee Auctions of the Dutch Trading Company 198
Mbeya, Tanzania 153
Meru, Kenya 148
metal filters 95
Mexico 228-31, *229*
　growing regions 230
　taste profile 229
　traceability 229
MH/ML (Mbuni Heavy/ Mbuni Light) grades 147
Mibirizi 156
micro-mills, Costa Rica 250
microfoam 120, *121*, 126
milk 87
　right temperature 120
　steaming milk method 121
　whole milk, skimmed and non-dairy alternatives 120
Mimaropa, Philippines 196
Minas Gerais, Brazil 277
Mindanao, Philippines 196
mocha 177
Mocha Java Blend 202
Moka Bar, London *118*
moka pots 102-3

Monsoon Malabar 180-1, 183
Montecillos, Honduras 245
Mundo Novo 24
Muramvya, Burundi 165
Murang'a, Kenya 148
Muyinga, Burundi 165
Mwaro, Burundi 165
Myanmar *186*, 186-7
　growing regions 187
　taste profile 187
　traceability 187

N
Nakuru, Kenya 149
Nariño, Colombia 263
National Coffee Board of Ethiopia 137
National Coffee Park, Colombia 262
National Coffee Research Centre, Colombia (Cenicafé) 25
natural process 34-5, *36-7*
　drying speed and storage potential 35
Nestlé 184
Neyba, Dominican Republic 225
Ngozi, Burundi 165
Nicaragua 246-7
　growing regions 247
　taste profile 246
　traceability 246
Nilgiri, India 182
North Central Region, Venezuela 259
North Santander, Colombia 265
Nueva Segovia, Nicaragua 247
Nuevo Oriente, Guatemala 235
Nyeri, Kenya 148

O
O'ahu Island, Hawaii 216
Oaxaca, Mexico 230
Oceania *174*, 174-211
　Australia 210
　Hawai'i 214
　Papua New Guinea 20

Old Brown Java 202
Opalaca, Honduras 245
Organic Trade Association 49
Oriental, Congo (DCR) 160
Orinde Farmers' Cooperative Society, Kenya 149
Orosi, Costa Rica 253

P

Pacamara 27, 239
Pacas 27, 239
Pacas, Don Alberto 239
packaging 73
   gas-flush sealed foil packaging 73
   sealed packaging 73
   unsealed craft packaging 73
Palheta, Francisco de Melo 272
Panama 213, 254-7, *254*
   growing regions 257
   Hacienda La Esmeralda 254-5
   taste profile 256
   traceability 256
paper filters 95
Papua New Guinea 175, *205*, 205-6
   grading 206
   growing regions 207
   taste profile 206
   traceability 206
Paraná, Brazil 277
parchment coffees 181
PB grade 45, 147, 152, 181
peaberries 19, 45, 147
percolation 90
Peru *268*, 268-71
   growing regions 269
   taste profile 269
   traceability 269
pests 18, 214, 215
phenolic coffee 33
Philippines 194-7, *195*
   growing regions 196
   taste profile 196
   traceability 196
Pink Bourbon 25
Planalto de Bahia, Brazil 277

plantation coffees 137, 181
post-harvesting techniques 40-1
potato defect 155
pour-over brewing 90-2
   bloom 92
   key principles 92
   method 93-4
   pouring kettles *90*, 90
   troubleshooting 94
   types of filter 95
Prestige Cup, Burundi 162
price of coffee *see* trade in coffee
processing 33-4
   bagging 41-4
   decaffeination 46-7
   depulping 33, 38, 39
   giling basah 198-9
   honey (MIEL) process 39
   hulling 41, *41*
   hybrid processes 39
   natural process 34-5, *36-7*
   new and experimental post-harvesting techniques 40-1
   pulped natural process *36-7*, 39, 274
   semi-washed/wet-hulled process 39, 198-9
   shipping 44, *49*
   sizing and grading *38*, 44-5
   washed process 35-9, *36-7*
PSC grades 206
Pueblea, Mexico 230
Puerto Rico 219
Pulney, India 182
pulped natural process 36-7, 39, 274
Puna, Big Island, Hawaii 217

Q

qesher 177
quenching 65
Quindio, Colombia 262
quotas 228, 273

R

Rainforest Alliance 49, 263
Raymah, Yemen 179
relationship coffee 50

Renacimiento, Panama 257
resting coffee 72
Réunion 170
Richard, Jeanne 104
Rift, Ethiopia 140
Risaralda, Colombia 263
ristretto 115, 125, *128*
roasting *60*, 60
   acids in coffee 65
   aromatic compounds in coffee 65
   cooling and quenching 65
   fast or slow, light or dark? 60
   home roasting 130-1
   stages of roasting 62-3
   sugars in coffee 64-5
   types of coffee roasters 66-7
Robusta 12, 15, 26, *44*, 45, 170-2
   Congo (DCR) 158, 159, 160
   genetics of coffee 12-14
   Rwanda 155
   Tanzania 152, 153
   Uganda 142, 144
   Vietnam 190-2
   West Africa 135
roya (coffee leaf rust) 18
Rume Sudan 25
Ruskey, Jay 219
Rutana, Burundi 165
Ruvuma, Tanzania 153
Rwanda 135, *154*, 154-7
   coffee's role in Rwanda's recovery 154-5
   growing regions 156
   local varieties 156
   potato defect 155
   taste profile 155
   traceability 155

S

S795 27
Sa'dah, Yemen 179
San Marcos, Guatemala 234
San Martin, Peru 269
Sana'a, Yemen 179
Santander, Colombia 263
São Paolo, Brazil 277
scales, digital 86
Scott Laboratories 147

semi-washed process 39, 198-9
Shan State, Myanmar 187
Shevaroy, India 182
shipping 44, *49*
Sidama/Sidamo, Ethiopia 140
Sidra 26, 266
Sierra Del Escambray, Cuba 221
Sierra Del Rosario, Cuba 221
Sierra Maestra, Cuba 221
Sierra Nevada, Colombia 265
Simbu Province, Papua New Guinea 207
sizing and grading *38*, 44-5
   common size grades 45
SL-28 24, 147, 250
SL-34 24, 147
slave labour 150, 222, 224, 226, 258, 72
SOGESTALs (Sociétés de gestion des stations de lavage) 162
speciality coffee 6, 50-1
Speciality Coffee Association of Panama 254
Specialty Coffee Association 82, 96
St Helena 172
staling 72
steam wands 117, 120, 121
steaming milk 120-1
steep and release brewing 100
   method 101
Steiner, Rudolph 276
storage potential 35
storing coffee at home 70
stovetop moka pot 102, *102*
   method 103
Strecker degradation 65
strength of coffee 84-6
   guides 67
strip picking 30
Sudan Rume 25
sugar 87
   sugars in coffee 64-5
Sul de Minas, Brazil 277
Sulawesi, Indonesia 203

Sumatra Mandheling 202
Sumatra, Indonesia 202
Superior grade 45
Supremo grade 45, 224, 261
sweetness 19, 76
Swiss water process 47
Switch 101–2
Swynnerton Plan, Kenya 146

T
T grade 147
Taiwan 211
Tamil Nadu, India 182
tangential roasters 67
Tanzania 135, *150*, 150–3
   growing regions 153
   taste profile 152
   traceability 152
Tarime, Tanzania 153
Tarrazú, Costa Rica 252
tasting coffee 74
   acidity 76
   balance 76
   bitterness 77
   comparative tasting 74–7
   descriptors 70–1
   flavour 76–7
   mouthfeel 76
   professional tasters 74, 77
   sweetness 76
TDS (total dissolved solids) meters 83
temperature surfing 123
Tepeca-Chinameca, El Salvador 241
Tepi, Ethiopia 140
terroir 22, 34, 30, 60, 250
TEX grade 152
Thailand 188, *189*
   growing regions *189*, 189
   taste profile 189
   traceability 188
thermal shock 40
thermoblock machines 122–3
Timor Hybrid 26, 208
Timor-Leste 208
Togo 135, 171
Tolima, Colombia 262
Tomoca coffee shop, Addis Ababa *111*
tourism 250

traceability 51, 71
trade in coffee 48–9
   advice to consumer 51
   auction coffees 50
   Fairtrade 49–50
   speciality coffee industry 50–1
Trans-Nzoia, Kenya 149
Travancore, India 183
Tres Ríos, Costa Rica 253
TT grade 147, 152
Turrialba, Costa Rica 253
Typica 22–4, 26, 27, 261
   Bolivia 278
   Peru 268–9

U
Ubico, Jorge 233
UG grade 152
Uganda 142–5, *143*
   growing regions 145
   taste profile 144
   traceability 144
UN Development Programme 184
United Fruit Company (UFC) 233
United States
   California 219
   Hawai'i 214
US Agency for International Development (USAID) 154

V
vacuum pots *104*, 104
   method 105
Valdesia, Dominican Republic 225
Valle Del Cauca, Colombia 262
varietals 22
varieties 22–7, 156
Velasco, Juan 268
Venezuela 258
   growing regions 259
   taste profile 258
   traceability 258
Veracruz, Mexico 230
Vietnam 190, 190–3, *192*
   growing regions 191
   taste profile 190
   traceability 191

Villa Sarchi 27, 252
Visayas, Philippines 196
Volcan-Candela, Panama 257
volcanic soil 239
   Cauca, Colombia 262
   Central Valley, Costa Rica 252
   Chiapas, Mexico 230
   Chichontepec Volcano, El Salvador 241
   Flores, Indonesia 203
   Fraijanes, Guatemala 235
   Kirinyaga, Kenya 148
   Murang'a, Kenya 148
   Nyeri, Kenya 148
   Tres Ríos, Costa Rica 253
   Visayas, Philippines 196

W
Waikapū, Maui Island, Hawaii 216
washed process 35–9, *36–7*
water for brewing 81
   better brewing water 82
   guidelines for perfect water 82
   how do I know if my water is good? 82
   how to get better water 83
   role of water 81
   TDS meters 83
   water hardness 81–2
water to coffee ratio 84–6
   AeroPress 98
   cappuccino 126
   electric filter machine method 96
   espresso 109, 115, 125
   French press method 89
   ristretto 125
   stovetop moka pot method 103
   vacuum pot method 105
Wayanad, India 183
WDT (Weiss Distribution Technique) 110
Weiss, John 110
Wellega, Ethiopia 139
West Central Region, Venezuela 259
West Harage, Ethiopia 141

West Valley, Costa Rica 252
Western Highlands, Papua New Guinea 207
Western Region, Venezuela 259
wet-hulled process 39, 198–9
World Aeropress Championships 98
World Bank 166, 184
Wush Wush 25

Y
Y grades 206
Yemen 175, *176*, 176–9
   growing regions 179
   mocha 177
   qesher 177
   taste profile 179
   traceability 177
   Yemeni varieties 177–9
Yirgacheffe, Ethiopia 140
Yunnan, China 185

Z
Zambia 135, 166–7
   growing regions 167
   taste profile 167
   traceability 167
Zamora Chinchipe, Ecuador 267

Picture Acknowledgements

Alamy Stock Photo: Archive Photos 69, Anders Blomqvist 191, Bertrand Rieger/Hemis 27r, Boaz Rottem 26l, Eddie Gerald 108, Efrain Padro 218, Ethel Davies/robertharding 215, Fernando Llano/Associated Press 259, F. Jack Jackson 178, Franck Guiziou/Hemis 110-111, Greg Balfour Evans 189, Gregory Gerault/Hemis 251, IMAGO/Godong/BSIP 17r, IMAGO/Xu Qin 209b, INTERFOTO 64, Jake Lyell 41, 149, Jan Butchofsky 206-207, Jacier Garcia 228, Joerg Boethling 204, Joshua Roper 250, Juan Karita/Associated Press 279, Nathias Putze 138, 141, Oleksandr Rupeta 166l, 166-167c, Painting 8-9, Penta Springs Limited 222, Phil Borges/Danita Delimont 266, Pulsar Imagens 24l, Radius Images/Design Pics 32, 232, Rob Crandall/Stock Connection Blue 258, Ron Giling 163, 194, Stefano Politi Markovina 114, The Africa Image Library 155, Ulrich Doering 151, Vespasian 23b, Wes shinn 25r, WorldFoto 146, Xinhua 184, 185; **Dreamstime:** © Sasi Ponchaisang 188; **Enrico Maltoni** 107; **Getty Images:** Alex Dellow 54-55, Andrew Aitchison/In Pictures Ltd./Corbis 145, Andrew Renneisen 34-35b, Bettmann 10-11, brandstaetter images 56, Brent Stirton 159, BruceBlock 152, Chaideer Mahyuddin/AFP 199, Edinson Arroyo/Bloomberg 264-265, English Heritage/Heritage Images 58-59, Godong/Universal Images Group 137, HUM Images/Universal Images Group 132-133, John Coletti 31b, Jonathan Torgovnik 144, Juan Carlos/Bloomberg 239, 241, Keystone-France/Gamma-Keystone 48-49, Kurt Hutton/Picture Post/Hulton Archive 118-119, Leon Neal 173b, Monty Rakusen 52-53, Philippe Colombi 247, RyanJLane 61, Sepia Times/Universal Images Group 47, STR/AFP 221, Tomas Ayuso/Bloomberg 244-245, Ted Aljibe/AFP 197, Tom Knudson/Sacramento Bee/Tribune News Service 42-43; **iStock:** Alfribeiro 275, Andrea Lopes 276, AnnPQ 17l, BROTEstudio 267, ByronOrtizA 15, DanRamirez 235, Dennis Alberto Gonzalez Salas 252-253, Dennis Wegewiis 142-143, dimarik 246, Emily_M_Wilson 34-35a, EyeEm Mobile GmbH 256-257, Gianfranco Vivi 248, Gummybone 227, hadnyah 28-29, Ianalyko 243, José Eduardo Dos Santon Martins 186-187, Rodrigo Pardo 230-231, Shelyna Long 209a, sheppardpk 261, Todd Sanchez 224-225, wsfurlan 31a; **Niall Kennedy** 26-27c; **Panos:** Philippe Lissac/Godong 164-165, Sven Torfinn 157, Tim Dirven 158-159b, 160-161; **Reuters:** Darren Whiteside 200-201, Kham 192-193; **Robert Harding Picture Library:** Arjen Van De Merwe/Still Pictures 168-169; **Shutterstock:** Alfredo Maiquez 255, Athirati 30, bchyla 270-271, Fabio Martinez Delgado 24-25c, Florian Kopp/imageBROKER 223, Gianfranco Vivi 20-21, HappyTime19 23b, Lano Lan 226, Lu Yu Jen 211, Manan Deb 183, Max Zvonarev 180, Media Lens King 173a, Stasis Photo 17c, Sydeen 203, trappy76 16, Zach Way Photography 217; **Sweet Maria's** 236-237

Author's Acknowledgements

Researchers: Ben Szobody, Michael Losada and Alice Groser

Research assistance, translation and motivation: Alethea Rudd

I'd like to thank Ric Rhinehart and Peter Giuliano for their astonishing generosity of time and wisdom. I'm extremely grateful to everyone in the Square Mile Coffee Roasters team, past and present, for being constantly inspiring and supportive.